MEMOIRS OF A COLLEGE PROFESSOR

BOOKS BY VERGILIUS FERM

The Crisis in American Lutheran Theology, 1927
What Is Lutheranism? (ed.), 1930
Contemporary American Theology, Vol. 1 (ed.), 1932
Contemporary American Theology, Vol. 11 (ed), 1933
First Adventures in Philosophy, 1936
First Chapters in Religious Philosophy, 1937
Religion in Transition (ed.), 1937
An Encyclopedia of Religion (ed.), 1945
Religion in the Twentieth Century (ed.), 1948
What Can We Believe? 1948
Forgotten Religions, Including Some Living Primitive Religions (ed.), 1950
A History of Philosophical Systems (ed.), 1950 (translated into Japanese — Vol. 1 and Vol. 11, 1956)
A Protestant Dictionary, 1951
The American Church of the Protestant Heritage (ed.), 1953
Jonathan Edwards, Puritan Sage (Collected Writings) (ed.), 1953
The Protestant Credo (ed.), 1953
Their Day Was Yesterday (A Novel), 1954
A Dictionary of Pastoral Psychology, 1955
In the Last Analysis, 1956
An Encyclopedia of Morals (ed.), 1956
A Pictorial History of Protestantism, 1957
A Brief Dictionary of American Superstitions, 1959
Classics of Protestantism (ed.), 1959
Inside Ivy Walls, 1964
Toward An Expansive Christian Theology, 1964
Basic Philosophy for Beginners, 1969
Memoirs of a College Professor — Telling It Like It Was, 1971

MEMOIRS OF A
COLLEGE PROFESSOR

Telling It Like It Was

By

VERGILIUS FERM, B.D., Ph.D.
Compton Professor Of Philosophy, Emeritus,
The College Of Wooster
and currently Professor of
Philosophy, Ashland College (Ohio)

THE CHRISTOPHER PUBLISHING HOUSE
NORTH QUINCY, MASSACHUSETTS

COPYRIGHT © 1971

BY VERGILIUS FERM

Library of Congress Catalog Card Number 74-125924

SBN: 8158-0246-3

PRINTED IN

THE UNITED STATES OF AMERICA

To the Memory of

Olof Wilhelm and Mathilda Ferm
and
Jacob Odin and Marie and Augusta Nelson

our beloved parents
pioneer Scandinavian Americans
who in their youth
chose America as their homeland

PREFACE

Fifty-seven continuous years on campuses of colleges and universities ought to qualify one to have something potentially of interest to relate. It certainly reveals the changing scenes of the decades especially in the mores and the cycles of thought that come and go. Longevity is not an attainment which can be equated with achievement; longevity is very much a gift of grace that life bestows on some and withholds from others. If life is a good thing — no matter how difficult it is at times — then I have been extremely lucky.

In fact I am convinced that one has to have a heap amount of luck not only on the life-span one experiences but on such important matters as the character of one's parents, the companion who shares one's life whose importance is beyond measurement either to make or break you, the people whom you happen to meet (certainly without intention), lucky if they twisted you around somewhat and steered your course out of a potential rut, places where you lived and the conditions that go with such places — and a thousand factors. Whether life is interesting or not depends on adaptability to whatever comes and more often than not upon one's dissatisfaction with the limitations of place and the desire to move out into other spheres of experience. All this has been mine. I consider myself fortunate in parents, in the circumstances of an age which went from the horse and buggy to air-condition-ed Skylark Buicks, from kerosene lamps to fluorescent lights, from a family of immigrant parents speaking freely in a foreign tongue and learning the American form of English and the American way of life, from small denominational college campus to universities, from a disciplined home with norms all over the place to the breakdown almost completely of all social stand-ards such as have come to the present age, from con-servatism to open-mindedness to other opinions and traditions, from frugality of living to the enjoyment of some measure of affluence.

Luck, in short, is a big slice of life. And the theologi-cal term for good luck is "grace." And the essence of true worship is certainly not the worship of man nor is the essence of the good life the sense of pride of achieve-ment — but rather all life is a gift of grace which makes one thankful and appreciative and certainly truly hum-ble in having been generously blessed with its oppor-tunities.

As I look back in the recording of my own journey through the years I believe I see — beyond the fortune of luck and grace — certain idiosyncracies which have dominated me as a person. I am not sure they are virtu-ous nor am I certain that they are vices. But I am now aware of them — with the perspective that comes in reviewing the many years. Where I have got them, whether by the influence of a person or a home or a teaching, I do not know. But certain characteristics seem to have persisted.

One is a drive to move along and hopefully forward.

Ambition is another name for it although it was never clear to me toward what that ambition was directed. It seemed to me, as far back as I can think, that I always seemed to want something more than I had. If it had been financial success or fame or some form of heroism I must confess failure. I would be hypocritical to denounce such ideals. But it was not expressed that way for me. My ideals were not far out somewhere beyond the horizon. Rather they were grounded in whatever situation I found myself and to be colored and motivated by wherever the scene lay. Since academic life came my way, my ambitions and drive lay in these channels. As a youngster I wanted to win spelling matches or be the one who when he joined an adventure wanted to find himself trying to see it through — beyond what satisfied many others. This drive has characterized my life all the way. I could easily forego some passing pleasure if it meant that such pleasure would interfere too much with what I wanted to do most at that time of life. To flunk a course or get a passing D grade — to put it into academic vocabulary — would have disappointed me so much that I would have taken such grades as a kind of curse which never must happen to me. Where does one get such drives? I do not know. Once in the system, they seem never to leave.

Another characteristic which seems to have played a dominant role may be summarized by the current song-hit. The ballad is entitled "I've Gotta Be Me" and the words go: "Whether I'm right or whether I'm wrong, Whether I find a place in this world or never belong — I've gotta Be Me, I've Gotta Be Me" and continues "I'll go it alone, That's how it must be, I can't be right for somebody else if I'm not right for me, I've Gotta be free, I've gotta be free, Daring to try to do it, or die, I've Gotta Be Me." I do not quote these lines as Scripture but I bring them here as a mirror which reflects myself to me. In other words, I would have been a failure as a politician or social climber or as somebody popular if this meant the threat of myself as me. This characteristic has closed many doors and I am aware of a good many of them. Where does one pick up such a drive? I don't know, I just don't know. It has its virtues and its vices. To me — on the long pull — it has been a virtue.

In this self-analysis (psychoanalysis) I may add another characteristic. If there is a word such as "stick-to-it-iveness" I am not certain. There should be a word like that. Maybe the synonym is determination, stubbornness, consecration (a nice word), do-or-die. Such synonyms are indicative of what I mean without saying wholly what I mean. My temperament has been the opposite of lackadaisical and this is the negative of stick-to-it-iveness. It is ambition with a plus. Is this a virtue or a vice? In a sense it is a vice since it tends toward worry and strenuousness and in that respect not altogether healthy. As a virtue it has seemed to pay off in an experience of self-satisfaction that comes only with work — plain drudgery — work which is the only real work I know.

I have in mind, now that I have written this book, several groups of people who might read my story. First, the academic folk who will recognize in my account much that is in their own experience as people in the privileged spot of campus life. They will perhaps appreciate the story of one's pilgrimage in the fierce battle toward recognition by the professional people who already know by experience what it means to plug along toward certain academic goals. Second, I think of those who are young who have some spark of ambition in whatever field, that they may profit by the reading of an intellectual biography and how the obstacles have been met and dealt with and what others may be expected to endure in securing some niche in life. And thirdly, I think of those people who are interested in what may be called "Americana" — the life in America during the early and middle twentieth century when changes brought about, more or less radical, departures from the culture of the immigrants who came to these shores to rear their families and how their children played their role in the typically American culture of the melting-pot which cancels out so much of the heritage into a new kind of ethos — a change which has been cataclysmic in nature. I am glad to have gone on the wave of this change intellectually and that I do not have to leave the scene sorry that I didn't try to make adjustments to the newer insights of life which critical thought has brought about and which is here whether we like it or not. In the area of religion, theology and philosophy my story moves and on the whole — as I look back — it seems interesting enough to remember and relate and share with others who may profit from the reading of spiritual autobiographies.

And, I hope, it is a fun book — where the reader will see that life cannot only be fun but even funny at times, and at most times. Deity, in my thought, has a sense of humor or else patience would have been pre-empted long centuries ago toward man even in his most serious moods.

My thanks to my companion throughout the fifty and more years we have been together — this time for typing out my manuscript and who has helped me in spelling and exposition. Not her first experience. She has been the silent partner in all my publications.

Vergilius Ferm
Wooster, Ohio

CONTENTS

EARLIER YEARS

They tell me that my parents bought a grave in or near Chariton, Iowa for me some time during my early days. They tell me that I was a sickly child, that I had about every disease going the rounds. The prediction for survival was negative. My memory, of course, is blank about all this but I am dimly aware of some later earlier years. I recall my frequent visits to a physician who seemed quite rough on me as he treated my eyes. I was told later in life that the strong medicine given me was probably good for that day; but I suffered long after this experience. I recall vividly that sore throats were frequent and my wearing raw pork-slices around my neck held together by a flannel cloth. I literally smelled like a pig at school. (This remedy was not unusual in that day!) I recall after a long illness my father giving me a high-ride on his broad shoulders around our yard after a long bed convalescence; I can almost now smell the invigorating fresh air and recall my blinking at the extreme light of the sun. I can easily remember nightmares which plagued me (not regularly) but when they came it was in the depth of sleep.

Our family invited to our household a "Sister" Ingdina (a consecrated deaconess of the Lutheran Church) who served the large congregation in Sioux City where my father was minister and where I was born and she was like a mother to me, babying me even after I had grown toward young adolescence. I remember the fright that came over me one night when I met her in the hallway — she without her "white cap," the insignia of her deaconess order (headquarters, Omaha, Nebraska). When the cap was replaced by her on her head I was relieved to know that I was "safe" again. It may all add up to a kind of congenital nervousness which ran in my family on my mother's side. My mother was warm and compassionate but strict. There was order in the home. (The Swedish word is "reda.") We were taught manners: many of which (I still think) are not outmoded. For example, as children we were not to interrupt adult conversation and we were to take seriously a "No" as well as a "Yes" from our parents. My older brother, Julius, always seemed to me to be the "fair-haired" boy by his being allowed to do things many boys did, such as "carry" papers and accompany his age-group in unscheduled rounds while I was not permitted such freedom. This brother relationship persisted and I grew up to accept it as a kind of natural phenomenon. We turned out to have quite different interests and points of view which persisted throughout life. My only sister, Judith (who was also older than myself), was a ladylike creature and always feminine in her ways, simple and sweet without any special flair or attempt at self-display. Her death which came in adolescence left an imprint on our family, especially on my father and my mother which never left them. My father would take me to visit her grave years later and unashamedly let the tears fall in my presence.

I recall the passing of the 1800's into the 1900's. It was New Year's eve and my mother, Dad and I stood before the open window and looked out into the cold, dark night. My folks said something about how important it was that we greet the New Year, this one especially. I was very young. But I recall the curtains blowing in the open windows and the cold, crisp December air. I knew something special was going on. (It was January 1, 1900 — the turn of the century!)

I still recall the ten-cent bag of candy that always came to us as a "surprise" gift when my father came home from his "district" meeting. It tasted like Peco-py (now purchaseable in m a n y grocery stores), very sweet, hard candy with peanuts and cocoanut mixed and hard to disengage from the teeth. We wished he would go to these meetings of the clergy more often.

I recall the sad farewell when we moved from Sioux City to Davenport, Iowa. Half of the large congregation (so it seemed to me) was down to the depot to see us off and I must have received a couple of dozen boxes of candy as a going-away present. There was a lot of crying and I remember the dingy railroad car vividly. Why? Soon after the train had started and we stopped waving I settled down to contemplate the uncertain future. I was tired of crying and weary. Suddenly I stood up in the coach and began to sway my legs in the aisle holding on to the armrests on each side. The train was humming along and I was swinging rhythmically. Then it slowed down and almost suddenly stopped. According to the laws of physics my body lurched forward and my chin caught the floor. I yelled in pain and there was blood on the carpet. My front teeth had penetrated my lower lip. And to this day I carry a lower lip with a swelling that cannot possibly be eradicated without some kind of surgery. I was a messy looking boy when I arrived in the new parish.

We moved to Davenport (I later learned) for three reasons. The church in Sioux City was a big order for my dad and the bilingual problem was just beginning to emerge. He spoke excellent English but he seemed to feel uneasy in the pulpit unless he spoke in Swedish. He read his English sermons but talked freely on his text if it was in Swedish. I slept on my mother's shoulder throughout the long discourse. (The large church building still stands on Fourth and Court Streets. Many a time I walked with him to his office in the basement of the church, practicing his type of walking which consisted of one foot pointed toward the street and the other toward the houses along the way. I do not know the term for this type of walking except that it was the opposite of pigeon-toed. My mother detected this new accomplishment on my part and hastily put an end to it by a few positive commands.) A smaller church would give him more time to the preparation for the new day. The second reason was his health. He had had a hard life, coming to this country as a young immigrant on his own. His education at "Örebro" in Sweden was of the best for college preparation. (We visited Örebro in Nerike and were quite impressed by the stature of the university.) He had worked in his homeland as a young apprentice at hard labor in a small smelting works (we saw the remains of this place on our Scandinavian tour) and then in South Chicago at the steel mills which offered meager financial prospects. It all had hurt his heart physically and his spirit. He wanted to become a Lutheran minister in the land of opportunity. He registered as a student at Augustana College, graduated with a bachelor's degree and then on to seminary, supporting himself as best he could. His first parish in New Britain, Connecticut was difficult. It was there he set up his home and married and the years of hardships had worn him down. And the third reason, he had already become a minister of national stature since he somehow had gained the reputation of being a good financier. At the small parish in Davenport he could give more time to his position as national treasurer of the Lutheran Minister's Pension Fund (Augustana Synod) and a central place for the national board to meet. Davenport is across the river from Rock Island, Illinois and Augustana College at Rock Island was a central meeting place for the American Lutheran clergy of the synod in that day.

It was at Davenport where I finished my gradeschool training. In that day there were nine grades, the ninth consisting of a course in beginning German (Davenport then being a German city) and a course in ancient mythology in which we had to learn the names of the gods and goddesses of both Greece and Rome, starting out with Zeus, Jupiter, Hera, Juno — and for years I could identify these gods and goddesses by their specific professions. (I will admit this helped me no end in my later reading.) In my first year at Davenport my father bought me a wagon. It was very expensive. I recall it cost $4.00. I felt sorry that he had spent so much money. I rode that thing down and up the East 6th Street sidewalk for miles and miles — back and forth. And to this day, this wagon is in my possession at our summer place, intact and ready to go.

I recall the frugality of our home. One instance: A circus had come to town and I spent the whole of Saturday morning listening to a barker coax customers to step up and see Hugo the Alligator Boy, the only one in captivity. It cost ten cents! I walked the long distance home for lunch and pleaded for a dime from my parents to see the monster. It was debated at the table. Both my father and mother decided that this was of no necessary part to my education (I had argued that it was) and, accordingly, vetoed my plea. I spent the whole afternoon watching people who looked at Hugo. No one felt philanthropic toward me. And to this day I have, regretfully, to confess that I have never seen Hugo! The Ferm estate had a plus ten cents with interest to its credit and a disappointed boy.

One of the tragic experiences which I keenly remember is the night I had a nightmare spell and my father came in to soothe me. He always seemed to be able to help. When he left my room he took a wrong turn in the hallway and instead of stepping into his bedroom he stepped into the front stairway. I can still hear the thump, thump, thump as his body went pell-mell into the open darkness. It cost him a broken shoulder from which he suffered to the end of his life. I heard no whimper out of him but I recall the long convalescence: arm in a sling.

My parents encouraged me to join the German boy's club *Verein* and each week I would trot from home to the downtown gynmasium to take exercises in jumping on and off and over the padded horses, drill with Indian clubs and dumbbells and jump hurdles. This was the extent of my academic athletics except for high school later when I wore a white shirt with the VF initials sown on it and raced my classmates in some kind of contest that was approved by athletic sponsors.

Ninth grade gave us a chance to excel in our studies. I, on special occasions, proudly wore one of the silver medals given out by the high school. Inscribed with my name, it said something nice about achievement in studies, deportment and initiative.

During the summers I was taken to Chicago's South 22nd Place near Wentworth Ave. This was a kind of Appalachia without tenants complaining to anyone. My widowed Aunt Lou lived in an exceedingly modest house with no backyard. I learned to follow the penny ice-cream cone man and his pushcart and played with the kids of the neighborhood. I was parked there for at least two weeks while my parents went on some kind of vacation and tour. I saw my first movie in a nickelodeon and I recall how I laughed seeing a clown shaking his head back and forth with tongue out like the pendulum of a clock and later I saw there my first Charlie Chaplin movie. (It was a sin among some of my people to go to movies but my aunt was a Roman Catholic and she didn't bother too much about the sins her church pointed out since each Friday she was squared away in confession.) Each afternoon she would take her little tin pail and go to the back of a saloon and come home with a generous supply of fresh lukewarm beer. I tasted it with her urging and decided it tasted like something is

supposed to taste when you grow up! South 22nd
Street and South 22nd Place are, of course, still there
and no doubt under some kind of Federal assistance
since it is now Appalachia-gone-mad. The far Eastern
people have moved in among the Irish Catholics and
America here has melted the pot. I liked my Aunt
Lou for she was a human being personified and nothing
but joy both to herself and others. She had come over
along with my mother's kin as an immigrant and instead
of going on to Iowa and the farm country, preferred to
throw in her lot with the city. She married an Irish
Roman Catholic and joined the clan. She was the
merry sinner among the relatives. Her therapy was
sought by everyone since she had no theory but only
a kind of life which was contagious. Even I as a kid
felt better after two weeks of joy in her home.

Speaking of Puritanical notions. Although a minister's son was not supposed to go to shows, my mother
gave me a quarter on occasion to see the show at the
Palace in Davenport on Saturday matinees. I recall how
my "conscience" bothered me. I would run across
the street hoping that no parishioner would recognize
me. I chose a seat in the back of the gallery and slid
down when the lights were turned on. I dreaded the
intermission with the bright lights. What if there
should be a fire? Imagine the newspaper headlines:
"Minister's Son Perishes in Theater Fire." I was uneasy and even glad when the show was over. I chose
the fire escape for my exit and disappeared in the alley —
my conscience quieted. To this day I am uncomfortable
in a theater and look both ways as I enter and despise
the lights turned on!

Davenport looks out on the Mississippi River. Between the two states of Iowa and Illinois lies an island which the government has taken for itself to engage in some more or less secret work, called an arsenal. Over the length of this island is a bicycle path reserved for bicyclers only. It is paved as it seemed to me with some kind of semi-soft preparation — in that day. I used to ride my bicycle over it, crossing over on the large bridge. I was old enough for such daring trips and to ride through the woods on the private and curved paths was an exciting adventure.

I do not recall how I got on to the business of raising pigeons but I did have a special coop made for them attached to the house and went into the business of selling squabs to affluent people who ordered from me. My mother always helped to make the wares look like food, seeing to it that they were clean and devoid of feathers. Pigeons are notoriously dirty and I had the never-ending job of cleaning their nests and everything adjacent to them. I still can hear the "paternal" pigeon coo and it got to sound like music.

One of the big adventures of mine was the Saturday walks with some boys' organization (not the Boy Scouts). The aim was to go the whole length of a small river which began somewhere and emptied into the Mississippi. We walked so many miles each week and the next weekend we began the walk where we had left off the week earlier — and so on until the whole river had been followed through. I recall I was the only one who saw the whole course of it. But I have now no idea what the name is of this "creek." Perhaps it did something to keep me fit.

We moved to Knoxville, Illinois, to a small parish.
I do recall that my father was failing in health but had
no idea that it would be only a few months before he
would be suffering a heart seizure which occurred at the
large parsonage in that village. The Reverend Olof
Wilhelm Ferm died in 1911 at 58 years of age and I have
always taken pride in being one of his sons. His books
were awarded to me by my mother and I found out later (when I could appreciate it) that his reading was of
the heavy type: philosophy, theology, dogmatics, many
of the volumes in Swedish.

His funeral was a kind of state funeral with many
dignitaries of the synod present, both at Knoxville and
Davenport. My brother was then a dental student at
Northwestern University in Chicago and he came home
from his studies. The long cortege followed his body
to the Oakdale cemetery in Davenport where he, my
mother (who died many years later) and my sister are
buried.

Funerals were at that time always conducted with
pomp and circumstance. I recall many trips I had in such
corteges while we lived in Sioux City. I sat with my dad
in the second car immediately following the horse-driven
hearse. It was always to me an interesting afternoon and
I enjoyed it. A privileged first "hack" seat in a long
parade! The large bell in the steeple of the Augustana
Church would toll mournfully spelling out the number
of years of the deceased. I would count the beats of the
hammers against the iron, a sound which could be heard
far and wide in the city. There were such things as
"wakes." The deceased was always honored by relatives
and close friends, keeping watch throughout the night

while awaiting burial. And the flowers were always profuse. (I still associate the smell of roses with burials.) I am pleased with my decision when I wrote an account of the history of the Augustana Lutheran Church in America—the section on the Swedish Lutherans—to include a brief account of my father and to have entered his portrait, a fine-looking gentleman—in my *Pictorial History of Protestantism.*

Speaking of horse-drawn funeral corteges reminds me of my first automobile ride which occurred in Sioux City, Iowa. The girl (I recall her name: Grace Hedenbergh) who picked me up for a ride was the daughter of the wholesale grocery man in the city, a man of some financial stature, a member of our church and a close friend of our family. There were no paved highways. I recall how her hair blew in the breeze while we were hurled through space at twenty miles an hour. It was my first taste of "class." I survived the trip and bragged about it to my friends who had never ridden in such a vehicle. (The date I do not recall but it was before 1910.)

My father was not stingy. He was frugal. He knew the value of earned money. Evidently he knew that on his very modest salary-plus-parsonage he could never get ahead financially in life unless he did something a-bout it early. His solution? He asked that instead of a manse he be given a salary raise commensurate with the cost of rental. In this way he saw that he could create for himself and his family an estate. I do not know what the terms were with this church but I do know that he bought a rather substantial house on a corner lot with an added cottage next to it (Sioux City). He moved into the large house and rented the cottage. This was the beginning of his real estate endeavors on a modest scale. When he left Sioux City to go to his next charge there was a parsonage to move into. With a mortgage still on his Iowa property, he sought and found a piece of property in Chicago; an apartment building for four families. He gained in the transaction sufficiently to be able to carry a new mortgage on the metropolitan property. Evidently, he envisaged the day of his retirement as a return to the Chicago area. Meanwhile, his rentals carried him forward in reducing the mortgage as the years passed. An agent collected the rents and dispersed the expenses. On his death, my mother moved into one of the six-room apartments they "owned" on Chicago's north side and continued to collect rental from the other three tenants. This gave her a home, a place to go with her belongings, furniture and child.

He had great trust and belief in life insurance. This paid off after his death. Although she was pressured somewhat to invest the money in stocks, my mother wisely decided to use the insurance to pay off the Chicago mortgage. Meanwhile, property values increased and my mother had a home.

We lived frugally since it was a tight squeeze to keep apartment intake in balance with apartment expenses. I recall that a few winters we heated only one end of the "flat" during cold weather; my mother herself tending a coal furnace two and a half flights down to the basement. I banked it at night on occasion and under her usual direction. She kept close account of our credits and debits and she watched carefully lest a foolish expenditure would bring chaos. I was then in high school and remember the lunches I carried: fish sandwiches (What could be worse than two slices of bread with a dead fish in between?). To this day I am not a sandwich man. I walked thirteen blocks to Lake View High School and the same in return five days a week. (Would students and parents today pressure for a car or a bus?) All this led to the inevitable: I must find a summer job to help toward clothing and also perhaps college.

Many years ago my mother (who turned out to be a first-class business woman on her own) was a lady nurse (not licensed) to the Sprague family in Chicago which brought her into affluent society. Each summer the Spragues went to Martha's Vineyard on the east coast and for a number of summers my mother (before she was married) accompanied them as guardian of their children. She spoke with delight of this family whose name was then well known as one of the major grocery distributors in the city of Chicago. So . . . when the day came that I needed a job my mother contacted the Spragues (how, I do not know, but indirectly) and I was given a menial job at the Sprague-Warner Wholesale House located west of the downtown area.

Thus began my earnings: $8.00 per week and the inevitable fish sandwich.

Thinking back on these summer jobs during high school, I recall two others. One was an appointment to be a statement clerk and licker of stamps at one of the downtown Chicago banks. This, of course, was the day before stamp machines and computers. We had to balance at the end of the month or "stay after school." More than one month's end we "stayed after school" checking and rechecking. The other summer assignment was an appointment at the new YMCA (skyscraper) Hotel on South Wabash Avenue. I was among the first appointees when it opened up—a hotel with 1800 rooms. I began as a baggage smasher (checking guests' baggage) in the basement. Then I got to run the elevator which was kind of a promotion. Then: a key clerk. This latter job I held until I became very certain that I wanted to go to college and move out of this monotony!

When I took my first piano lesson I do not recall. I knew that when we were living in Davenport I had come far enough to do simple piano duets (taken from the *Etude*) with the church organist on dull Sunday afternoons. At least I could umpa umpa on changing bass chords. Moreover, I can remember one of the first lessons: sitting at the dining room table with the teacher giving me an introduction to the so-called "Virgil method." This consisted of raising the fingers alternatingly and keeping the wrist steady and parallel with the table (never turned) with a penny on the wrist to assure the correct position. Then count: one, two, three. Then all the fingers of both hands. My first lessons consisted of sitting at the dining room table and then performing before the teacher as "his lesson." I finally told my mother that I wanted to go to the piano to make music, that I no longer cared for this kind of thing. To my surprise my mother agreed! Something was said to the teacher after my complaint and then the lessons continued at the piano. I still don't know what was accomplished and I often wondered what one did with an advanced course in the "Virgil method." Did one eventually get to a piano?

Practicing scales was tiring (as for all normal kids).

And later — in the fulness of time — I was assigned melodic pieces and even came as far as those dreadful sonatas which sounded like the old Singer sewing machine — up and down and cross over without rhyme or reason. I still feel a bit of sicknes when I think of that rather thick yellow Sonata book which lay on the top of the piano. These lessons went on with teacher succeeding teacher (most of whom have left my memory-cellar).

Somehow I perked up with my interest in piano. What perked me (I believe) was the current ragtime rage and the new love ballads which were coming out at ten cents per copy. I spent noon hours at the music departments of The Fair and the Boston Store — two of the well-known department stores in downtown Chicago. I just loved to watch and to hear the girls demonstrate the new songs to hopeful mothers of darlings and the "new" music charmed me. I know my lunch was sparse and the hour went by in a flash. I recall how mothers would return with the music they had purchased and complain that when their darling played the notes appearing on the sheets, the songs didn't sound at all like the way the demonstrator had demonstrated. This gave me the cue. Of course the little darlings didn't get the music the demonstrators got out of the sheets (and this included the present darling who tried too to emulate the demonstrators). My mother, of course, paid no attention to my frustration and certainly did not complain. Her role was to see to it that I spent time practicing, practicing, so many minutes each day except Sundays.

Then, I noticed one of the major tricks of the trade!

No one ever told me. I just saw these gals perform. They just didn't follow the sparse notes on the sheet. They improvised! How? Well, each one did it in her own peculiar style. One basic trick was to roll the left hand (the bass) into what in music harmony (I later learned) is called a "tenth." Instead of an octave on the bass clef, make it the tenth (instead of the eighth). This cannot be done by stretching: one holds the pedal down and then roll with the left hand. When it came to the treble clef, use the octaves and fill in with the keys that go with the major key. (One does this on a guitar if one has some musical sense: one uses the fingering for a ninth if the music calls for a seventh (in certain situations) and one uses diminished chords (the kind that make you cry) when possible and appropriate and end a song with a sixth instead of a major — and all that. (Simple tricks!)

I do not pose as an authority. Heaven forgive such a thought. I just learned to play jazz music by watching what was going on "magically" at the music demonstratrations in Chicago's department stores. Soon I was doing some of them and the music took on a richness which the score does not suggest. (I learned later from courses in music harmony how performance rests upon established theory.)

To this day I love to toy with a piano. I still buy melodic ballads and pay little attention to the silly lyrics. If there is a good tune available I am eager to include it in my dilly-daddling at the keys. I go over the music as it is printed a few times to get the backbone of it and the rhythm. And that's about all. If it is in G (or any other key) you go one path with your augmenteds, sevenths, blue notes, minors, rolls, and what not. And with practice you have it made. Soon you are improvising — and even making your own melodies.

When I hit college I had this going for me. Most college student pianoplayers read music much as one reads the music from a hymnbook or folk-song. I would take any of that stuff and give it a swing which amazed most of my contemporaries (even myself) and I probably shocked the "musically cultured." I was invited out to more than the average number of parties and spent a good part of the time at the piano (if it was in tune). If pianos are out of tune I shun them as witches. And I curse in a polite way the fathers and mothers who ask their darlings to try to learn to play an instrument that is either out of tune or cheap (it would be easy to name such pianos made with beautiful mahogany or walnut finish which I would consign to the city dump). I like a brilliant piano. I began with the family piano "McPhail" (now in my summer cabin) and then went on to other levels. I never reached a Mason and Hamlin nor a Steinway nor a Baldwin but finally settled for a Chickering which is a B (minus or plus depending on good luck). I expect a better piano in heaven (if I make it there!).

To this day I find relaxation in tickling the ivories as an amateur. I took more private lessons at college but they seemed to cramp my style; besides, I had no ambition to become a classical performer. Classical music should be performed by professionals otherwise it sounds like coming from a place lower than purgatory.

Lake View High was my high school in (north side) Chicago. From it I graduated in 1913. My memory of this portion of my formal education is not too generous with events to recall: the long walks to and fro; frequent visits to the swimming beach at Lake Michigan's northshore (then unpolluted) at Foster Avenue where the Edgewater Beach Hotel used to stand. My only extracurricular activity besides amateurish "track" was a short course in Swedish. My instructor noted that already I had a working vocabulary (hearing it around the house especially when company came and having been confirmed in Swedish, learning Luther's Little Catechism by heart and part of the Large Catechism in Swedish) although I spoke the language haltingly. A club was organized and I was elected to my first office — president. I was a rather shy person and had (for some reason or other) a dread to make speeches.

At Lake View High there was an English teacher who scared the daylights out of me. I can still see her: fat in the usual as well as the unusual places, loud-mouthed, eyeglasses which fit loosely over her awkward nose and held by pinchers of some sort, wabbling when she became excited; her eyes so non-parallel that I could never figure out upon whom she focused her attention. When she called on me to recite (her method) I usually went blank. I went home early one day and told my mother I was quitting school. She turned me on my heels and I went back. I had no counselling, no conferences, no Spock-book mother to consult on matters dealing with psychosis, no — nothing. I sweated it out and came to hate Chaucer, Shakespeare,

Wordsworth, Dickens and the rest of the "classical" writers. This same teacher threatened to flunk me because I did not seem to respond and what was worse: I was a senior. I still think something wonderful happened to her the night she made out our grades: she gave me a "D". (Maybe she found a boy friend.)

To this day, I feel sorry for college students who have a big dose of self-consciousness when they are called upon to speak. If the class is large this, of course, increases the embarrassment. If my class is organized in such a way that students must appear up front with some sort of oral report, I immediately invite anyone suffering from the same malady which I suffered for years to let me know confidentially after class. I tell them they will hand in a written report instead of an oral and their confidence will be respected and their grade not suffer. To make it easier, I tell them how self-conscious I was in my earlier days and how I came to lick it. There are almost always one or two students who respond to this invitation. (My remedy for overcoming it [which I tell such students] goes something like this: never say before you come into a lecture room: "Today I'll speak up." Never! This increases tension. However, if some day you feel as if you would like to say something in class or at any public meeting, just blurt out. To raise your hand is to give enough pause to invite the psychosis. By blurting out enough times wears the thing down.) I suppose many people who know me wonder why I sometimes appear rude or unorthodox in the manner of oral expression. They do not know my problem and my therapy. And I don't care. I recall that Martin Luther once commented on his own nervousness at the Diet of Worms: that he licked his own self-consciousness in speaking before priests, bishops, archbishops, princes and what not, by taking time to smell a rose at the rostrum (or pulpit) and then saying to himself: You bunch of blockheads (his own term) I'll tell *you* something. I don't know about Luther's therapy but I can say that my remedy works and many students have expressed their appreciation of the sympathy of a once-fellow-traveler in similar suffering.

COLLEGE AND SEMINARY DAYS

And so off to college. It was but natural for me to head for Rock Island, Illinois where was located the alma mater of my dad and to a church college of our own denomination. I did not even consider any other possibility. Moreover, the dome of Old Main I had seen easily from our home in Davenport — a skyline marker of the area. I never asked about tuition, scholarship or even took any entrance tests. I am sure I would have flunked any such tests. (Happily, in those days there were no competitive scholarships nor College Entrance Board examinations.) I just got on the Rock Island Railroad train (main line from Chicage to Denver) and got off at the depot not far from the campus and went to the proper port of campus entry. I lived off campus (at an instructor's home) on the strong suggestion of my mother who felt I needed continued sheltered protection of someone already connected with the college.

My monthly allowance was thirty dollars (which was generous on the part of my mother whose own finances as a widow were very limited). I somehow got along on this sum, beginning a system of budgeting which system (with many revisions) I have continued to this day. At that time each and every nickel had to be accounted for to myself so that at the end of the month I could attain balance. No student had a car.

We walked or took the streetcar which was then a nickel a ride with transfer privileges. We had at that time no dues to pay to any organization that I can recall. The first surprise that met me when registering was the suggestion that I should try to do college in three rather than four years. (With nine grades in Davenport grade school this would give me a year to catch up — although my chronological age didn't need such catching up.) So I registered by taking one or two more courses.. And so I did graduate in three years (Class of 1916) and without any fanfare of special study.

We were not grade-conscious in those days. I knew I was doing acceptably well and that was that. There were no special dangling tuition scholarships to tempt one to excellence. As a minister's son I had one already going for me — clergy discount! My mother must have paid the tuition since I do not recall worrying over it. There really were some "green" students in those days. One from Galva, Illinois on arriving at the railway station immediately called up the president of the college and said, "Ay am here now." (He expected the president to meet him. A true story.) He is the same fellow who in the college library was seen with his head at an appropriate slant standing (arms folded behind him) reading the newspaper on the rack. Someone told him he could take it off the rack and sit down at the desk and read it comfortably. When grades came out he went around flashing his "U" grade. He thought it meant "Utmärkt" (Swedish for wonderful, excellent) when it sadly meant "Unsatisfactory".

One fellow who went all the way through with my

class had an odor which I have never smelled in duplicate form anywhere in all my life, here or abroad. It was not a stink but somewhere between that and polluted vinegar. Moreover it changed from week to week but never got on the side of either neutrality nor pleasantness. Nobody sat near him if one could help it. There were no deans of men nor counselors in those days to have a conference about it. He just went on smelling infamously. One theory was that he didn't change socks from semester to semester. And there were other theories. No one was Christian enough to tell the guy, including myself. Another peculiar specimen was seen in the shower one day naked as a Gentile. For years he had not seen fit to wash his total body. Had he been an Orthodox Jew he would have been more hygenic and perhaps more civilized. But there he was — and we saw to it that we made our exit when he came in. (I hate to report this but it is a true story.)

I suppose we all have our idiosyncracies. One was forced on me. I came to college with a suitcase so old that it no longer had square corners. It was approaching the senility of bulges. When the streetcar stopped it would suddenly "take off" down the aisle and I would have to run to recover it. People laughed and so did I. But I had no substitute and lived with it learning the trick of control by either sitting on it or putting some block underneath it. (Really, this was not my idiosyncracy. It was the suitcase's!)

I had not been on the campus very long when someone who knew my family in Iowa came to see me and asked me to join the college band. (Maybe he had heard

that I was an amateur jazz piano player.) At any rate,
before I could say no or perhaps yes or tell him the
truth that I had never played a band instrument in my
life, I was at band practice with a short cornet in hand.
The professor of physics was band director and he
looked over at the new "member" and gave me the
signal to tune up. I blew into that d—— (the word
is dowlderdash) thing with all my might and nothing
came but returned spit. The professor didn't crack a
smile but just turned away and ignored me. I went
to my room and my Iowa "friend" (who had found
the instrument laying on the floor in the band room)
came over and taught me my first lesson: squeezing
the lips tightly and letting the pressured air come out
as if my mouth had constipation and then showed me
the fingering with only three buttons to push down. It
was a large order for a beginner and I nearly had lip-
paralysis (which is no good for a trumpeter) that night.
It took weeks and weeks to do the C major scale and I
attended weekly band practices with the professor
still ignoring me. The sheet music given to me was
marked "fourth cornet" (that is fourth or lowest from
solo cornet — lowest of the lows). The cornet looked
like a piece of circular plumbing under the kitchen
sink, only it had a flash of brightness when one shined
it with a shoeshining rag. The cork cups leaked spit
and I continually had to keep it drained dry during my
frequent rest periods.

But weeks followed into months. On the positive
side I could read music (not with flash but with study)
and I knew what sharps and flats were — two-four
time and waltz time and all that and I was not embar-

rassed if I made a mistake when everyone else was
playing. I knew that I could be a tragedy to the band
if I came in with an off-tempo toot. So . . . I watched
the tempo cautiously and avoided being a nuisance to
the organization. I held on and on until one day the
conductor gave me the signal to tune up and I proudly
answered by the proper amount of spit and mouth-
tension.

I write about this at length since band and orchestra
were pretty much a part of my college and seminary
life. Little did I realize as a Freshman my destiny as an
amateur in extra curricular activity. As semesters piled
up on semesters I found my participation in this business increasing. We had a small dance orchestra that
played for small money and really for fun. It got us
into a new kind of environment quite different from
our own hothouse-plant existence. I was promoted to
first chair among the trumpeteers and now had come to
own my own trumpet: a Holton with a gold-plated
inner bell and one of full trumpet stature. It looked like
one and blew like one. I was extremely proud and I took
loving care of it. It was purchased in Chicago directly
from the factory and is still in my possession.

We had quite a concert band going. The peak was
reached just before World War 1 and we were also
in fine uniforms. Our director was excellent and one
who demanded discipline. Then the inevitable happened — off to war — everyone. It was somehow made
possible for the band members to enlist as a group (at
least this was the "deal"). So one by one the members
signed up. The promise of playing band music through

the war sounded especially as a gift of the gods. I was one of the few who did not enlist.

In that day anyone who was in the draft age who did not enlist was called a "slacker." It was a term of the most despicable reproach. For me it was a difficult decision. I suffered no end of anguish when most of the band members marched down Seventh Avenue and then on to the station to go off to war. It was a parade of utter enthusiasm and patriotism. I tried to hide my shame in solitude and utter dejection. There was no one who pressed me either way. I just had the feeling that I would have to suffer ignominy and learn to live with it — just as one had to do with an incurable disease.

The fact of the matter is that I was already classified as a pre-ministerial student which was legal and above-board. Furthermore, I had a physical defect which would have classified me far from the top eligible draftee. (I had never overcome the effects of too strong medicine given me by a physician in my earlier days when there were no antibiotics. I have written about this condition earlier in this book.) It was either 4F (army flunk) or ministry. I had made a decision before there was any talk of a band marching off to war — and possessed that classification.

What really happened was that this band was disbanded almost immediately at a boot camp somewhere in Illinois and the members scattered to the winds. Some arrived back home as 4F's or for some other reason. Some of the members found themselves in seminary halls with me and I never asked any of them the history of their strange odyssey.

Meanwhile, the SATC moved in on the campus. This was the Student's Army Training Corps (I believe this was the title). And in moved an army lieutenant in full charge. Our dormitory was taken over and there were the inevitable drills on campus and students even marching to the library. Then came the quirk of fortune. The lieutenant wanted a band. The lieutenant was a rough sort of guy who was not in the habit of giving orders and taking No from anyone. The president of the college, Gustave Andreen, called me to his office and told me that he thought I should take over the band, reorganize it and that I would be put on salary of $100 per month. This was hard to turn down — even though I knew I was not qualified for the job.

One of the first things I did was to have all the instruments belonging to the college (stored away in the men's old shower room) shipped to Lyon and Healy's in Chicago to be changed over to the new pitch which had become standard among bands. I was authorized to spend this money. Also, I wanted to have the kinks taken out of many of the instruments. And so, with months passing, the thing was reorganized. With SATC on campus and a lieutenant desiring a band I had it made with reference to SATC band students. He ordered them to practice and I could even take attendance. To supplement with other needed players was more difficult for they were scarce (war situation). We managed quite well. The summer before I had watched the band director in Long Beach, California in concert performance and thought now that what he did I should try to do. So without batting an eye I played solo trumpet and led the organization without a baton — for the simple reason that we were short of manpower. We played on assignments of the lieutenant, playing very much like amateurs. Our unprofessionalism was overlooked by most everyone since marching band music is, for the most part, martial and noisy and needed not the delicacies of a symphonic band. I can still feel the thrill of turning my face and trumpet to the large gymnasium hall audience and playing the melodic lead while the members filled in background music. To me it was a moment of achievement in the light of my total inexperience only a few years back. I was emulating the professionals but without portfolio.

Then the crash of excitement came. It was November 11th, 1918. The day of the surrender. The lieutenant sent his lackey to my dormitory room and ordered me to get the band out hastily, that we were to celebrate with a parade on the streets of Rock Island. In the joy of the occasion there was no urge to demur; I sent word for the non-military boys and the lieutenant ordered his boys to be ready at a given time. So, the march. It was quite a walk from the campus to downtown Rock Island and return. When it was over I had blown myself out physically and spiritually. I was dead tired and sat almost in a coma in my room. About 6:30 p.m. there was a rap on the door. One of the SATC boys had come to tell me that he heard we were to march again that same night, lieutenant's orders. I assured him this would be quite impossible since everyone was dog-tired. Then he broke into tears — a nervous wreck not only from his own marching that day but in deadly fear of the lieutenant. I had never seen a college boy cry before and it really moved me. (This same boy soon after suffered an untimely death by gunshot, having been mistakenly taken for a night prowler of which he was quite innocent.)

The lieutenant's lackey came just before seven o'-clock. He told me the orders. I was to take the band on a second march to downtown Rock Island as "they" were to bury the Kaiser. A funeral dirge all the way. I told the lackey to tell the lieutenant I was physically dead from the ordeal of the afternoon and that I would not go. The message was delivered and the return order was sent me. (I knew I was not vulnerable since the lieutenant had no command over me.) I returned the same negative answer and went to bed.

That night the band was ordered out by the lieutenant minus a leader and minus a few non-military players. And the march was on and the funeral ceremonies celebrated in downtown Rock Island.

On the following Monday I came to the usual practice hour to find not a single SATC student there. I enquired, "How come?" And the reply: "The lieutenant had ordered his boys to the library for study period." Then I knew that the lieutenant was out to get me. I had lost my band, the great majority, and I told the few who were free to come to practice that this looked like the end and that they should not worry.

I had my resignation written the next day, directed to the president of the college. Before I could deliver it in person there was a knock on the door and opening it, there stood President Gustave Andreen! I was ready to hand him my written statement when he said in his usual excited way, "No, No, No. You must stay on. No, You must stay on. The war is over and we will soon be back to normal." He did not sit down nor stay. He had checkmated my next move and there was only one thing for me to do: to obey *my* boss and wait.

I was kept on salary and rehired — even though I was a student in the theological seminary (on the same campus). Furthermore, I was appointed a member of the college faculty with the title of "instructor in cornet."

And I actually had students taking trumpet lessons from me — unpredictable, indeed! A seminary faculty member got on the streetcar one Sunday morning to find me in the car loaded with band members and instruments. He frowned and asked where I was going on this Sabbath morning? I looked him in the eyes and said that we were on our way to Moline to have a band picture taken. "On Sunday?" he asked. "Yes, it was the only time we could get together," I replied. (I myself think he was jealous rather than religiously disturbed. For it was this seminary professor — Södergren by name — who was seen to frequent a certain saloon north of the campus for his intermittent nocturnal and pleasant rendevous with beer!) He did not frighten me although I was certain he had intentions.

During my college days seminarians were regarded (in terms of our contemporary language) as "kooks." On Sunday mornings some of them came to breakfast carrying Bibles and clothed in Prince Albert coats. (Our standard diet at breakfast in the dormitory was one monotonous breakfast-food still found on family tables called "Cornflakes" which we called "Elephant

Dandruff.") Considering the ministry myself, I wondered then how in the world I could get myself to join
any seminary class. (The seminary was on campus and
used the same buildings and dormitories as did college
students.) As a group they were insipid and delicates-
sen. Some who came from Sweden expected their
shoes to be shined by someone and set their shoes outside their door at night thinking perhaps that a mere
college student would polish them. Some owned parlor organs and when we could get away with it, we
would stuff their organs with whatever was available
and then screw the back on again. This didn't seem
to help. There was nothing in the world (I thought)
more melancholic and sickly than a seminarian playing and voicing hymns to the accompaniment of a
self-pedalled organ.

I was elected to membership in the Wennerberg
Chorus which was an "elite" (male) group of singers
who made tours each spring and wore tuxedos. Some of
the members were pre-seminarians who already got their
religious message from somewhere to the effect that
they were no longer human beings. They were jolly
for the most part but hard to live with. I remember
one time being reprimanded by one of them for
saying "gosh" as it sounded as if I were saying "God."
Such a word was swearing and a form of desecration.
(I might have substituted "Bowlderdash" as students
did on the Wooster College stage when the script called
for "damn.") To get the best "call" (salary, large city
church and perquisites) was the height of seminary
achievement in those days (except for missionaries
whose prospect promised free world travel and ser-

vants). Of course, not all pre-seminarians and theological students were Christian villains but, on the whole, Seminary was regarded on the campus as a peculiar place set apart and somehow peculiarly sanctified. Speaking of the Wennerberg Chorus, this membership gave me the first chance to see the world including the east coast and even to sing at the Capitol (my first visit to Washington). The politics of the organization got so bad in matters of election of membership I finally sickened of it and resigned my membership after three or four years.

Hazing was a part of the student ritual at college. In my day the Sophomores would try to prevent Freshmen from painting their class numerals on the high chimney stack and Freshmen were supposed to fight to the finish with fists and wrestling if their class was thwarted in any attempt. The annual Senior class banquet was a secret matter and the idea was for the Juniors to kidnap the Senior class officers, especially the class president, and hold them captive overnight thus preventing their presence at *the* banquet of the year. All fall semester there was tension, whisperings, alarms. A Junior would even be called out of class to join a company of bandits bent on capturing some Senior class officer planning his early escape. This was a tradition handed down to successive classes and we must keep it. I recall in our Senior year we had the secret word that our banquet was to be held at the Black Hawk Hotel in Davenport across the river. How I ever got there I do not recall. My partner was told to go by herself on her own and "pray" that I would somehow not be captured. I was not a potential grand prize for the Juniors to capture and hold incommunicable for the night. I had a much lesser office, such as secretary or treasurer (I don't remember which one). But I know I disappeared on early Friday and hid somewhere in Davenport for the day and arrived safely at the hotel. I was on the program to make a speech. My girl friend was there looking lovely (she is the girl I married and still my girl friend). We were then a little on the "romantic shy" level and I suppose we were trying slyly to impress each other. When I rose in my chair at the table to give my speech, the zipper on my trousers caught in something and I heard the zip. I still compliment myself as one who at *one* occasion (at least) in his life had a built-in emergency complex: to adjust automatically to a new situation of frustration. Automatically and without any philosophical thinking, I grabbed the large napkin at my place on the table and held it with my left hand throughout the speech and only hoping I would not be so carried away with my home-grown oratory to start waving both arms. This is about all I remember from that important occasion — except the experience which was then common in the new fashion of Zips of "how do you get a zip to zip when it no longer seems to wish to zip." But this was a matter to learn later on in life as one gets older and has more zip experience!

We were called upon as college students to supplement our income in any respectable way. The common calling for such work and income (if successful) was to sell Bibles and-or aluminum (kitchen kettles, pans and the like — aluminum was then "the thing").

Concordance Bibles offered summer financial potent-
ials for college students as everyone must have God's
Word cross-indexed. Not being much of a salesman
I stayed away from that. But I do recall working on
Saturdays for the Rock Island Gas Company.

I was under contract to sell gas heaters (moveable
by some kind of flexible hose). I sold only one. And
may St. Peter help me through purgatory for this
sinful act! The lady was interested in a heater for her
upstairs bedroom and how would she connect it with
the gas? I asked to see her basement. She led me down
the stairs. And then I looked. I couldn't tell a water
pipe from a gas pipe — never having had a course in
this subject. So I asked her where the front stairs were
relative to where we were standing in the basement.
Then she pointed to a spot. There I saw a pipe! "Why,"
I said, "it would be simple: drill a hole in the floor at
this spot, connect the hose with the pipe (already
there!) and run the flexible hose up through the floor
and along the bannister and up to the bedroom."

I could hardly believe my eyes when she signed
the contract which I later turned in and received a
30% commission. All my long life I have thought of
this poor woman — how she made out and what her
husband said when he came home. Did he beat her? Did
the family die of asphyxiation? Was the cellar flooded
with water? What did she say to the company when
she madly consulted them about the phoney salesman
or was she a commited Christian believing all things and
hoping all things? Had I been a Catholic I would have
confessed some Fridays to more than one priest. And
whatever conscience still operates in me it operates at this

point. But I have no address and cannot write her or apologize or include her in my will.

Miss Pearce was our speech teacher. A little, prim thing with a smile like the moon at crescent, dipper up. She taught us to accentuate the vowels rather than the consonants when we spoke. So we practiced aaahs, ooohs, iiiss, yuusss, eeeeeesses and then supposed to take our turn up front of the class and read from our class text. My turn came eventually. When it came it ended the class session and my last course in elocution. I was reading aloud with great concentration, such as roosees aah reeeeeed and in the middle of whatever the passage the plaster from the ceiling came down knocking the book out of my hand. "Mr. Ferm, are you all right?" she exclaimed witnessing the horror scene. I picked the chunks off my torn book and turned toward her and showed her my still living physical organism. I still have this book in my library and if anyone doubts it the torn page is still there. (I learned later from another professor of speech — though I never took his course, heaven forbid! — that the new method is to emphasize consonants and not vowels. So today it is with a bang TTTT, DDDD, WWWW, KKKK [try it sometime — at least it's fun at some crazy party]. So theories change with further research!)

The one grand party I attended at college lasted all night through. (There were then no deans of men and women.) My roommate's girl lived in Geneseo, Illinois and she gave the party. About fifteen couples left on the train about 5 p.m. and rode a distance of about fifty miles to Geneseo and the Swanson home. We dined. We played games. We dined. We walked the snowy streets

— then back for more lunch. The party ended about eight o'clock the next morning when we returned to Rock Island by train. It was my first grand date with the girl I married who stayed with me beyond fifty years!

The valedictorian of our class was "Squeaky Benson" who with the highest grade-rank was predestined to to give the valedictory at commencement. There we Seniors sat on the platform in Old Main with the governor of the state, some state senators and candidates for honorary degrees. His (the valedictorian's) turn finally came. It was memorable. (He was an excellent student in Greek and I believe became a noted archaeologist. But he was not particularly strong on the social and platform side.) These were his words (without a record player so I cannot give them literally as my classmates will recall): "Farewell, Mr. President; Farewell, Honored Faculty; Farewell, Parents"; (some more oratorical Farewells) and, turning completely around on the platform and facing us, his highpitched voice got to its peak: "Farewell, Classmates — May we all meet in Heaven" — then dropping into a plaintive pianissimo he added hesitatingly: "At least I hope so." (These last five words are exact quotes — and I never forgot them!)

When I returned to the campus of alma mater as a seminarian in the fall of 1916, I was greeted by my fellow classmates with "So .... *you* are here!" I replied calmly "Just for this year." They were sincerely surprised since I had given no public declaration of my interest in the ministry. I had avoided campus prayer meetings and campus church fellowships (not services) as places not to be seen in public. I avoided seminarians as infectious people whose germs I did not want to catch. And what is more: I was uncertain that I should come back. But I did. And it happened again the second year: "So you came back," and I replied "For the year." The last round brought no further surprise comments since it looked now as if I had been "tagged" (their word was "had a calling").

The most eventful of my seminary memories were the summers spent in what they now call internship (a fancy word taken from the more professional medics). One summer in Calgary, Alberta, Canada and the other in San Pedro, California. Both were far enough from homebase not to disgrace the seminary! Both were assignments which called for preaching in Swedish! I couldn't handle the language too well so I took with me *"postillar"* (or canned and approved sermons in Swedish). The congregations did not know my plight until it was too late: there I was and they were stuck with me for three months.

I still shudder at the sign on the little downtown Swedish Lutheran Church in Calgary: *in Swedish* it said that Student Ferm will preach tomorrow at eleven. Believe me, I could read *that* and understand that I had bitten on too big a cow. But I prayed about it and Jehovah was kind to help me in the foreign language, although without proper accent. My "bishop" boss lived in Winnepeg eight-hundred miles away. He traveled as a home missionary on a railroad pass and enjoyed himself. I had never met him but heard that he was tough on seminary students. I was happy to learn that he lived so far away.

Meanwhile, I got along with the situation tolerably well except for Sundays. All the members naturally spoke English (some with accents) and I didn't need an interpreter to express my daily wants and views. My salary was $50.00 a month (with free room-rent). I did not collect until I returned to the States but I lived on loans.

I had heard of the famous "Banff" resort located where the eastern Rockies begin — about seventy miles from Calgary. I disappeared two days and took the passenger train to Banff. My suitcase was marked by me to be delivered to the Grand Hotel (Banff Springs Hotel) some five miles away. I handed it to the uniformed boy at the station. I had no money for hotel. I remembered then how generous Christians are supposed to be about hospitality. So I looked up the village church. It was marked "Methodist" — good enough "Christians" I thought. About 7 p.m. I tried the lock. (It was unchristian.) Then I used some tool and quietly forced the door. I spent the night on a church bench and said my own mass. Fortunately, I woke at the break of day, bummed a ride to the hotel and took a day's look around. When I got back to the station, I called the hotel and asked them to send my suitcase to the evening train which they did. I returned to homebase that night. One should never miss Banff — even if he has to go to church.

After seeing some of the Canadian Rockies I became restless. (After seeing Paree how can you go back to the farm?) So I planned another trip. Some of the church people suggested a way. Take a carload of cattle to Vancouver. You get free fare going and coming. So be it. I got permission from the church to be away one Sunday so off I went (after a little politicking at the Canadian Pacific headquarters). With a battered suitcase in hand, I boarded the top of my assigned freight car and was told to hang on until I was attached to the main train. I sat for hours on top of this thing, hearing the pigs squeak below me. My orders were signed, sealed, and delivered. By early evening my car was hooked on to the main freight train and I was called down to get into the caboose. So I had three days of caboose riding past the most magnificent scenery in North America at snail's pace, seeing ahead, behind, north and south in the cupola of the caboose. At night my car was switched to a side track for feeding and watering the fifty-nine head of hogs. I was afraid that I would get bitten so I hired a bare foot boy at the little station (another one at a later station) for a quarter to go in and dump the sacks of grain in the troughs. It worked! I soused the pigs with water from the powerful hose available in the yards. And off we went. (I recommend this manner of travel to anyone who wants to enjoy a vacation — and it is very cheap.) At Vancouver I got the papers properly signed and away I went. Packages given to me by friends to deliver to some relatives in Vancouver I stuck in some locker at the station. I asked St. Peter to plead for me when my name is called "up yonder." But then my poor conscience doesn't bother me: why should people be so naive as to ask a guy to look up their relatives when he is sneaking away for the briefest of vacations?

How I got to Tacoma, Washington, I do not remember. But for ten dollars paid in Tacoma, I got a bus ride

to Paradise Valley on Mt. Ranier (or is that feud still
on: Mt. Tacoma or something?) with a memorable
day tucked away in my memory. I had but a few days
to get back for the Sunday appointment in Calgary.
Everything had to click. But the click didn't quite click.
At the U.S. border I got into difficulty. What was a
person my age, male and "fit" doing: leaving the coun-
try-at-war? So it was nip and tuck. Conferences. My
registration card made everything legal—but it just
didn't look that way to border guards. I almost missed
my connections—and a job a thousand or so miles away.

The deal was that I was to ride third-class on a passenger train back from Vancouver to Calgary. I missed
one train but got the next. Sitting in a dumpy smoking
car was not too inviting, especially when passing
through (again) the scenic Canadian Rockies. So . . .
I bribed the Pullman car conductor (having learned
this trick from the story of Adam and Eve and from
their genes in my inners) and with the promise that
I would wash up and "act the part" and behave I could
be seated with the affluent in the open observation car
at the rear of the long train. So I had two days of this.
I hobnobbed with the "Vanderbilts" (so I thought)
and ate my meagre lunch up front with the third-class-
ers. I took pictures of the rich. They took mine. It was
a ride deluxe, blue-ribbon in anybody's book. Then
"they" met me at the railroad station in Calgary.
("They": some of the members of the church board.)
It was Saturday night 10 p.m. "How are my relatives?"
and all that. But I had no need to find a white lie.
Already they had told me that my "bishop" was here
and would be in the church on the morrow. So, my

answer was: I haven't got the time to talk. I am in trouble with the "bishop." Please understand. (They were Christians—more so than I.)

When I got to my rooming house, there sat the bishop. I greeted him "enthusiastically." And he spoke Swedish. And I answered in English. (After all Canada is either French or English!) I told him how glad I was that he had come; the people were anxious to see him, especially to hear him preach. But I got the ruler on my hand on that one. Said he in Swedish (which I translate almost verbatim): "I have come all the way from Winnepeg to hear the student preach." I knew this was final by the pitch and strength of his coarse voice. "If so," said I, "I must be excused since I must prepare." I softened the answer by saying to him, "I understand you have a fine singing voice and play your own accompaniment. Will you please sing a hymn solo at the morning service?" This pleased him. I tickled him where he was most ticklish!

Most of the night I sat up reading a Swedish "postilla" (sermons from Biblical texts). I practiced anything that might be *ad lib* (such as announcements). When morning came I was a dishrag spiritually, physically, emotionally. But I prayed to Jehovah to carry me through. The people came in larger numbers to see the show (I guess). The word had spread. Since I was half-conscious through most of the service my memory of the details are quite beyond recall. All I vividly remember I have already related.

The bishop sang a solo pumping the organ with his feet in decent rhythm. Period.

Sunday dinner at the house came. I dreaded it. I still

kept my English going—with everyone at the table (except the children) speaking in Swedish. When the heavy dessert was finished, I prayed that the familiar family album would not come out and that conversation would lag. Each moment threatened the next. I became so high pitched that I suddenly said (and it was some "inner voice," since I was surprised myself), "Will Pastor Bergstrand (his name) come up to my room? I want to talk to him." To my surprise he said, "Yah." Moreover, as an answer to prayer, he added in Swedish: "I must catch the five o'clock train back to Winnepeg." (If there was any agnosticism in me it left immediately. Jehovah was on my side—so far!) I went up the stairs and straightened out my table-desk and threw some white clothes under the bed-cot and waited. In due process of time proper for a bishop to be summoned by a seminarian-layman I heard his heavy footsteps on the stairs. I opened the door and pointed to my best chair. "Now," I said, "let me have it. I was away from the parish with permission of the church. I borrowed the money. I haven't yet been paid. I am really no good. I am only a poor seminary student— trying to learn." The pastor was a man of experience with great responsibilities, especially over this far-off foreign field of the church's mission—an outpost. And so on. I told him that I knew my sermon was no good. And all that. And then, "What did *he* have to say? What would *he* recommend? What did my parishioners tell him I needed to know?"

What happened, the reader of these lines will never believe. Truth is sometimes stranger than fiction. He took aim at one of the flowers on the wallpaper and let go his tobacco spit, hitting one flower in the bud! This was too much for me. I have a first-class temper which with sufficient provocation operates on eight cylinders. Instead of my undisciplined reaction to give full vent to my tongue, I opened the door, fled downstairs, sought out the lady of the house and asked in almost perfect Swedish (Jehovah had taken over my temper: Billy Sunday would have said): "May I have a large pail?" She looked at me with the strangest look. "Please don't ask why. I'll tell you tomorrow," I blustered. She went to the basement and found a pail the size of a bucket and I hurriedly filled it with one third measure of water. I ran back upstairs. I put the bucket down next to the bishop's chair. I said nothing. I waited. I saw the roll of chewing tobacco gradually approaching ominous size. Then he let go—splash into the bucket. In the words of today: he got the message. In religious terms: Jehovah had called him to repentance!

Then he said in Swedish: I suggest that you visit the outlying parishes north of Calgary and I have arranged with Deacon So and So to make arrangements. This was his chastisement of me. I could hardly believe that this was the end of our conversation. He motioned to me to accompany him. The interview ended: I accompanied him to the train. I experienced a sinful joy when the cars pulled out of Calgary bearing the bishop in the direction of Winnepeg. I had jumped a hurdle and I was still alive.

The one chastisement which I performed "under orders" of the bishop was a visit to a lonely church up north of Calgary, a couple of hundred miles toward

Edmonton. (I never saw him again.) It was a service which began about 9:00 p.m. (still light). I recall the darkness which set in at the time of the sermon and how difficult it was to see my "postilla" and how hard I tried to remember the Swedish words: "Please, a candle or some light," and I recall how this was answered, after some pause, by a husky guy who stalked to the basement, found and brought a candle to me, lit it, and the discourse proceeded.

The summer ended strangely. I could never have predicted it.

I had heard of the possibility of being hired by the Canadian Pacific Railroad for a job on one of their supertrains, the deal being a free ride for service rendered. I had no money, only a mess of small debts. I visited the area manager of the CPR and told him of my plight. I needed fare-money to get back to the States—would he have a job for me? He responded by setting up for me an appointment as fourth-cook on the diner of such and such a train leaving Calgary for Winnepeg on such and such a night. Thus I made my final exit from Calgary (and have never returned to the scene). I never asked what a fourth-cook was supposed to do but accepted. I was told to board the evening train and walk through the cars to the diner. This I did after waving my farewells at the depot and not revealing to anyone my secret arrangement. I had my baggage in hand and walked toward the rear of the train, car after car looking for the diner. A colored man asked me what I was looking for and I said "the diner." "You just passed it." So I went back. This was no diner (I thought). It proved to be. I never knew that a diner at night is sleeping quarters for waiters, cooks and what not. On my enquiry of where the fourth-cook is supposed to be, a wave of the hand pointed to an upper berth and that was that. I peered out of the window into the darkness and waved goodbye to no one who saw me nor cared and the train moved on. Then I climbed the ladder and tumbled into the upper.

My sleep was intermittent but, at its greatest depth, I was awakened by a jerk and the covers pulled off me. I dressed quickly and soon found the place transformed miraculously with tables set in white linen and glistening plates, cups and saucers and silverware. I was waved toward the kitchen. I had absolutely no training for my job—no word, no teaching, no notion, no premonition—just a wave this way and a wave that way.

I landed in the kitchen and got my white rigging somehow. I didn't even know who my boss was nor did anyone ask my name. I was just waved to the kitchen sink and to a huge tin of potatoes and given a peeling knife. I peeled potatoes way into the sunshine of the day. When the customers' breakfast hour ended I followed the other kitchen cooks into the diner and ate breakfast. I was enormously hungry and decided that all those potatoes I had peeled were worth ham and eggs and all the rest. The food seemed to be ample and I served myself. Looking out of the window I saw the province of Saskatchewan: telephone poles, flat, flat fields and sky. Then back to the kitchen. This time I got an order from someone to start washing dishes. This I did as my mother taught me: cleanliness first, speed afterwards. By nightfall it was reversed: speed came first, cleanliness second. I was told to save the butter on the used plates which came back from the customers. There was a large tin can hanging up above the sink. I learned the art of using my forefinger on a customer's plate and with one swoop throw the stuff into the container. Butter untouched went back on the plate of the next customer. Those were war days and butter was at a premium. By nightfall I was in the swing—taking dishes six or eight at a time and processing them with the speed of a professional. No dishwashers in those days. The only rest I got was after the customers' lunch and the evening dinner hours and when "we cooks" were served by the waiters in the diner. (I recall I ordered corn on-the-cob which for the help was verboten. Only I, an idiot, had ordered it unashamedly. It was verboten since it was a high-cost item. My comrades-on-trip laughed when they saw me eat corn on-the-cob, looking over at the steward and expecting me to receive a reprimand.) It had been a long, long day and when I stepped off the train in Winnepeg I was "bushed." It was late at night and I waved my goodbye to my chefs, and cooks and waiter buddies. Somehow, I found my way in the dark to the large waiting room of the depot. Eventually, I landed in Ironwood, Michigan, to a happy reunion with my college girl friend and in the country I claimed as my fatherland.

My other summer experience I must relate with greater abbreviation. I was stationed in San Pedro, southern California. The "church" building was near the downtown area—a kind of shack. My assignment was "home missions" among the Swedish Lutheran inhabitants. I continued to read the Swedish postilla and I continued with *my* language except for services. One Saturday as I was playing the old Mason and Hamlin piano (which sounded good to me) someone entered the chapel. I turned the piano stool and faced him.

"Hello," is what I supposed I said.

His reply (I remember exactly): "Are you saved?"

"Well, now," I said, "this is so sudden."

Then he let me have it. If I didn't know it, I surely was unsaved. And hadn't I ever heard of hell? So I argued with him. Noting that I had some little background on the subject of heaven and hell and the rest —he said:

"Aren't you the janitor?"

And I said: "Not especially."

"Well, who are you, you sound like you have an adjukation."

"Well, I am a kind of student-preacher. This is my church for the summer."

"I am very sorry," he said, "I don't intend to try to convert preachers. I am sorry."

"Oh that's all right," I said, "I was just here loafing of a Saturday afternoon."

"Well," he said, "I'm a preacher. Shall we pray together?"

"No special objection," said I.

"Where shall we pray?" he asked.

"Why not up at the altar?" I replied.

So I showed him how and where to kneel.

Then he said: "You begin."

And I said: "No, *you* suggested it. *You* begin."

I waited in silence for quite a while. Then he began.

What he said sounded something like a Chinaman
would speak, then some mild moans and groans. I didn't
recognize English nor Swedish nor German nor French
nor Greek, nor Latin—about the extent of my reper-
toire. Then he began to shout and pull at the altar
railing. I got scared. I was hoping that no church officer
would drop in and wonder about their student-pastor's
goings-on.

When he finally got tired and quit, I waited for
more. Meanwhile, I found the church altar railing had
broken loose from its secure moorings to the floor.

He said to me: "Now it's your turn."

And I said: "Is there anything more to say? You
seem to have covered the ground."

When we arose, I asked him what he had been saying. He said calmly even though plainly and nervously
fatigued: "I spoke in tongues. I speak Chinese, Japanese
when the Lord permits. These people understand me,"
and he went on to testify that a true Christian can experience the gift of tongues.

We began our farewells. I told him he had his place:
It was downtown (as he admitted) on the street corner.
And perhaps I had mine (in the little Lutheran shack).
We shook hands and I met for the first time a first-
century Christian who was certain of his election by
his ability, through the Holy Ghost, of being a full-
fledged Oriental linguist who needed no highfalutin'
education by the secularistic world! We parted never
to see each other again.

I conclude with one further summer incident which
took place on the return trip that same summer.

Before leaving for my summer assignment I purchased a roundtrip ticket which would take me north through Salt Lake City and then down to Los Angeles and then I would pick up the return ticket by way of the southern route heading for New Orleans. It was a bargain. So I would take my stopover privileges and enjoy some sights along the way more leisurely. One such selection for a stopover was El Paso, Texas. I chose this because I knew that there was an international bridge across to Mexico and this would probably be my only chance to see a southern foreign country so close by. I checked in at the YMCA, not for an overnight stay but to have a stopping place between the long wait of suitable trains. Almost immediately upon arrival I strolled down the streets and the first man who came along who looked like a native cowboy I stopped and asked:

"What is the nearest route to the Mexican border?" He looked at me suspiciously. Then he began a series of questions.

His voice all of a sudden took on the note of command. "Follow me," he said.

I did. At an alley-crossing he took me by the arm into the alley away from the crowded street and then began to search me.

"What's going on?" I asked nervously.

He seemed to suspicion I had a gun. Then he commanded me to follow him into a nearby drugstore and told me to sit still and not leave. He watched me while he talked to someone over the phone. After a few minutes he came out of the booth and said: "Come with me." He commanded with more certain authority: "I am taking you to the Mexican border."

I thanked him and said sarcastically: "That's where I wanted to go in the first place."

We boarded a streetcar, standing in the crowded aisle. After ten to fifteen minutes he told me to get off. I did. Meanwhile, he sort of "took charge" of me, holding my arm and leading me down to a large building by the river. (It was the Rio Grande, I later learned.) We walked down a long dark corridor and things didn't look too good. I knew then I was hooked. He rapped loudly on a windowless door. A loud voice from within yelled: "Come." Inside there was some kind of an official sitting at the long desk, dressed in uniform. My new "friend" addressed him formally. I cannot recall the exact words but they went something like this:

I have apprehended this young fellow on such and such a street. He was carrying a collapsible fishing pole (which was true: my one treasured souvenir from California), a camera, some papers in a foreign language, and so-on and says he is a "preacher." He accosted me by asking directions to the shortest way to the Mexican border.

The lieutenant called in his lady secretary, commanding her to take full notes of my testimony. My draft card came first, of course.

"What on earth are these papers?" he asked.

"Well, sir, I have been working on my report to the church and these words are Swedish. I am supposed to report in the language of my church," I replied.

Now, I began to see the light. Here I am. Alone. No one knows me in El Paso nor within hundreds of miles. I am in the draft age. I am not in uniform. I am asking directions how to get to a foreign country. We are at war. I have a camera which I now will lose. I have a fishing pole which is collapsible into two sections and long enough to look like a shepherd's staff. I am dressed in a Norfolk suit, patch-pockets and ostensibly "sporty." And I am very young-looking — just very much so. I am a kid, dressed like a semi-dude and act like a nut (asking such a question bluntly of a stranger). And I claim to be some kind of "minister."

My testimony was forthright and honest.

"Where is this college and seminary located?"

I gave its name and where located. Then, of a sudden (as if Jehovah were coming in at the time of crisis), the secretary butted in saying that she had heard of this college and that they had a school for ministers. This was enough. The pieces finally seemed to fit. My registration card was like a gold certificate and my signature corresponded with other data. The Swedish didn't help especially when I honestly told him I could hardly speak or write it!

"Case Dismissed," he said, and then turned to the girl ordering her to keep the file on me.

"Your honor," I addressed the court. "Thank you. But two things I want to say. As an American citizen I have the right to know who apprehends me as did this fellow. I could have been robbed, beaten or murdered. He did not show any credentials. I make this protest."

"Sam, where is your badge?" the lieutenant enquired.

"Home, on my other trousers," said the secret officer.

"Sam, go home and put on your other trousers," he commanded. "Well, now, what was the other matter you spoke of?" asked the lieutenant.

"Your honor, may I take a picture of International Bridge?"

Answer: "You may."

With a final thank you, I picked up my pole and camera and strode out into the hallway. Down the long stretch I walked until I came into view of the river. There was, indeed, a bridge. It must be the International Bridge. It was. So I looked for a good position from which I might get the best picture. I pulled out the bellows of the kodak (one of the ancient Eastman models) focused carefully on the bridge and was about to press the clicker when a heavy hand grabbed my shoulder and loudly said "You are under arrest."

This fellow was burly and looked more like a Mexican than an American.

"Come with me" he commanded.

Then to my surprise he walked me toward the same building from which I had just emerged, led me down the long, dark hallway and stopped at the same door and rapped loudly. A familiar voice inside said "Come."

There I stood before the same lieutenant and judge. I heard a similar formal charge.

"Sir, I apprehended this fellow in the act of taking a picture of International Bridge."

And so it was — all over again. But this time, the pronouncement came quickly.

"Joe, he was just in here. I gave him permission. Case closed."

Then I stood squarely before the army lieutenant and pleaded my case: "Your honor, now I really want that picture. Will you not assign your officer to stand with me and give me protection?"

The reply was terse: "Joe, go with the young man, stand by him as he takes the picture and escort him to the streetcar."

So I took the picture slowly and confidently and the officer escorted me to the streetcar, waited until the car came and watched me enter, fishing pole, camera, sport clothes, notes in a foreign language, and all. I asked to be let off at the YMCA. I was motioned to get off after ten to fifteen long minutes. I got off and there was my haven: the YMCA. I went in and sat in the corridor lobby. I didn't dare to go out on the streets. I sat nervously until near train time. The depot was only a block away. But I called a "cab" and the driver gave me a funny look when I said: "Take me across the street and let me off at the railroad station."

THE TURN IN THE ROAD —
GRADUATE SCHOOL

When I came to my first pastorate in Cedar Rapids, Iowa in the fall of 1919, I knew then that my career was to be most modest. It was a small church but situated in a fine city — then called the "parlor" city of Iowa. It was one of the very few all-English speaking congregations of the Augustana Synod (Swedish) of the Lutheran church — long days before the super-mergers that were to come and national identity of the immigrants to be lost forever in the maelstrom of American integration.

I almost did not become ordained. To be ordained, one had to have a "call" (a legal as well as a spiritual call to a definitely organized congregation, member of the synod). There just were no churches available and I was too American to handle an immigrant church. Swedish, I understood fairly well. I never spoke it with ease nor had (at that adolescent time) appreciated the "class" of being the kind who was at least bilingual. To speak a foreign language in that day was to identify yourself as a kind of non-American. I had gone through the public schools and graduated from a typical American high school (Lake View) on the north side of Chicago. The college which I attended had Swedish courses, many of which I took. But the seminary served a bilingual church at that time — with few congrega-

tions all English. One major course (systematic theology) was given in Swedish with a Swedish textbook.
The professor was big enough to understand my plight
so he addressed me in my language (in his Swedish-ac-
cented English) and gave me a good grade to boot. But
there were no churches in the synod for me. To go over
to another synod was a kind of betrayal and it certainly
was no promotion. So my fellowgrads were politicking
for big churches and there was enough of Swedish heritage in their blood to perform the liturgies and preach
the Swedish Word of God.

Conveniently (or was it an act of God?), a young
middle-age Lutheran minister died suddenly. He was
pastor of the all-English church in Cedar Rapids, Iowa.
The political machinery began to move fast enough to
get me a "call" and thus I could apply for ordination
in time with my class. Thus, I too, had a "call." And
with my young bride of fifty years ago, we moved into
a large and convenient parsonage, minus much furniture
but with a lot of togetherness and love and all that sort
of thing. We, at least, were young. We had that kind
of virtue thrust upon us.

With my classmates settled in large parishes in Minneapolis and Chicago and parts East and West with salaries much larger and the world already expansive, I
felt the loneliness of the disinherited. Bravely we set
out. Meanwhile, I knew there was something wrong.
I just couldn't quite take the little minutiae of a parish
ministry: such as the woman who called me up on
Monday mornings after a battle with her Fred over
the weekend (Fred is a fictituous name but not the
man), telling me her troubles and adding reprimands

toward me for not preaching about the Book of Revelation and the impending end of the world. I told her
that when the pericope (selected texts for particular
Sundays) came to that Book I might try a sermon;
meanwhile, I assured her I was young and inexperienced
and did not yet come to fathom the mysteries of Revelation. (Had I done it at that time I suppose I might
have played fast and loose with history in interpreting
the allegories in the Book of Revelation and made up
some catastrophic prophecy of the end of Cedar Rapids
and parts near and far, including her Fred!) The ladies-
aid bazaars were never funny to me, nor even pleasant.
I had already served as an auctioneer in a sanctuary in
Canada one summer, standing at the center of the chan-
cel and auctioning off things I knew little about such as
"shifts" they call them now and "bras" (another new
term) and such. (The terms for many items were whispered to me as I shouted out for bids.) I never liked
bowling in church basements (I should say: bowling,
period.) But the day was soon to come when I was expected to do that with the he-men of the church once
a month. To this day I do not like the smell nor the
looks of geraniums which were often prominent in
sickrooms and local hospitals. The smell of roses in funeral homes leaves me with a kind of feeling of intesti-
nal flu to this day even when I smell them at weddings.
Moreover, to this day I can hardly eat cake - *any kind
of*. I was supposed to be the supreme taster of cakes at
every church supper or bazaar. Church suppers I despise with righteous hatred, not because the food was
bad but because I hated to shake hands while I ate, mixing sweat with sweat and getting my hand bruised by

some stalwart male Christian. The gossip in the parish
I enjoyed but never let on. I came unexpectedly upon
one of my deacons (whom I thought was a saint) when
he had a fit of swearing, using the toughest words I had
learned from alley kids: he was loading a truck in the
lumberyard and he didn't see me coming around the
corner. He didn't so much shock me as reminded me
how close the good life can slide into the pit of hell —
and I supposed I knew that I too was a candidate for
that kind of hypocrisy. The little things that go on in
congregations were not typically Iowan; they were
going on all over the country including Connecticut
where I eventually was to land. Somebody has to be a
pastor or shepherd. But I felt myself losing that "call."
I felt letdown — putting it frankly and irreligiously —
and I wanted to get up. My classmates were successes
and I was feeling the ghost of failure stalking in the
shadows of my mind. And so I found the way: it was
to be "my" way and *my* type of "call." I do not think
my decision was so much a personal ambition as it was
an escape from the thought that life must have something more to offer than presiding over little affairs of
communal living such as a small parish seemed to offer.
Perhaps I was looking for some escape.

Thus it was, that by the fall of the same year I was
riding the interurban from Cedar Rapids to Iowa City
(with the permission of a generous church board) and
taking on graduate school. I had no idea who was there,
what I was to do, nor the money to do it with. All I
world beyond the monastery of a confining parish. The
had was a growing and burning passion to take on the
manager of the interurban was interviewed and he re-

sponded generously with a ministerial "pass" to and from Iowa City. All I had to do was to get up at 5:00 a.m. on Mondays, Wednesdays and Fridays, light the wood-coal stove in the interurban as I boarded it at 6:00 a.m. (I being the only passenger for several local stations.) I was to be on the university campus for an eight o'clock class.

But the thing did not at first turn out as I had envisioned. I did not know how unprepared I was for this venture. Nor do many students graduating from small colleges and small denominational seminaries know today how unprepared they may well be even though their grades had been good enough all the way through. (I much later found out that my grades were good enough for membership in Phi Beta Kappa and the college alma mater chapter honored me in 1953, with that recognition—soon after the college received its Zeta chapter.) I swear we were not grade-conscious since it made little difference. One could get into the ministry simply by passing courses. There was little academic rivalry. Our day was very different from that of our present generation who are grade-conscious in a world of increasing competitive struggles.

And so I registered at Iowa University Graduate School.

In those days one need not go through the routine forms concerning one's parents, income, life insurance, recommendations from respectable citizens and IQ tests nor performance scores, et cetera, et cetera. One needed only a transcript showing previous formal education. I seem not to remember even such mundane matters as grades in high school. (They were probably entered with transcripts which I never saw.)

The main event in registration at Iowa University was the scheduled personal interview with the dean of the graduate school. I did not know then what an important man he was academically. He was none other than Carl Seashore, internationally-famous psychologist whose musical-score tests were standard over many years. He knew my alma mater well (he being of Swedish blood). And he knew then much more about Augustana College academically than I ever pretended to know. I found out almost immediately what he thought of my alma mater.

In effect, he said: "You must take introductory courses before you go on with any other." I protested. I reminded him that I had some seven or eight courses in philosophy (including theological seminary) and some courses in psychology, and so on. He asked me about our text in psychology at alma mater. I remembered it: Putnam's. He laughed and reminded me of the definition of psychology in that text: "Psychology is the science of the mind or soul!" (I knew sooner than I wanted to know, that he was right: the text then was about twenty years out of date.) So .... I must register for introduction to philosophy, introduction to psychology, introduction to sociology and that would be sufficient to get me moving. The interview involved a test for my musical potentiality: some tuning forks, some machinery, etc. (He gave this test as a friendly gesture.) I was told that I had near perfect pitch and that I had potentiality in the musical field. I was impressed by the man but altogether humiliated by such advice: here I was a graduate with a B.A. and a B.D. from an accredited college (though seminaries in those days had no creditization, being denominationally acceptable only, that is: orthodox).

I left his office and took the interurban home. My class-schedule called for Monday, Wednesday and Friday lectures in the courses *he* chose. The only respected opinion I had received was to work in the general fields of psychology or philosophy.

For over two weeks I refused to register. I came down on my ministerial "pass," sat on the bench in the then city park (not too far from the campus) and fed the pigeons. They seemed to look for me on Mondays, Wednesdays and Fridays since they were there ready for my offerings. Some of them sat on my shoulders. Students came and went, passing by without a hello or even asking about my problems. Nobody asked. No one cared. And the days went on. It was the day before all this business of personal counseling and I have come to believe that I missed little. (Not all academic counselors are mediocre — if not idiots; but — let's be frank: many are semi-psycho cases. To this day I have an antipathy for them and work on my prejudice with little success.)

Then the day of awful choice came. Either I must show up at the eight o'clock hour or forget the whole thing. I thought of my wife and her sacrifices in sharing her life with me. I thought of my low status in life in comparison with my fellow college and seminary graduates. I thought of the lady who had married Fred. I took a look at the future. And it was very dim. Nobody from the university had enquired if I had become deceased — not even an official of secondary status. Certainly the dean could care less about my Putnam psychology. And there (happily?) were no other deans.

I still recall the day I entered Professor G.T.W. Patrick's classroom. It was completely filled with some 75 or 100 students. I was motioned to a special chair.

"And who are you?" he asked.

I told him my name which meant nothing at all, absolutely. He consulted some sheets and some notations.

"You are a seminary graduate?" he asked.

I bloated out my chest and bravely acknowledged my accomplishment.

"Then you have had Greek?"

I bloated some more.

"Well," he said "translate the sentence above," pointing to the blackboard. I was stunned. I hadn't even seen it yet. But there painted in black and in cursives the words stared at me ominously: οὐ φιλοσοφία ἀλλὰ φιλοσοφειν. (I had had a stickler of a Greek professor in college who made us learn vocabulary no end. We despised him because he scared us to death. Moreover, he was an insurance salesman—on the side—and lacked humor. His name: I.M. Anderson [we called him "Eye M" from his initials in remembrance of the O.T. Jehovah "I AM."] His ghost took over my lips.) And without even thinking I said "*Not philosophy but to philosophize*". And to my amazement, Professor Patrick smiled and complimented me. (I gather that no one else in the class could have done it and he, no doubt, had some impressions about me.) I was "in," even though almost three weeks late! Cause of my lateness: stubbornness.

I had a common illness without knowing : I was a

college graduate and even postgraduate of three added years in theology and *therefore* I thought I was educated. This was my major psychological disease and it was a long time being cured. (To this day, I am not impressed by plain academic degrees. *Where* and *when* and *under Whom* are far more important. And may I add a personal prejudice: What is worse — in my day — than a B.A. from Oberlin College with a major in psychology: a character omniscient, strong in assurance of knowledge and know-how but weak in structure and unknowingly pontifical?)

My conversion set in, at first slowly and quietly and in another month in a violent upset. I came upon a whole new world which I had no idea existed. I was motivated to ask questions which I never had thought worth the asking. I was rudely awakened to the immense areas of knowledge and the awful ignorance that man possesses about his Universe because he is so very little and the Universe is so awfully big. I lost "V.F." (which to the unwary reader are my initials). I found it harder to preach on Sundays. Evolution was taken for granted at the university (some form of it) and I was wrestling here with the Devil when I found that word (evolution) to be commonplace. I bought books on the subject though my family needed new clothing. I found out that I was thirty years or more behind the schedule of academic time. I couldn't handle philosophy, religion and the sciences with my theology and religion. They wouldn't mix. Genesis could be eras rather than days but even that liberal interpretation didn't satisfy my growing curiosity: why *seven* days unless it was just a holy number? And so on and on and on. And my preaching became wild. I was afraid to make statements without more substantiation. I was becoming a "worldly philosopher" who had been set free from institutional orthodoxy—but at that time I could not diagnose my intellectual difficulties. I knew then that my ministerial commitment was in difficulty but I had too much sentiment to shake it off.

I wrote articles for the Seminary Journal and complained about my seminary education. And my name soon became mud. I wrote articles for a journal called *The Lutheran Companion* suggesting that the doctrine of original sin be updated! (My argument was — and I still think it a good one — why save something thoroughly rotten? If you save something there must be some measure of potentiality for good, worth saving. But Augustinianism had overtaken Lutheranism of that day and both Luther and Augustine called themselves rotten. Augustine was a bad, bad boy and he knew it. And Luther had called himself a "stinking carcass." And the church held that there is no good in man, none whatsoever.)

Soon the Bible School in Minneapolis was to demand that the holy orders which came with ordination be taken from me (along with two others — Ferm was on their list as a questionable Christian and no longer should wear the cloth).

This went on for years — slowly I receded into the background, "prayed over" and blasphemed. I never gave up my ordination letter and doubt that I would even under pressure.

It is now only one month since the United Lutheran Church of America — Synod of Ohio — gave me a public testimony with a rose and golden ribbon and certificate honoring my fifty years in the ministry of the Lutheran Church in America — even though I had served foreign fields in America. I was a case of a foreign missionary on the homeland. They gave me a standing ovation (along with two others so honored). I told them in my impromptu speech that I had been received so warmly by my own because my own was a new generation with newer and more generous ideas. (The prodigal — I said to myself only — is the father in the story rather than the wayward son. I did not say this publicly. It was too frank a statement. Sufficient for me was the friendly applause.) It was one of my finest hours: at Oberlin College, about twelve noon, June, tenth, 1969, Ohio Lutheran clergy and as many laymen standing in applause in the great new School of Music Auditorium. The critic of my article on Original Sin who asked the church to "pray for the dear young brother" must by now have the news in heaven that his prayers were heard but in a very mysterious way: Time is of the essence, a great healer of both the oppressed and the oppressors.

Back to Professor Patrick. One of the greatest of all my teachers: informal, systematic, provocative, original, historically oriented and the writer of one of the best introductory texts in the field of philosophy which I had in lecture notes, a preview of his book. He gave me no personal counseling. There was too great a generation gap between him and myself. I needed only to be cooled by time. To have asked for his time would have been selfish on my part and even sacrilegious. A

stubborn know-it-all as I was then in my academic
ways had to be first tamed and replaced by something
else, much like anything else in nature. Nature is not
in a counseling mood but the teacher of patience with
the maturing processes. And as I write this I add:
Amen.

And there was another great academic figure at
Iowa University. I happened upon him. I had never
heard of him. But it was suggested by the front-office
that I should go on and take his course in logic and also his course in the psychology of religion. I was already chastened enough not to argue with the dean of
the graduate school. My first term courses had, in a
sense, been a nightmare: first: I had to learn how to
study (which I had not really learned at all in college and seminary though I thought I had) and second, I was so disturbed in my thinking that I began
to feel the need not so much of another academic degree as an intense desire to rethink myself and to explore this wonderful world of ideas — especially the
ideas of free men who were not subject to the brainwashing of some set of beliefs. It was then I came into
the classroom of Professor Edwin Diller Starbuck.

He was a handsome man: wavy white hair, a face
broad and symmetrical, eyes which looked through
you with friendliness, tall, masculine. He wore Oxford
glasses attached to a black ribbon around his neck
which ofttimes he would twirl around as he lectured
with a kind of charisma of a gentleman of blue blood.
His first class with us in logic went something like
this. We were there waiting. The professor was late.
Someone came in and did something up front which

made no sense. Some motions and walked about. Then disappeared. A little later a good-looking hunk of manhood came in with a broad smile. He bowed. He, the professor, handed us a sheet of white paper with the quiet command that we should write down after our names an account of what had happened since we had entered the room! This was almost too much for me. Nothing had happened! The professor had not shown up until now. We, the students, looked at each other while the professor sat at his desk relaxed and smiling and waiting. Then we got the message. He wasn't fooling. We actually were to write down what had happened after we came into the room. I searched my mind. I could think of nothing except this idiotic person who had come in and done some idiotic things which were unimpressive.

The professor gathered our papers after about twenty minutes. Some of us handed in blanks. Others had lengthy essays. No two papers, he was to point out (not to our surprise), had much in common. Then the rationale of the whole thing was told us. This was a course in logic, in thinking, observing. It was also a kind of psychology course (a major interest with the professor) to reveal how unobserving mortals are and how inaccurately they report events, how inattentive and irresponsible human beings are and how logic is a special discipline toward accuracy, observation and concern for concentration of attention and how hard it is to think carefully, et cetera, et cetera. The first class. And he made us aware that thinking, really careful thinking, is a sorry mess for most people and something few of us do. Logic, among other things, was a study to sharpen our wits of observation of the world and of the thought-processes themselves. We were humiliated and ready for anything he might tell us after our first unannounced lecture.

Professor Starbuck was a very disorganized person himself. His mind seemed set in a self-conscious psychological key, observing human behavior rather than performing systematically. (Most everyone of us tends to be unsystematic just like our very makeup as animals flirting about many unrelated interests and not given to coherence and to systematic effort.) His manner of teaching was altogether provocative and he never seemed to worry about results so long as we were aware of the kind of people we are: emotional, prejudicial, scatterbrains, intellectual hypocrites, disorganized, satisfied, daydreamers, pseudo intellectuals, parochial—in short: human beings sitting in formal classrooms with a kind of sophistication that makes us forget we are human beings with prejudices, unscientific and illogical to the core and members of the same clan of animals called "human beings" without portfolio and with little promise of training. I have never forgotten that first class. It was a laboratory which impressed me later: my own self-recognition as a pseudo-intellectual who doesn't think as clearly as he thinks he thinks and is plagued by his own careless observations and trapped in a mess of daydreaming and prejudices. It was basically a course in inductive logic with logic resting upon the precarious basis of human psychology. As it is *in life.*

I was a guest in his home for lunch one day. He picked me up at the university in his Ford car. The model was designated as "T." It was the kind that had curtains which admitted full ventilation. He drove slowly down main street in Iowa City and out came this child and that boarding the car as it continued its slow pace. These were his kids I soon came to learn and their friends. We had a car full before we turned away from Main Street. Any kid late did not get the ride. Arriving at the spacious home we were taken to the large dining room and I was introduced to the mother (a professor of music) presiding at the table. A colored maid brought in the food unceremoniously, amidst the din of chatter, chatter, chatter. At the table I recall the remark of one of the little Starbucks about the winter Commencement exercises: "Pa, you sat up there with the big boys on the platform. So you're a big boy, aren't you?" And the professor smiled approvingly.

But I must not forget the post-lunch incident. He said he had a book I must read. And directed me to his library. I passed a mess of clothing on the way: women's under-apparel lay strewn on the grand piano and there were kids' toys on the floor with all the hazards of an obstacle course. The walls of the spacious library were packed solidly from top to bottom with books, books, books. A dream world to me. He began searching. The book was not there where it was supposed to be. I noticed that Volume Two of a set would be missing here and there. Then I heard him grunt when, after pulling out a small volume, a bottle of catsup fell out on the floor. This was the chaos of the family situation and perhaps the professor himself. I remembered too, that he was a professor of aesthetics and my mind began to put some things together, such as art or a theory of beauty having something to do with feeling and feelings are supposed to be psychological rather than logical and systematic. Was that not tucked away in the first lecture in logic?

Professor Starbuck was already a national academic figure. William James of Harvard had a way of singling out people before their fame grew. (Charles Peirce is another case in point). In his famous *Varieties of Religious Experience* he gave page after page with full acknowledgement to Professor Starbuck's scientific (statistical) studies of conversion which any reader may check for himself. There was a certain correlation of conversion experiences to the physiological changes of early adolescence (so Starbuck). James' writing in the newer field of the psychology of religion had spotted Starbuck's studies and given him recognition. I was to learn later that there was some friendly rivalry between him and Coe, Leuba, G. Stanley Hall, Pratt and others. There was even the question of who was the first to publish in this new field of the scientific study of psychology in relation to religious behavior. Later, in my own publishing career, I decided to settle this "dispute" (if I could) by getting each man involved to write his own intellectual biography relating to religious studies. Starbuck, indeed, was the pioneer in the field which has been documented (later) in my own edited volume called *Religion in Transition* published in London by George Allen and Unwin in 1937.

His forte was in inspiring and directing graduate students toward master's theses and the earned doctorate. In my days at Iowa University he had three such students, each one being directed personally by him toward their degrees. I was one of them. The other two were Rachel Knight and Herman Hausheer. We sat together in the same philosophy seminar room and library and perspired. Miss Knight did not perspire; she simply exuded sweat. Her weight was enormous: perhaps three chins and a stomach which kept her spine many inches beyond a foot from the table. I felt altogether sorry for her. In those days, no one talked about diet and its relationship to longevity. She had a pencil only two or three inches in length which she held invisibly in her chubby hand. She poured over George Fox's journals (the founder of the Quaker religion). Her breathing was heavy and disturbing. Hausheer pored over Augustine and he, too, was short and fat. The lean one was myself who was reading Martin Luther like mad, searching out the psychological elements which played in his theology.

Miss Knight received her master's and doctor's degrees under Professor Starbuck and published a standard work on George Fox, the Quaker. Herman Hausheer received his degrees similarly at Iowa (but as far as I know his doctoral thesis lies buried in the University library). I had occasion later to have the help of Professor Hausheer in my own editorial work on the *Encyclopedia of Religion*. The last I heard about him before his early death was that he was teaching in a juvenile girls' school somewhere. Dr. Knight came to an early death. All three of us followed Professor Starbuck's thesis (which he had already set forth in some encyclopedia articles), namely, that there was a correlation between a religious genius and a mixed-up personality. The academic word for this mix-up is "crosscurrents." Each of us had a rich personality to work on: all three of our subjects, Fox, Augustine and Luther were religious geniuses (of some kind) and all three were psychopathic and mixed-up personalities which added greatly to their potential enriched interests in causes and in theologies which were not altogether harmonious. (My thesis was begun at Iowa University and Yale later honored me [1923] with a master's degree when I finished it there. It lies buried in two libraries: Yale and my own. I dropped the enquiry with the advent of the new psychology which was on the scene in high speed and altogether unsympathetic with the Starbuck approach.. We were silenced by Watsonian behaviorism—even at Yale.)

At Iowa, it was my good luck also to study under the well-known social psychologist E. S. Bogardus, a visiting professor from the University of Southern California. My life was becoming enriched as well as further disturbed by such good fortune of contact with eminent professors. No one could sit with these giants for any length of time before experiencing revolutionary changes of points of view and perspectives. I sensed soon that I needed to direct these changes which were involving my thinking into the larger areas of philosophy and theology and I wondered what to do and how to do what I seemed vaguely to want to do. And so began some new correspondence and another major decision of my life: to seek out new fields of exploration and contacts. I was luckier than I knew when another major door opened with full swing into another world—as big as Iowa and to me even bigger.

Major decisions, I suppose, come to most people. And

some come early in life. Underneath may lurk a secret ambition toward something which is not too distinct and defined. One then either avoids the making of them and this becomes itself a decision. Or, one just thrusts out—like the first step on the moon not knowing what will happen. I had now come to another major turn in the road and perhaps my luckiest break.

ANOTHER SHARP TURN IN THE ROAD—
NEW ENGLAND AND YALE

And so I began politicking. I had very few contacts to swing open the doors of new opportunities. But then I remembered that there was an important churchman out east—and East then was a kind of Mecca for the academically minded. There were some reputable gold-edged universities and I knew, of course, their names. But I had no special one in mind—except East and in the area of my interests. I knew now I must not turn back—I must go on. My mind was ripe for fresh stimulation but it must be philosophy and/or theology. Behaviorism in psychology had come on the scene and closed my door. I could not bear to think that I must deal with statistics, graphs, charts, animals, behavior. Starbuck had led the way as far as I cared to go. Starbuck himself was destined to go into psychological shadow since psychology of religion belonged too closely with philosophy for the biologically-minded behaviorists. And too, Starbuck's interests were turning to studies in character-training which led him to leave Iowa with a retinue of followers to the promised land of Southern California where a new institute was to be founded and which he was to head. With him an era at Iowa had come to an end; so also Seashore, Patrick soon to follow. There are such things as Ebb and Flow in academic life. When any one mentions his degrees he must say when and where and under whom (mentioned before). There are unfailing rhythms which include peaks and valleys. I had hit a peak. Philosophy was to become physics-minded at Iowa and I could at least see this (important as physics is, it is not metaphysics).

The "bishop" of the eastern seaboard among the Scandinavian Lutherans was none other than S. G. Hägglund. He was Swedish from ankle to forehead. At this time, he was writing articles on "Svenskheten's Bevarande" which translated says "For the Preservation of Swedish and the Swedish Culture." He was sensing the intrusion of Americanism and the English on the immigrant churches and though he was tolerant in many areas on this question he had a passion which exceeded true prophecy. I happened to know that he was a Brown University Ph.D. and this ought to mean something to a young fellow like myself who was trying to enter the gates of academic pursuits. Moreover, I knew that he and my father, a Lutheran clergyman, had long been friends and both had come out of the state-church of Sweden as emigrants and young men. So the politicking began.

I got hold of a Swedish dictionary and a friend and began corresponding for an assignment in the church in the bishop's territory—just anything that would sustain my family while I continued graduate school. His letters were properly paternal and always in Swedish. And one day a letter came: would I like to come to Ansonia, Connecticut, which was only some twelve miles or so from New Haven and perhaps I could commute between the two places on a part-time basis. And New Haven, of course, did not mean New Haven

Junior College nor New Haven Preparatory Institute: It meant *Yale!* "Could it ever be?" I asked myself. Frankly, I had no idea that Yale would be possible. I would even have been willing to settle for Harvard! (Harvard grads: please note.)

But I must come by March—so said the letter—since the parish must not be left vacant too long. Already I had started another semester at Iowa and the situation offered an awful dilemma. (It was a case again of choice [and for me another major decision] which Sartre, the existentialist, says in effect, is the essence of our lives: those lonely and awesome choices which make or break us.) Soon a formal "call" came from the St. Paul's Lutheran Church in Ansonia, in Swedish, signed properly and sealed, by the deacons: a modest $100. per month with no house and the privilege of part-time visits to New Haven for study. Again, I consulted the Swedish dictionary and my Swedish friend. My wife—bless her —was like Mary, who sat and listened and believed, and hoped, and agreed I should go.

It was a fateful decision. My whole life from then on took another sharp turn in the road. And I was scared. I recall vividly a bus ride down Sheridan Road in Chicago. My mother and I were seated on the upper deck. The long ride from Foster Avenue to the Loop, passing the expansive lake on the one side and the homes of the Chicago affluent on the other were symbols to me of exciting possibilities which lay ahead in my imagination: the expansive possibilities of new vistas of learning, on the one hand, and the affluence of being with academic royalty and the possibility someday perhaps (maybe! maybe!) of an academic career, on the other, made me almost deaf to my mother's entreaty to stay put where I was and be content with the comforts I now enjoyed. When I look back on it now I think, too, she was scared for me: such promise of financial poverty and sacrifice and my poor family caught in some kind of potential trap. She was right: hard living lay ahead and many a discouragement. I did have it well at Cedar Rapids and at Iowa University and I was already settled in my profession, certainly good enough for any man with a somewhat circumscribed horizon.

Word came to me that the little parish church in Ansonia had become bilingual, at least part of the time. There were enough young Americans to lay pressure so maybe I could somehow get by. (I counted on Jehovah to swing the door open wider.) The trolley ride (Toonerville trolley) from downtown Ansonia to the end of the line at some strange home where we were to be guests for our first few days, was a sad, sad bumpy ride. We were very much alone with our uncertainties. And we were awfully tired. It was a long trip from Iowa to Connecticut in those days when one's pocketbook allowed only the barest necessities without the luxury of Pullman cars. And we had a small child and another not yet announced.

"Which will it be this Sunday?" I was asked by a deacon. My first Sunday! "Swedish or English?"

I promptly replied "English," without a blink of an eye. So it was. The church was modestly filled. A choir had sung an anthem from their place in the choir loft at the back of the church. I walked up the stairs of a kind of wine-glass pulpit to preach my initial sermon. I lay down my notes and began to concentrate. Meanwhile, there was silence—a kind of awesome anticipation much as an audience is hushed at the first rise of the curtain at a stage play. I looked up. No choir —I noticed immediately. No choir. Had they suddenly and miraculously gone into oblivion? Not a human soul either at the organ or in the loft! There must have been at least twenty people there a few minutes ago. I was so upset with curiosity I couldn't think. What became of the choir? They couldn't have vanished or died or—what? So I waited. The congregation evidently thought I was scared. And they were only partly right. I was so d—— curious of what happened that I just had lost any vestige of a message. But long silence solved the problem. One by one a face peered up from behind the red velvet curtain that hung on the long choir rail in the loft. They, too, had become curious— what happened to the preacher? So curiosity begot curiosity. The routine had been broken! For years, evidently it was the custom of the place that when the sermon began the choir slunk down in their choir chairs and began their morning vigil: sleep. Who cares to keep awake and listen to a Swedish sermon which has to do with ancient sinners, Jews and Gentiles and Swedes? So . . . as the custom of the place had it and the hour was come: the choir had disappeared from view and the preacher was supposed to go on his own with his sermon addressing himself to the captive audience in the pews before him.

It was the last sleep of the choir at Lutheran mass— so said I to myself. I began with my appointment and I jazzed it up enough (so I was told)—and it was in

English—to preach a funeral sermon at the same time:
the funeral of choir sleepers during the preacher's turn
up front. It never happened again. One of the main
reasons follows: "What will it be next Sunday, Swedish
or English?" And I promptly said without batting an
eye: "English." And so it was and so it came to be. I got
my way, the choir lost some needed sleep and I began
to feel more at home. What a way to solve a problem!
Well, religious people might well say: "The Lord's
way mysterious is." All went well until a few of the
elders in the congregation got mad at their new preacher and this is the way it went.

There were very few people in the parish who had
the say. The one man—a generous giver and a Christian
and a business man—was church treasurer. Each Sunday
he went to the altar after the service and scooped up
the money from the collection plates and put it in his
left trouser pocket. No accounting nor auditing by
anyone at the service. He was the undisputed power-
house of the church. A fall out with him would spell
catastrophy. One of his first orders came as a mem-
orandum from him to me: a list of people whom I
should visit. He was a circumspect man and he kept
his power in ways exceedingly shrewd. One of the
most noticeable was his weekly visits in the parish
to take orders for his grocery store (a really fine, small
store which in that day had charge-customers and delivered). Geographically convenient, he had a kind of
corner on the market. It was the day when only afflu-
ency could spell out automobile ownership. So his contact would include ladies of the parish and information
in the area of gossip (making his rounds). It was but

a short time when I became aware that I was not his "fair-haired boy." He always spoke to me about what fine men the former ministers were, what wonderful personalities they had and what great preaching. Those were the days when the Lord smiled on their little congregation. And then the bomb struck.

One day I got a letter from the Swedish bishop saying that there were many complaints and that he was coming down to see me. Would I make an appointment, etc? It was the Rev. Dr. Hägglund, the savior of the Swedish language and culture in America. I knew I was licked even before I had got going. Yale looked like a place far off on another planet even though only forty minutes away.

And so the day of reckoning came. The bishop visited me at an appointed time and summarized the complaints. (Sure, it was a case of striking at Achilles' heel. I was to be wounded in my non-Swedish foot): I had introduced the English language into a Swedish church without congregation voice and I was a kind of dictator and the people longed to hear Swedish and I was young and all that sort of thing. So . . . I sat and waited for the pontifical pronouncement of the bishop: Ferm, get thee hence. He took me to Mr. So-and-So and we confronted each other. My accuser had a Swedish-English dialect but he was miles from being himself a Swedish patriot. His wife was a charming American lady (loyal to the core to him) and his sons were fully Americans like the rest of us. I never heard that they could even speak Swedish. But I was wounded where it could be fatal. My accuser mellowed somewhat in the interview, admitting that I was performing my parish work acceptably,that there were no complaints other than the longing to hear Swedish psalms and the Swedish liturgy and the Swedish God's word expounded. The older people especially were being left out. The church collections were dwindling and it was difficult to finance the situation. (Of course, the finances were dwindling by, at least, as much as the best giver! But who would know by how much, except Deity and the word of the treasurer himself?)

So the bishop decided. He took me aside at my home and said he knew my ambitions. He knew them well since he had gone the lonely trail of university study. He was with me heart and soul. There was a way. I could exchange pulpits with a Swedish "brother" living in Branford (near New Haven). He, the bishop, would arrange that for at least once a month. There were a few older people perhaps. But he knew that I was handicapped and he knew my father and he knew there were many young people in the church and he had heard some nice things about me and all that. So it was arranged.

I exchanged pulpits with "Brother" So-and-So on an appointed Sunday. He was a fine, conservative middle-youngish Lutheran with a lot of the state-church of Sweden in him. I knew he was a dull personality as I had heard him speak and I knew that the ultimate solution in my parish was immanent: back to English but this time—forever. He lasted one Sunday in Ansonia. And the pressure came: give us back our English (even if it meant Ferm). And so it was. I must add: we had many dear friends in Ansonia and we still hear from them. Many were good to us. Many understood our predicament. The end of that church came recently: the church was altogether absorbed into another synod and now only the building remains with the basement where I used to come and bowl with the men and thus praise the Lord and keep the peace.

And so the story moves on to New Haven.

My first bodily contact with Yale was in an appointed interview with the dean of the Divinity School in the old building on the northeast corner of the New Haven green. (This was the day before the new and elaborate complex of buildings beyond the old campus.) Charles Reynolds Brown was then dean. I had no idea that he was one of America's distinguished preachers (I being beholden to Lutheran circles); and I can underline this statement for I heard him at every opportunity. He was a Methodist and an artist at homilies. He always started out with scripture but he traveled the highways of everyday human experience and ended with something which I can only call a "lift." His sermons were widely distributed in his books and even now have a freshness about them. I found him most congenial.

Little did I realize that I brought with me a sentimental contact: I had been at Iowa University, his alma mater and that let me into a receptive heart. As the weeks rolled by, he seemed to single me out as if I were an adopted son. He hosted me to my first varsity football game: a cold, cold November day: Harvard vs Yale. I recall that my overcoat was a bit shabby but no one minds such situations except anxious wives. We were wrapped in blankets and my initiation into academic fellowship had formally and pleasantly begun.

When, after my academic work had come to its finish, and I marched with the young doctors of philosophy to the Woolsey Hall commencement platform in June of 1925 (the only grads who were privileged to be singled out to receive their diplomas on the platform publicly and personally from the president of the university, the others receiving their degrees in wholesale fashion by one swoop of formal declaration)—Dean Brown was there on the platform and he rose from his seat and came over to shake my hand just before President James Rowland Angell handed me my sheepskin. I was very proud indeed!

And unknown to me, Dean Brown was the person who worked behind the scenes to urge my appointment to the faculty at The College of Wooster in Ohio which came as a surprise in the spring of 1927. (Many of the better appointments seem to come when the oiled machinery operates quietly and undisturbed by one's own manipulations.)

His homiletics class was always filled to the full and always exciting. Since I was not a student in the undergraduate School of Divinty, I was marshalled into strictly graduate courses where homiletics had no place.

While I was there the deanship changed hands. And here is where another paternal friend came into my life. Dean Luther Weigle was or had been a Lutheran clergyman of Gettysburg style and he took me under his wing. His counseling was strictly academic and he knew his way around the university. The fact that I was a Lutheran and he, like I, a kind of "wayward Lutheran" (he had come under the spell of the viewpoint of the great Horace Bushnell) made the way easier for me, although politicking at Yale never entered into strictly academic relationships—certainly not in student-faculty relationships.

The friendship of these two leaders, Deans Brown and Weigle, made me feel more than ever responsible for the work being cut out for me and the worst sin seemed to me to betray them at any point. Professor Weigle's psychology of religion class was tops—his lectures well organized and down to earth. His seminar for Ph.D. students was a rigorous exercise each Monday from four until six where, toward the close of my residence, I was subjected to his sharp criticisms as were the brethren in the same class under the same suffering. My first book would never have seen the light had it not been for his urgent pressure with the Century Company of New York which took it on the face of a potential financial loss. (Long out of print [*The Crisis in American Lutheran Theology*, 1927] this book did take fairly well and some Lutherans castigated it—until recently when they write for copies for their libraries. There is a sinful satisfaction in writing back to them: "sold out.")

The Plato seminar over a full academic year (of about eight or nine students) in the professor's book-lined office, remains one of the highlights in my memory. Professor Charles Bakewell had his reputation made in ancient Greek philosophy and his love for Plato spread itself thick upon us in his informal comments on our papers. It was presumptuous for us to write "learned" papers on Plato for him to criticize but this was the price we had to pay for academic credits. A state senator, he practiced what Plato taught: activity in politics for philosopher kings. He was distinguished looking, gray hair, fine features, masculine, relaxed. Our class consisted of potential professors of philosophy and with many of them I kept contact through the years, each one going his own philosophical way but under the skin eternal admirers of the one and only Plato as Bakewell had introduced him to us. What a privilege to sit under great scholars.

Then there was Professor Benjamin W. Bacon. The tough examiner for the potential Ph.D.'s, he was an international figure in New Testament criticism, himself not the owner of a Ph.D. I did not take his work since it lay outside of my field. But my contact with him was rigorous. It was he who gave the green light or the red light (flunk) on our capacity to read French and German. And his seminar on sight-reading in these languages was no Sunday school picnic. He had the knack of translating faultlessly (so it seemed) idiomatic language and this flair had his novitiates baffled. This seminar was a weekly affair and we never knew how to prepare for it since it was understood we had already had basic French and German and needed only to practice under a professional. I squeezed through, thanks to my French professors at Augustana College (Martha Foss and Carl Esbjörn) for being sticklers with us as to grammar, vocabulary and sentence diagramming. Had they not been of the strict breed of teachers I would never have made it under Bacon at Yale. (Miss Foss set the passing grade in her course at 100 for the section of conjugation of verbs which I was lucky enough to pass after the first attempt. It meant memorization to the point of insanity.) And for the German, fortunately I had this language in the ninth-grade public school (Davenport, Iowa, a German city then, plus college courses); and all the Swedish I had learned by absorption and under the strict Professor Jules Mauritzon at Augustana (who scared the daylights out of us if we seemed to bluff). German and Swedish have much in common. I was thankful for this at a critical time.

When I come to report on Professor Wilmon H. Sheldon, I come upon memories of a rare philosophy seminar which stands out *primus inter pares*. I had never heard of Sheldon. But there he was up front sitting in a somewhat slouched manner at his desk in a small classroom and peering down upon us as if to ask "What are you doing here? Why have you come?" He had certain mannerisms difficult to describe. Some people when they really think make all sorts of faces, some amusing, some horrible, some fantastic, some haunting. He was the thinker's thinker, the philosopher's philosopher. It was a free-for-all seminar and why I took it I do not recall. At this point I could believe in a providential predestination for I experienced something that has never left me. He has remained to me an idol—if I could choose to be what I regard highly I would choose to be like him. The course was a seminar on the English philosopher James Ward: the text was Ward's *magnum opus: The Realm of Ends*. There were six of us—I dimly recall. And each, in turn, was assigned a paper covering a chapter: expository and critical. To understand Ward's book meant to know the history of Western philosophy—a very large order!

Yale had some visiting professors while I was there but I had no classroom contact with them. Among the younger men whom I came to know as a student sitting in class were Roland Bainton, a first-rate historian who specialized in the Protestant Reformation period with a specialty on Luther. He loved to translate the off-color passages in Luther's writings which, for the general public, remained in unintelligible Latin. He was an earthy person who enjoyed the mundane tidbits of historic and contemporary characters. He was also a bright cartoonist who liked to draw his students as they read serious papers in his seminar. (I still own a Bainton cartoon of V.F. which was realistic rather than flattering.) He must have passed me on my M.A. thesis since he sent me a carbon copy of his estimate of it—presumably as a member of some committee. (It was his estimate of my estimates of Luther and he was incisive, critical and Baintonian.) The psychology involved in the thesis (which I had begun at Iowa University under Professor Starbuck) was not his forte so, I suppose, the psychology men on the university faculty (unknown to me) must have had a look at the thesis and given approval. (One of my major regrets is that I did not find it feasible nor did the opportunity come to have my thesis published. The thesis still seems sound and does open an approach to the study of a great personality. Someday some lonely scholar will look it up in the Yale library and maybe find it of some academic use.) Professor Bainton was a fine human person and a devoted scholarly professor and a credit to his university—even the bicycle he rode added distinction to his person.

Then there was the young instructor Robert Calhoun —fresh out of his Ph.D. program, coming from a first assignment at Carleton College. His course in the history of Christian thought was a triple "A" course, full of detailed information which students, to pass his course, must have recall at an instant demand. He was systematic with every detail fitting into every other— and an excellent lecturer. Being young, he was tough and not too charitable with boderline-academics. A bluff in his course was soon spotted and eliminated. Good students flunked his courses and no one seemed to complain. No counseling. Just learn the stuff—that's all. He was highly scheduled. Most of his professional life he suffered from the impairment of hearing so that if a question was posed by someone with raised hand he would march politely down the aisle and the questioner talked into his microphone. His answers were always to the point and exactly clear. I was pleased to hear, many years later, that he had seen fit to use my doctor's dissertation to potential candidates for the degree as one which had the organization of its material fully satisfactory to him. Though he never said a word to me about it —this was a compliment full and running over. He published little. He was, I think, too conscientious to have something in print when there might be the possibility of an immediate revision.

Although Professor Porter's field was outside my academic highway, I did audit his course on Paul. Porter and Paul were synonymous names at Yale in those days. And, moreover, he thought that if one knew Paul one was in direct acquaintance with the earthly son of God (*The Mind of Christ in Paul*—his one and only major work). He came into class each time—a short dwarf-like person—balancing a huge pile of unassorted books of different sizes. We could not see his face. He ceremoniously juggled them down to the level of his desk and arranged them before his lecture began. They were in poor gravitational order: a little book at the bottom, size 95 on top, with some other odd sizes in between and perhaps an encyclopedia resting precariously. In my memory he never spilled the stack. He always made it. (I wickedly thought he belonged to Ringling's circus—act number 47.) Then he looked at the class and smiled. His teeth were store teeth, immaculately white, large and even. One thought one saw a corpse laughing. When anyone asks me about the Apostle Paul I quickly say: I have met him! And indeed, I have: Porter was Paul and Paul was Porter. (He must now be having some fine chats with the Apostle to the Gentiles.)

Tallest among the academically tall pines stood Professor Douglas Clyde Macintosh. He was a typically dour Scotsman, of medium build, impeccably dressed and always dignified. He almost never smiled although his eyes on occasion took on a twinkle. He was what one would not call a good lecturer; he mumbled his words and he was not too easy to follow. Only those took his courses who dared to face the quiet lion of them all. We knew he knew his stuff. We respected every word that came from his formal lectures. He was deathly systematic. He wrote books which never would make the drugstores nor even paperbacks. His sentences were chiseled out as a sculptor would carefully touch his mallet to bring out fine differences of detail. He was logically cold. His interviews were always scheduled. I used to see him once a month by appointment which would go something like this: "I'll see you a week from Friday in my office at 2:34 until 2:55." I would have my question-notes ready and check the answers off as he gave them. His counseling was purely academic. He never asked about my health, my family, my ambitions or the like. He was writing books and preparing lectures and this was his calling in life.

They say he mellowed with the years (after my time); that he joined the Moral Rearmament Group and took part in personal religious testimonies. This was not his nature as I knew him but it was altogether consistent with his religious philosophy. For, as a Baptist, he held to religious experience as the ground not only of the personal religious life but also as the cornerstone to his basic theology. God for him was a possible personal experience if one had the proper religious perspective. Theology was an empirical science insofar as it rested not on a series of propositions but as it lay embedded in a personal encounter. (He would have liked some existentialists—but we never heard such a term in those days.) One sentence I may quote from him from a memory of it which never, never fails. The reason: I seemed never to comprehend it; my buddy found it opaque; and morever, the professor himself when asked about it, took quite some time before he gave his own version of it (It had something to do with the philosophy of the German philosopher, R. H. Lotze). The sentence comes from page 50 of Macintosh's *The Problem of Knowledge*. I hope the reader of this page enjoys it as much as we suffered under it: "Moreover, the ingeneous dialectic by means of which a numerical ontological monism is supposed to be established through a synthesis of the empirical actuality of interaction with its theoretical inconceivability, also fails to convince." Let this stand for what it's worth. Believe me when I affirm: it really means something.

This is the way he wrote and lectured. And to get the full impact of his lectures one sat up front and one took down every word and then went back to his own room and brooded. I took two of his courses over again not because I flunked them the first time (please believe me) but because he was then the tall man I had to hurdle in order to satisfy the requirements of my doctorate. I was very humble before him and I am sure it paid off; for the day of reckoning came and I was soused in his viewpoints and could have been an Aaron had Moses suddenly passed away.

Honoring his 60th birthday, there was a quiet celebration at Yale. I was one among his graduate students invited to come. There was a formal dinner upstairs somewhere in Woolsey Hall. The president of the University was there and some deans and the editor from Harper's publishing firm (New York) and then the authors of a *Festschrift* (and their wives) and a formal presentation by admiring students. Professors Julius Bixler, Robert Calhoun and Richard Niebuhr were the co-editors of the book entitled: *The Nature of Religious Experience* (1937). The eleven contributors were: Eugene Bewkes, Vergilius Ferm, George Thomas, Julius Bixler, Richard Niebuhr, Reinhold Niebuhr, Cornelius Kruse, Robert Calhoun, Filmer Northrop, Hugh Hartshorne, D. S. Robinson. Each contributor took his own free measurement of the professor's philosophical and theological stance. There were words of appreciation from the honored guest. Little did he then know how naughty some of us were: we were now in the freer position to critically evaluate his theories and I, for one, took the occasion to question his initial thesis, namely, that emotions are cognitive. All this later provoked an attack upon some of us in a series of articles by our teacher in some journal (which one I have forgotten).

Professor and Mrs. Halford Luccock who hosted my wife and me in their home during this Yale visit commanded me to speak in the Divinity School Chapel the following day. I accepted reluctantly. My memory of my speech is hazy—something about my good fortune as a student in coming to Yale though I had never heard of any of their professors (true it was because I just hadn't been in the proper places). I still vividly recall seeing Professor Macintosh sitting behind a post and nary a word about my speech from him afterwards.

One and only one time was I a guest in Professor Macintosh's New Haven home. We were seldom, if ever, invited to homes of our professors at Yale (at least I never heard a student speak of it). It was a rather formal dinner with Mrs. Macintosh at one end of the table and the professor at the other. It was a very dark room and I seem to remember that the maid who was as dark as the environment appeared so suddenly from behind, that she actually scared me. While we were conversing (both hosts were extremely congenial without being a bit hilarious) the buzzer seemed to buzz and buzz and buzz. I wondered why someone didn't answer the phone. I could hardly follow the run of the conversation. Then Mrs. Macintosh leaned over and said politely: "I think, Mr. Ferm, your foot is on the buzzer." I had no idea that such things were hidden away under the rug. Well, things went on and on and then the buzzing began again. Evidently, I didn't know where to put my feet. I thought I had learned my lesson. I finally found some awkward place to hang my feet and finished the dinner without further mishap. My theory about it all: is that the maid had left the house; that there was more than one electrical contact under that Bolderdash rug. Mrs. Macintosh was amused but the professor gave no sign of an unusual response.

I never knew how I stood with him. He never gave a word of compliment. He just was one of my best professors without the embroidery of an outgoing personality.

After my stint at Yale was over I went back to take some education courses. Professor Calhoun gave one in the History of Religious Education. He started with the Pithecanthropus and I quit. (I could quit now—being already academically decorated and no one could *ever* rob me of that one.) I sat in another course in Religious Education but I have forgotten the professor's name. He talked about the various methods of teaching (Socratic, etc.). I was assigned to write a paper on the following topic:"Abraham ready to slay his son Isaac" according to the Herbartian method as taught to twelve-year-old boys. I wrote the paper. It was returned to me with a "90" at the top and I quit. I never went back. (This is about what I still think of many education courses—methods gone mad with so little content.)

My stay in Ansonia became financially precarious. So I pleaded with the bishop to help me find added work in order that my family could continue together. An English-speaking church of the New England Conference became vacant in West Haven and I was "called" there, with the understanding I would commute each Sunday and continue at Ansonia. This I did. My salary increased at least by one third. We moved to a second-floor apartment over an automobile salesroom in a building directly back of the Hotel Taft in New Haven. It was there I worked on my "prelims"—commuting to Ansonia and West Haven in an old Franklin car (down-payment of $100. which was loaned me by a deacon). This car became a familiar sight—so they said in New Haven, Ansonia and West Haven: wagon-like wheels, curtains with broken isinglass flapping in the breeze and with parts irreplaceable. One day driving midway between my two assignments I heard a fearful noise, so I stopped and parked. There it lay: a part of my car! I knew I was in trouble. Could I make it to the garage in Ansonia? So I turned back and drove slowly to the haven of my Franklin. Engineer Josephson (mechanic, deacon, fine fellow, salesman) saw me coming. I stopped in front of his garage, opened the door, called to him and said "Well here it is. I saved it. Made a fearful noise." I brought a large piece of iron pipe (from the back seat) which I had picked up on the street when I stopped and showed it to him. He looked at me in utter surprise and disgust: "That thing was never in or on your car" he said.

This is not the end of the tall stories circulated about this little innocent episode (much as the New Testament stories must have circulated about little innocent incidents—perhaps, perhaps, perhaps). One version was that this fellow V. F. picked up a piece of sewer pipe and went back to the garage with it; another had it that a long pipe had dropped out of some truck, and so on. Finally my name got lost in these stories. Then, one day, at a minister's conference where stories were bandied around, I heard this one: Have you ever heard the story of the preacher who was riding in an old Franklin toward New Haven and of a sudden heard a crash? He stopped and went out to look. There it was: part of his car! He brought the thing back to his garage-man. Said the mechanic: "That's never been on your car—that's a manhole cover." And they all laughed and I walked away.

My wife walked our little girl back and forth on the New Haven green each day while a friend of mine and I studied for our prelims. It was a day of trial. How could any normal woman live with me? I was as tense as a cable on a cable car. I had two churches. One had a building program on and I was supposed to attend commitee meetings. I still had to bowl with the men in Ansonia. I still had to send in reports to the Swedish bishop. We had sickness and death in our little family. Our son became infected with a contagious disease in the house where we lived and all the professionals at New Haven hospital could not save him. We were in mourning. Some humanitarian stuck an envelop in our mailbox at Christmas time and in it was a check for $100 as an answer to prayer. I cannot possibly name all the commitments which I had that piled up on top of each other at the very same moments that the faculty at Yale were to give me a thorough scrutiny of my familiarity with such subjects as epistemology, contemporary metaphysics, history of Christian thought, systematic theology and one or two others—one week of writing in which there are only two grades which result: P or NP (Pass or Not Pass). Not to Pass meant at least one more try—a year hence. And maybe a command-exit from this campus forever.

AND SO BEGINS THE PROFESSION
OF COLLEGE TEACHING

It was almost impossible to find a college teaching appointment back in 1925—unless one had actual teaching experience. Here I was with my four academic degrees, with six years of actual professional experience in the parish ministry, and some mighty fine people, well qualified, endorsing me by word of mouth and by written recommendations. Of course, I was not ready with academic experience; the big jobs were waiting (as usual for those of maturity and excellence) and the little jobs were few and far between. A natural would be to turn to some small denominational college—even of my own Protestant lineage. One by one the doors were shut in my face. Reason: I had written too frankly and too often in the religious journals revealing my own pilgrimage away from the ecclesiastical orthodoxy. I name them: Augustana was unwilling; Upsala College in New Jersey was unwilling; Gettysburg also; Muhlenberg; Wittenberg; names mentioned since I knew that I was being considered. So I placed my name with a New York Teacher's Agency and waited. Experience in college teaching? Reply: None. Period.

So I stayed on in the New Haven area holding fast to my slender income—until the day came when I could stand it no longer. I had had a breakdown during the last days of my work on my dissertation and I was actually led with human support into my doctor's oral exams by one of the professors. (The previous Sunday I had fainted in my pulpit in West Haven. What the diagnosis was we never knew since we were not in the habit of calling a physician each time illness struck.) A summer had passed and there was a slow recuperation.

But now patience had run out. I resigned my pastorate. My parishioners asked where I was going. My answer, though it was not believed, was "I just don't know." Neither did my family. Where I would have gone had nothing turned up—makes me wonder to this day and shudder. There were no social programs for the unemployed in those days. (That would then have sounded like some form of socialism—God forbid.) The closest thing I could think of was the Salvation Army's program for the disinherited. I had no business in resigning. But my spirit was just broken down. There was no plus left in me. All this effort, effort, effort—and NOTHING.

Then one July day there came a telegram. Would I come to New York for an interview? And tomorrow morning?

My salvation lay in the hands of the then president of Albright College in Myerstown, Pennsylvania, who after an hour's interview offered me a position for the year 1926-1927 as professor of the social sciences. Without any questions whatsoever I blurted out a quick "Yes." It was arranged that we would move into a few rooms in the girls dormitory and I would teach sociology, economics and one course in philosophy.

"Do you not know that philosophy is on the way

out?" asked the president. "The new and coming thing is the field of the social sciences."

To which I sadly asked: "So?" I would have agreed with anything he said. I was that desperate.

And so I became a college professor. (I don't even recall the rank.) I was to be put on salary—modest, of course, but satisfactory to anyone used to living close to the poverty line.

My memory (as I now write) is my first meeting with the dean of the college after our arrival in September. He was post middle-aged and a little stooped. He came strutting hurriedly across the campus (I can vividly see him). He had something in the palm of his hand from which protruded what seemed to be a pen or pencil. After self-introductions I asked him what he was carrying.

"Oh *that*," he chuckled, "is my fountain pen. I keep it moist and sharp in this here potato."

And that was that. (How ingeneous, so I mused. And now as I write I am sure he had something going there.)

I recall this same dean announcing a concert pianist at a formal concert in the little chapel. "And now we shall be favored by Mozart's opus on the piano——*far*—*far*—on the piano *fur te*." (I had come a long way from New Haven's Yale.)

I never have had a course in economics. My sociology was only that of social psychology. There were lots of texts in the field. In sociology the texts were eminently readable and required little critical thinking: e.g., so many people (a study has shown of the gold-coast area in Chicago) have alcoholic problems, divorce rates, income per capita, families of such a size and so on and on. I could bluff this. Economics was something else. I recall the textbook I had chosen, by the authors Fairchild, Furniss and Buck. I kept one day ahead of the class. When questions came up which I could not answer, I simply said: We shall defer these until a little later (and then I would pray [to myself]). On one of the exam papers a student answered my question: Name the authors of the text. His reply: Farechild, Furnace and Buick. And that was that.

One day it was announced that a couple of Union Theological Seminary graduates would speak in chapel and that we should give them extra time—thus excusing classes following chapel. I met my classes as usual but my morning post-chapel class had no students. They had gone to chapel and I came to learn that they had been greatly impressed by this couple. It was reported to me that the speakers had asked: "How many of you young people wear jewelry?" All hands up. "Well, Jesus Christ wore no jewelry: Sell all and give to the poor." Their consciences were hurt to the bone. And some of them came forward to the platform and offered their jewelry to the couple. "Look at us," the speakers said. "We own nothing. What we have we have from the Lord."

Thus, the report. I told my students later in the week that I had seen this couple on the campus and it looked as if the Lord was very stingy. They did not even have shoes nor socks on.

Colleges are the haven of many religious and social-economic crackpots and this little Pennsylvania denominational college had its share of itinerant visitors earn-ing their keeps by some kind of religious gimmick. (This was back in 1926. What about today?)

The only time I spoke in this college chapel was the time that a cat somehow got on the platform and competed with me with several loud meows and I could hardly compete. So I said in Scriptural terms: "Get Thee Hence." This brought the students down in howling applause and willing to listen to my poor message.

Myerstown was a very small and quiet village of some few hundred people. There was a large Lutheran church situated strikingly along the highway leading to Lebanon, with its cemetery hugging it closely. When I was there, the minister suddenly died; and knowing that I had certain qualifications the church officials asked me to come and supply. I stayed on seven months. We lived in Lebanon in an apartment building in the downtown area. I commuted not only to the college each day but now on Sundays. When I came to the church before 11a.m., I met most of the members going out (home)— they were used to attending Sunday school which preceded the morning mass. They had musical instruments of all sizes and shapes and I imagine they had a musical whirl before services. (I never heard them, but my imagination kept telling me how they must have sounded as amateurs.) Each Sunday *right after the sermon*, the choir rose en masse and chanted with gusto: "Thanks be to Gawd." I didn't appreciate it since I took the hint that they were supremely glad I had finished. (I later changed all that when I got enough nerve.)

I recall one funeral which was held at the church

cemetery, I officiating (the funeral director giving me the know-how of the place). After the burial, the congregation and mourners marched into the church for full mass, I delivering some sort of English sermon and a retired German Lutheran finishing it off with another forty-five minute discourse in German. After it was over, I prepared to leave for Lebanon. The undertaker got ahold of me. "You must go to the restaurant. It would be folly to go home without a meal with the mourners." I went to the village restaurant. It was a chicken dinner to end all chicken dinners with the chief mourner (the widower) going from table to table dishing out potatoes and gravy and insisting that we eat more and more. I was ready to be hauled away when it ended. The most cheerful person was the host, the chief mourner. (I wondered about his sudden happiness.)

I recall a wedding I had. I never quite understood it. The groom came over to Lebanon one dark night and said "Ssh," and added in so many words: I want you to marry us next Tuesday night about 9 p.m. Nobody must see you coming into the brick house on Main Street in Myerstown. If you see anyone, walk around the block. I noted down the appointment and the place. The night was dark and Myerstown's "sidewalks had been pulled up for the night."

The house was pitch dark. I rapped on the door. "Who's there?" came a peepy voice from inside. "I'm the minister," said I. Quietly the big lock was turned and through a slit-opening I was let in. There they stood—the potential bride and groom. All the shades were down and the cracks sealed by some kind of white cloth. I asked for the license and it was presented. I looked suspiciously at it but it did say "The Commonwealth of Pennsylvania" and so forth, and I took it that it referred to these two characters. I pronounced them man and wife after reading the Lutheran liturgy and they hurried to the door pleading me to leave as quietly as I had come—not suggesting that I stay and at least taste their cake. I never saw them again but I felt that there was something weird about the whole process and for weeks I followed the tidbits of the local newspaper hoping for some information about them. But never a word. She was extremely cute and he was on the declining side. Some shenanigans were involved but I didn't worry since it was legally proper, liturgically sound and I got my five-dollar bill (about fifteen dollars in today's money). Besides, I was never called before a judge as having commited a legal impropriety and further my conscience didn't bother me. It was just one of those queer things which happen without too much rationale except an understanding of the psychology of male-female attractions which keep going on generation after generation not always with social approval.

The Lebanon area is one of the most picturesque in all of Pennsylvania. The houses are immaculate. German is widely spoken. No front yards. The town clock. The horse and buggy of the Amish slowing traffic. Wholesome people who like food and drink. A quiet campus. Beautiful countryside. And then: Hershey.

Just as you go over the city line of Hershey you smell the chocolate factory and it is superlatively sweet. The Inn in the town is the last word in atmosphere (at

least in those days). It was a programmed city with
events (sports, concerts, lectures) going on season
after season. I heard Will Rogers one summer afternoon. The price of admission was high so I settled for
a dollar seat in the highest part of the large auditorium
(called by a term not now printable). I came alone. It
was a long trek to my gallery seat. The Western cowboy came upon the platform with his lasso and his
famous grin. He stopped short at the front of the large
stage. "Hey," he said, "What a peculiar place! Down
here in front is a small crowd of you. Then blank
seats all over the place. And way up there you birds
roosting on the rafters. What's the matter with you-
all? Mad at each other? Hey, you guys way up there,
come on down here so I can talk to you. Sit here with
these money-people. Let's get together and have some
fun." Did I ever run down for a front seat. So did the
others, the proletariat. Next to me was some important
citizen in town and I soon got the message: What's this
little specimen of *hoi polloi* doing down here with us?
And I rubbed my right arm and shoulder and crowded
him to the very edge of my seat and over and made
him uncomfortable throughout the show. And show it
was. Washington politicians taking the usual ribbing
and all that. His humor bounced forth like the popping
of corn and you just couldn't keep laughing at the last
joke since you were still working on the one of several
minutes previous. I was drained at the end and glad to
go back to Lebanon and the quiet little apartment.

And so one day in March 1927, a telegram came

asking if I would be interested in a teaching position at The College of Wooster and would I reply immediately. Then began a search for an Ohio map and each member of the small family took a section of the map to find where this place lay. We had never heard of Wooster in any manner, shape or form.

I was met at the station by the college car and taken to the president's office. The secretary (Miss Leila Compton) tried to make me comfortable and kept apologizing for the long wait. It dragged on through the morning hours and I was then told to attend the trustees-faculty luncheon in Holden Hall. Here I met the president most casually, some unknown trustees and a few of the faculty. Then began the long afternoon wait. Discouraged and righteously angry I told the secretary that at 5:30 my train left for the East and on which I had reservations. (I learned later that this was the president's *modus operandi:* keep 'em waiting, "play it cool," not be over-anxious and, moreover, this was a lowly matter: the hiring of a low-status faculty member.) College presidents in those days were semi-gods.

Almost in the nick of time the president came and the conference began. He talked about himself and his battle with William Jennings Bryan over evolution, "convincing" me that he was not a fundamentalist but a liberal. He asked few questions about me even though I had my obituary ready. He had the secretary make out a check covering my railroad fare and made no suggestion whatsoever of his interest in me as a candidate. My report at home was quite negative. And I wrote off the deal as I had written off other nibbles.

In his good time, Mr. Wishart evidently dashed off a
letter inviting me to join the faculty as an assistant professor of philosophy (which, at least, was a step up
from instructor and already I was a professor at Albright).

It was a tough decision. Albright had been good to
me. We liked it there in spite of its modesty. Wooster
seemed neutrally promising but without any special
glamor. Who was I to make a choice when the alternatives were not too clear? How would we get along with
Presbyterians, especially Calvinists who had fought
Luther (and vice versa)? I had no emotional overtones
and could just as well have joined Sears-Roebuck College, if there were such a place.

But to Wooster we went in September, lock, stock
and barrel. We rented a three-room apartment with the
front room serving as the sleeping place for the Ferm
tribe which had just been increased.

This decision stuck. We remained at The College of
Wooster for thirty-eight years until the rules applied
irrevocably to retirement when the final top age of
active service was reached. We have not regretted it.
After all, one has to live somewhere and the somewhere
is generally quite unpredictable. The place did not suit
us at first. There were many things we disliked and we
hoped to change this by moving away some time. We
continued to rent on the theory that the moving van
some day soon would be dropping by to take us and
our belongings to more promising pastures. Opportunities did come—but these did not seem to have the
gravitational pull strong enough to take us away from
our own orbit. As time comes, things change and if one

is alert and patient enough one can remake his job. I did mine. In the latter years my position at Wooster was pretty much the way I had hoped it would be—no matter where in geography or in what environment I would happen to be. (I note now that even my sons, who in their early professional careers seemed to scoff at my position and locale, came to show envy and wondered if they, too, might strike it as lucky.) All small colleges have much in common both as to virtues and vices. And universities with their metropolitan hugeness gobble up individuals and personalities until the paradise changes from *philosomegethos* (my word for love of bigness—out of the Greek) to a yearning for a more neighborly environment if it still is academically respectable. Thus, the small liberal arts college of academic stature still remains something of a dream in anyone's academic ambitions.

Dr. Wishart was a distinguished looking president. And he was—for his day—a good preacher. His reputation was wide in denominational circles and especially among Presbyterians. I became quite amused by his style of preaching: it began with potential heresy (always open to philosophical rather than homiletical style) but somewhere about the middle or two-thirds through the *tide* would shift: "but on the other hand," (he would seem to say in retreat): "the faith of our fathers still remains and we as their inheritors do not bury them but continue to follow in their steps and praise them." The sermon thus always pleased the liberal and the conservative and thus he weathered certain critical storms of churchmen and faculty. (He had defeated Williams Jennings Bryan, the arch-anti-evolu-

tionist of the day, for the moderatorship of the Presbyterian Church in America and he never ceased to remind himself and others of this victory.)

He once told me how he happened to invite me to
Wooster. Frankly, he said, he didn't want any more
Presbyterian preachers around the campus. He had been
in so much controversy with small-town operators in
the church—missionaries and clergy and notorious and
conservative and wealthy laymen, that, come what may,
he would reach out and pick from the outside field
(especially in the field of philosophy). This is where
Dean Charles Reynolds Brown came in to sponsor my
name (unknown to me) and moreover I was a Lutheran (a foreigner) and still moreover, I was at least
academically qualified and extremely unknown.

He was on the whole kind to me. But he treated me
much as he did others on the faculty—always at arms'
length. I never quite got to him and neither did others
on the faculty or others whatever their relationships.
This back-fired in his retirement days. He was an ex-
extremely lonely man with few personal friends, if any.
Maybe this is the price one pays for one's self-protec-
tion. (I recall my own mother once saying that she had
a right as a minister's wife in the parish to have her own
personal friends—no matter what the congregational
chatter would be about. And she had them: even a select
social club (in and outside the parish) which partied up
in their own way. Her idea was that you need not be all
things to everyone and thereby lose your own self. And
this has stuck with me as a sound social principle.)
When an officer sits close to the moneybag and determines salaries of others, he unwittingly gathers a large

cohort of hangers-on. As soon as the cord of the bag is taken from him almost immediately his friends forsake—as they did in Wooster with alarming rapidity upon his resignation. This is the way of all flesh—I suppose.

At one time in my career (1940 on)—during the late depression years—he called me to his office and shocked me by asking me to become dean of the summer school. "It is bankrupt." he said, "and the trustees will have no more of it. But I think you might make a go of it. We'll furnish the equipment as usual but will guarantee no salaries. You run it as you wish, hire and divide however you please. You will report, of course, to the treasurer and myself. And you will print your own catalogue at the summer school expense. Your salary is not promised but you will divide the earnings in proper proportion. Will you take over?" I never realized that I looked to him anything like a businessman but I guess he had sized me up as a live option—after looking over the roster of his faculty.

I accepted. Instead of bankruptcy, we made money. The faculty I chose was on the basis of required courses, personalities who could attract students and few in number. We did it on a split-basis, with the president approving a proportion for the dean's pay. My appointment was renewed. And for four years—beyond the usual three-year stint—I remained on the job. And this is how I got my summer home started—although it cut my vacation down considerably each year. (I suppose I must have taught some twenty-five summers in all in order to keep the family finances on an even keel.)

So far as I can recall, I made only four motions at faculty meetings over a period of four decades. It is incredible but true. Those motions were after my report of summer school as dean: "I move, Mr. Chairman, that this report be accepted." In each and every case my motion was accepted. One wonders why I was a Quaker at faculty meetings—and I attended hundreds and hundreds of them. As I now see it I can think of several reasons: 1) We had a big proportion of chatterboxes, especially one who always asked for the floor since he seemed not to understand the motion and he wanted to explore the maize of implications. So I sighed (with others) and came to see how stupid much of the discussion was; 2) I had learned early that the administration had a way of getting its own way—if it really wanted to—in spite of faculty motions; 3) Being somewhat philosophically-minded, I could always see alternative views and that led me to hesitate in expressing an opinion with so many reasonable arguments on the other side—especially when it didn't seem to matter one way or the other; 4) I found that if one stuck his neck out, one invited himself into some committee assignment (which always seemed negative to me).

On the latter side, I recall my first assignment as a member of a committee called "public relations." The chairman called me one day asking me to meet an early train to escort a college guest to his hotel. This I thought was an imposition. So I laid it gently aside in my memory-bag and just didn't show up. I got a telephone call from the chairman asking me about the success of my hosting. And I told him I lost the item in my memory-bag. The same chairman asked me to see that so many chairs were in a lecture room at a certain date for some special event. This, too, I failed to do since my professional conceit suggested that there were paid-workers for such assignments more experienced and probably more physically fit. Being such a poor member of such a committee gave an almost certain assurance that I would secure the kind of reputation I coveted: namely, a poor committeeman. Once I was a member of the library committee. President Wishart came to the meeting. The issue was: should the library be opened on Sunday? I spoke up in favor of it suggesting that the campus went into a complete paralysis-shock on Sunday afternoons and would it not be nice for the students to have a place to go? I recall the president's flashy retort: "Over my dead body will the library be opened on Sunday!" (He was a United Presbyterian who was extremely puritanical on Sabbath-observance and, incidentally, loved to read the Psalms in chapel like a United Presbyterian and give them his sonorous vocal interpretation and read long excerpts from the Old Testament—typical of a brainwashed Calvinist.)

So it went. I know deep down inside of me that committees are important (even in a theoretical democracy). I despised them (having been to many ladies-aid societies and church committees in my day) and further, I was an unregenerate graduate-student who had learned to budget his time perhaps to the point of *ad nauseam*. But it worked! For many years I was a classroom teacher plus a student at my home and there was little time in between except for the things I chose. My study was never at the college office since it was for me impossible to concentrate with and under unpredictable interruptions. (Students were counseled by me by appointment.) It was easy for me to see that the major academic problem of most students was that of a low grade and for that there was only one answer: study, study, study. Beyond that, I had no information about the things which only psycho-therapists may see fit to conjure. I never regarded the academic profession as that of a pastor, counselor, psychiatrist, good Joe or campus VIP. I interpreted my "calling" as that of a teacher and a student in the field of my specialty. This did not mean a kind of hermit life. I think I could be as social and extroverted as anyone but I disliked just plain time-wasting over chit-chat. Gossip I have always loved. But not chit-chat hobbygoodoo-licks (whatever that is).

When I came to Wooster I was asked to visit Professor Elias Compton who had just been retired as professor of philosophy and psychology and the dean-ship, after many years. He was regarded as one of "the old, old, guard." He was a quiet little person and at the time I met him was plagued with illness which eventual-ly caused the amputation of a portion of one leg and then on to greater disability and death. Looking me over he asked me my philosophy.

"Well, sir," I said in so many words, "that's a hard question."

"But are you not a personalist?" he asked.

I knew then his philosophy.

Personalism was then reigning at Boston University under the tradition of Borden Parker Bowne. To be a personalist in philosophy meant an assurance that you could be a philosopher and a Christian. (William James —so the story—sometimes came to his class in a fit of boredom and malaise and at such times he would most likely dismiss the class with some remark about his own poverty of ideas and therefore no sense to sit up front. One such day when ideas became fewer and he was about to quit the lecture for the day, he suddenly turned to the row of books on his lecture desk, took out one of the newest books [which happened to be Borden P. Bowne's most recent] and then remarked: "Well, let's see what God has to say.")

In my earlier day it was personalism which reigned in small denominational college philosophy departments. It was middle-of-the road, fairly Christian and not subject for campus heresy-hunters to complain about. God is the great Person. There are persons (of higher and lower degrees) including man, angels, sticks, worms, molecules, et cetera, et cetera—persons everywhere in the Universe of the Person. And so on. It used to be said that when the president of Ohio Wesleyan (Methodist) College needed a philosophy instructor, he picked up the phone and called Boston University (not Yale nor Harvard) and put in an order for any of their philosophy graduate students of their recommendation. No worry about possible radical heresy.

When Mr. Compton (he had an honorary Ph.D. from Wooster College, I believe) got on that subject, I smelled a mouse. I knew then that this had something to do with the less-trusted Yale philosophy graduate department.

And so I said truthfully: "Mr. Compton, I am very young. It is too early in life to say that I have settled on one philosophy."

This seemed to gratify him. At least, it was an honest and humble statement of my philosophical status at the time. I suppose the word then passed on to the hierarchy on the campus that I had the patriarch's blessing.

We went through a long period at Wooster when the Compton name was golden. I myself eventually held the Compton Chair of Philosophy (established by the alumni) over many years. We knew Mrs. Elias Compton quite well—an unusual woman of warmth and common sense and homemaker *par excellence*. She became the Mother of the Year in America (the year I do not recall)—and mostly deservedly. On the occasion of the death of Senior Compton, I came into contact with the Compton sons briefly and perhaps my only personal contact with them. They came to the campus often at the height of their careers with their wives proudly in their company.

I recall one incident which I never seem to be able to erase from my mind. I give it now. It was at the modest Compton home when the funeral procession was forming for the elder Compton. I could not believe my eyes when the famous sons in very proper dress came out of somewhere "rouged up" (cheeks and lips and forehead) with a kind of stage make-up, in white gloves and impeccably dressed getting in line for the campus-state funeral hardly a block away. I still see in my mind's eye the stately march down the long aisle and I wondered if perhaps some of the wives had taken this occasion to present their well-known husbands to the Wooster townsfolk and got their cue from Hollywood or a New York stage. I sensed an incongruity in the scene which was held to honor a modest man and father. But it is a part of the record. I slunked away into some corner of the chapel wondering about the strange ways of the world, strange, strange.

We had tenure at Wooster in those days. It was not easy perhaps to come by but it came to me. The appointment to the chairmanship of the department eventually came to me after having been twice passed by—given to the more suitable (campus-minded) of the Presbyterian royalty. Meanwhile, I began to "dig in" more than ever into my solitary study at home. It was the best thing that could have happened to me: for it left me freer to do the very thing I secretly wanted to do ever since my graduate school days at Yale: a hankering after authorship which disease I already had and probably would never have been cured of anyway. And the time came in its full swing—and thanks to the Wishart regime—to amend many little hurts. Of course, I was still a Lutheran at heart (sentimental perhaps—my clergyman father having been a stalwart in that church) and, moreover, I was not a personalist and I came more and more to realize it. I would have to earn recognition in ways other than being Big Man On Campus; and in due time, the shadows disappeared and the sun came out and I became, unwittingly, another candidate for the status of honored "old guard" which retirement has now conferred upon me—for better or for worse.

A PUBLISHING CAREER — EARLIER
PERIOD I

Shortly before I left the Yale campus, Dean Weigle took me aside and said in effect: Now when you go into this college teaching business, you will face two major alternatives about which sooner or later you must make a choice: on the one hand, the administrative and/or the social side of academic life or, on the other, the strictly scholarly. You just can't do both.

This alternative became crystal clear after a few years' round of experience. My choice was somewhat made for me: I had the fresh imprint of first-rate graduate-school teachers who were all scholarly; I was fed up with chasing after little things of a parish such as committees, ladies-aid societies, Luther Leagues, men's clubs, reports to the bishop and others, riding interurbans, a complex schedule which had continued since the year 1919 (and it was already 1926); and further, I noticed the gap between scholars and academic administrators who always had to defend something, to be beholden to public opinion (churches, preachers, synods, heresy hunters, moneyed people, alumni). The administration people seemed to recede into the distance of my respect. Diplomacy and accommodation did not seem appropriate on academic campuses where solid truth is supposed to be quested. Hypocrisy at any level (including the teaching profession) has always seemed to me a major offense. I now understand Professor T. V. Smith (philosophy of the University of Chicago) who once counseled me and pointed out to me: remember politics (he was engaged in Illinois politics) always spells accommodation; no one can ever succeed at it without the plasticity of compromise. And so I gradually withdrew from certain areas of the campus—where words must always be weighed. I did my work in social communication where I honestly could be myself, in the preparation of lectures, seeking the minimum of committee work. Perhaps my nature lacked the flair of political maneuvering and my temperament more suited for quieter places.

Dean Weigle had nursed me through the publication of my first book, not only in the matter of inducing a New York publisher (The Century Company) to take it in spite of the promise of a financial deficit but throughout the whole process of manuscript preparation, revisions, organization and even style. The mechanics I came to learn on my own later—also my own tricks of the trade in the dull preparation of book indexes. I suppose at heart I am a kind of perfectionist. This is the major reason why I never trusted any of my writings to a secretary. (My one major exception: my wife who is the best speller of the English language I have ever known and who has been, for me, an excellent critic of both style and content.)

And so years of writing began with the preparation of *The Crisis in American Lutheran Theology* (published in 1927) to number 27, which is the number the present book carries. All my "chillun" have their own personality and character and life history. No two books are alike. Not one gave their author fame. There were a few book club selections but never on the best sellers' list. Just about all of them are out-of-print and I myself am the best potential buyer if I can now get ahold of an extra copy. My own library has them all—and when I leave the scene I can envision no conceivable person interested in its physical fate.

In this chapter I set down some random notes on the birth and the delivery of the books—those of earlier years—since each one has a kind of life story (from conception to delivery) perhaps of interest to literary-minded people. For others, books will simply be books lacking personality. To this day I myself look at any book and wonder about its author: his type of personality, his health, his biography, his temperament and how he looks and dresses and behaves. I have always been of the school which holds that ideas belong to people and to understand them you really have to know something about the *persona* and the contextual situation which lies back of the writing. We shall never know fully about Plato and his Platonism without digging up some more reliable information about him. Was there a Mrs. Plato? (Behind every man is a woman to make or break him, be it a wife, a mistress or loneliness.) Ideas do not float around. They are all grounded in human beings: their experiences, their culture, their geography, their pocketbook, their frustrations and a thousand other factors.

I give my account without concern for strict chronology. I give it as the mood comes as I sit here in a northern Wisconsin hideout relaxed on a cool July day with chipmunks darting here and there and a mild breeze blowing through the pines and a peaceful sky-blue lake below me with not a human being on it at the moment. It is idyllic in a strife-torn world. And I sometimes wonder if I should forswear my life's earnings which gave me this modest place of quiet luxury and turn to work in the ghettos "where the action is." I rationalize and say: we are all somewhere (as I have said elsewhere in this book) and we take it from there. Others have their somewheres and they take them from there. When the somewheres get to be a universal Somewhere then we will do what others do because we are a part of the Absolute which is the sum-total. Meanwhile, here I am at this spot and at this particular stage of life. And like all older people I tend to reminisce and tell tales which interest the teller a great deal more than any theoretical listener.

A lot of hard work was involved in the making of my first book. It involved trips to Gettysburg in an old Franklin car none too dependable. They were amazed in New Haven that I was allowed to cart away so many hundreds of pamphlets and books from the historical library there. Many of them were unclassified—in today's terms of classification. Some amateur librarian had marked his or her own identification number—and that was all. My car was filled almost to its roof with this precious cargo. And I was told in no uncertain terms that this was an unusual privilege and that I must take super-care to see that every scrap of it was returned.

Professor Abdel Ross Wentz who had written a general history of the period on which I was writing had some kind of authority to let me into the library in the basement of the old seminary building at Gettysburg. I was in an historic place—which, as everyone knows, had to do with the Civil War and the take-over (for a time) by the Confederates of this old Lutheran college. Professor Wentz did not seem too anxious that I undertake the job; but Dean Weigle had given me a letter of introduction which was not to be easily by-passed.

It is strange that the human mind remembers trivial things as the past comes to memory. What I recall immediately from my first visit to Professor Wentz's home is a most trivial thing but, for what it is worth here it is: I had just left the large and expansive house, well furnished and historic and beautiful. I had forgotten something and remembered it after I had reached the road—quite some distance from the porch. It had been snowing and the drifts were deep. I called to him at the door saying I had forgotten my gloves (or whatever it was). Instead of coming down the swept path and meeting me part way and delivering the article(s), I recall that he threw them out into the deep snowdrift which necessitated my detour into the drifts. He failed to apologize. I always thought of this as a kind of discourtesy. But at the time, I remembered I was only a student begging for help and a professor may have certain privileges appropriate to himself. I always thought of it, however, as a case of bad manners—even to a person of non-status.

I had visited Mount Airy Seminary in Philadelphia for help in my research and there met the well-known church historian Henry Eyster Jacobs, venerable at that time. He gave me no encouragement. I remember his saying, in effect: let the dead dogs lie. In other words, my topic was full of old controversy. Why stir into it? It was a dark chapter in the history of American Lutheranism. (This, I thought then and I still think, was a strange utterance coming from an historian!) At any rate—I kept at the job and my first book is the result.

It was not warmly received by the Lutheran historians and churchmen. It was an account of the heretic Samuel Simon Schmucker, who wanted to make a more American church out of the Lutheran heritage and was even willing to compromise with the simple Augsburg Confession to promote the cause of ecumenical and fraternal relationships with other Protestant denominations. It is a sad story. The accepted books treated Schmucker as a kind of villain, his own son turning against the father. He died a lonely man—unaccepted by his time. Conservative Lutheranism won the day—thanks to the new and overwhelming powers of ultra-conservative Lutheran immigrants from Germany and Scandinavia—an explosion by numbers from abroad burying the growing American type of Lutheranism of the heritage of the Muhlenbergs and ultimately causing the capitulation of Gettysburg Lutheran theology to the conservative Mount Airy Seminary in Philadelphia. The two were recently merged into one. The Schmucker tradition was already buried at the time of Professors Wentz and Jacobs—both of whom were more denominationally conscious at that time. I was innocently caught in the middle and I think Dean Weigle must have enjoyed my predicament (which really had been his own in his earlier career).

Thus, I became identified with the Schmucker liberalism in the Lutheran church as my book circulated. The reviews were much better from outside Lutheran church circles than within. Church historians have the same frailty as systematic theologians: being sufficiently apologetic (that is, defenders of something rather than scientifically oriented to facts and to their philosophical [larger] interpretations).

1930 was in the offing. And it came to me that this was a big anniversary in Lutheranism: the 400th anniversary of the adoption of the Augsburg Confession, the Mother Symbol of Protestantism. It would call for commemoration festivities of one kind or another. How about a volume published for this occasion: one treating a reappraisal of the unique character of Lutheranism in the light of representative dissident groups in America? Would not such a volume be appropriate and perhaps appreciated? To this task I assigned myself as editor. (I did not believe in any one organization sponsoring it since there would be an open invitation to a loaded bias.) I invited twelve contributors and asked Dean Weigle to write the introduction. The book appeared in that year. It was a volume which invited almost immediate negative reaction from the synodical churches. With the ultra-conservatives were the liberals joining together under the bound covers of one volume: *What Is Lutheranism?* (Macmillan).

Professor John O. Evjen of the Hamma Divinity School (Wittenberg), the Reverend C. A. Wendell of Minneapolis and I were the bad boys of the book. The first named got under fire by the powers that be and I recall Dr. Tulloss, then president of Wittenberg College, contacting me by telegram and arranging some sort of interview in Wooster, Ohio, relative to the delicate situation on his campus because of the Evjen heretical views over which I had no control. There was some sort of panic going on, the details not now too clear. But I heard later some of his trustees came to Evjen's defense and the wrath of churchmen quieted. In the case of Wendell and myself, we were under public censure in the church press with pressures coming from my former professor at Augustana Theological Seminary and from the dean of the Lutheran Bible Institute in the St. Paul-Minneapolis, Minnesota area to bring us to trial and the possible termination of our status as accepted clergymen of the Augustana Lutheran Church. This was quieted down by the synodical president and some others who were not too happy about the Augustana professor and the dean and head of the Bible School. The church press continued to call for heresy summons but the boys in power stayed it off.

Some years later, the new president of the synod wrote me that there were murmurings among some clergymen concerning my philosophical writings and asked that I make a written statement as to my loyalty to the Lutheran Confessional books (doctrinal statements longer than any New Testament and dated in the sixteenth century). I wrote the president of the synod a short note in which there were two parts (I remember them well): 1) If you ask if I honor the Lutheran Confessional books in their historical setting as satisfactory for that perod of theological reformation my answer is: historically they have a place of respect for the Lutheranism of confessional development and that this is to be the only way to understand them and to give proper evaluation. Meanwhile time and experience

and study suggest reformulations according to a continued developing theology and that my position lay on
the side of a growing and maturing appreciation of what
may be called *essential* Lutheranism. 2) And my short
final paragraph referred to the close fraternal relationship which my father and the president's father had had
in their earlier ministries and such long mutual associations would suggest that their sons might find room
within the same church, that is, room for the Bersells
and the Ferms. This letter was never replied to and I
assume was filed away into a presidential file for naked
oblivion.

In my early years of teaching at Wooster I conducted
a seminar on contemporary philosophy using as a basic
text the two volume work called *Contemporary American Philosophy* edited by G. P. Adams and W. P. Mont-
ague. These volumes were the counterparts of
Contemporary British Philosophy edited by J. H. Muir-
head. Both sets followed the pattern of some of the
similar German series. I came to be impressed with the
fact that philosophies come out of the personalities who
espouse them: their culture, geography, training, time
and many other factors. Autobiography is certainly
not foreign to one's philosophy. Carl Murchison had
done a series on the psychologists revealing much about
their various psychologies. One such (I recall) was
Psychologies of 1925 (1927)—which reminded me at
the time of Broadway's Follies of 1930 and the like.

So one day the thought came: why not do a series on
American theologians, autobiographical accounts by
representative men? I decided that, if I undertook it, I
must ask the advice of some key-men as to selections

but I must be careful not to be drawn into some kind of super-editorial committee which would cramp my style. (One gets this urge after so many years of graduate work trying to please professors and committees. For once: on my own.) There were some reservations on the part of some potential contributors, one of which was my lack of status—being young and inexperienced and without too much portfolio. I decided then and there that I would stand up to such hesitant people oversensitive to a Freshman editor and omit them if they so chose. I believe I lost no one of importance as I later reviewed the scene. I regretted that I could not, by the limitations of space, include all worthy of a place in such a volume. Variety was desired: including even the most conservative.

The project developed into much larger proportions than at first anticipated, necessitating at least a two-volume series. A large batch of manuscripts came into my possession after heaps of correspondence. (I had to outline the purpose and format and all the little details which an editor must assume.) I had no secretary except the gratis help of my faithful spouse (who now knows as much about galley sheets and indexes and proof reading as any editor in a New York publishing firm). "We" acted on our own with all the risk involved. I was protected from the phone and given a private room in the attic where papers were never disturbed by friend or foe. This venture—after my Lutheran volumes—was the beginning of many years in dealing with printer's ink, the smell of which to "us" by now is as native as the smell of the pines is to us at our summer place. My mail began to mount. I lived from mailman to mailman and I am certain the postman believed he had some kind of wicked curse upon him when he was assigned our route of delivery.

My project almost died in stillbirth. I had no publisher nor a promise of one. Our country was in a financial depression and no publisher would be so foolhardy as to undertake a work of autobiographical essays by academics, especially a two-volume thing. Such a work would need subvention and where do I turn for help? I knocked on many publishers' doors. The answer was always curt (short, snappy "rejects" and "no's")—in spite of the distinguished company of scholars represented. Men such as: Benjamin W. Bacon, Edgar Brightman, Rufus Jones, E. F. Scott, W. E. Garrison, J. G. Machen (ultra conservative), H. N. Wieman, S. J. Case, D. C. Macintosh—to name some from the first volume; and from the second: E. S. Ames, John Baillie, William Adams Brown, Shailer Mathews, Luther Weigle, Eugene Lyman, Frank C. Porter—and others. All these men were leaders in the theological thinking in America of that decade.

There must have been some maneuvering behind the scenes because all of a sudden—after so many discouraging contacts with publishers—one day a letter of interest in my project came from New York. A publisher, unknown to me, was interested in it. We came to terms and got as far as the galley sheets. And then—silence, a long silence. Somebody, at least, (I thought) had already made a large financial investment in it and I need not worry. But the weeks passed—after I had read the proof —and weeks went on into months. My enquiries became increasingly anxious and there still were no replies.

What had happened I did not know. And to this day I
cannot recall the details. I later learned that one of the
co-owners of the new publishing house had jumped
out of his office window high up in a New York skyscraper never to circulate again. His partner after many
months seemed to reorganize and began publishing
under his own name—a name which did develop into a
modest reputation.

Meanwhile, page galleys began coming from still
another publisher whom I did not know. In the process,
I visited him in New York to see for myself what the
prospects were. We met for the first time as the door
opened, he at his desk and I a frustrated editor trying
to get some beginning acquaintance with these peculiar
people called "publishers." We both sighed at the same
time. He sighed (he told me later) because he was so
surprised to see such a young guy as editor of his forth-
coming publication. He said he envisioned me as a
human being, a stubby and fat person with a little pencil between my thumb and forefinger, hunched over.
(I do not have any idea now of how I looked then but I
guess I was a disappointment because I might have appeared somewhat vigorous and dapper [whatever that
means].) My sigh was my disappointment at his appearance: The thing was mutual. I had figured on meeting
another type of person—probably more businesslike and
formal. All we knew of each other as physical beings
was our handwriting and this is what gave us our impressions. We laughed about it loudly and long. It turned out to be none other than Charles W. Ferguson who
had written an enormously successful book on the
various religious isms and cults—a book well-informed

and jazzy *(The Confusion of Tongues*, 1927). I found it a fun-book and recognized it to be more: extremely well-informed. The Round Table Press was the name of his new firm and my galley sheets had found their way to his desk and to his liking and (as he said) this book would give his firm an entree into certain circles he coveted. So it was then. My two volumes were published under the title: *Contemporary American Theology* (1932, 1933).

Charles Ferguson seemed to have left his own firm (or those who underwrote him) a few years later. His name reappeared later on the list of the higher echelon of editors of *The Reader's Digest* and we have been in intermittent correspondence ever since. His literary work continued not only behind the scenes of the *Digest* but in authorship of serious and careful writing. My second volume in this series made a Religious Book-of-the-Month Club Selection which must have pleased Ferguson enormously as it did me then. For many years both volumes have been out of print. The reviews were extremely favorable as they should have been, considering that the contributors were top men in their several fields in America and of wide influence.

I was in a state of depression when, about this time—I began another major project. I felt at the time that my teaching assignment—although it was pleasant—was not panning out as I had hoped. The administration (which makes decisions of policy) seemed to be somewhat neutral towards me and I guess I had deserved it. My life did not gravitate toward the status of BMOC (Big Man On Campus) and those who then belonged to the campus Order (or Garter) of Administrators did not in-

clude me among their fair-haired boys who watch to
do the bidding as expected from the center of power.
I did not like the crowd. Every campus has its hangers-
on and I seemed to get the message since I was not
elected to the circle of the elect. I "holed in." To me,
at the time, the world outside looked a lot bigger than
the campus (as it really was) and I knew then that to
get going academically I must contact the world.

So I set myself a goal. My hero in this matter was
Professor Patrick at Iowa (already mentioned in this
book elsewhere) and I thought I would like to try an
introductory philosophy text along the line of his
(which incidentally had become a classic). How could
I improve over him? I had no such ambition and if I
had thought so I would have failed. But, why not try
a hand at it?

I recall a hot, hot summer in the attic of my home
on Beall and Wayne Avenue—an old house which we
rented cheaply. When the nearby campus became deserted, I put myself on schedule and worked long hot
and sultry hours up there near the hot tin roof—full of
ambition to contact the outside world. (No one thought
of air-conditioning in those days. Had it been available
we could never have afforded such luxury.)

So it went. On and on during the long summer. After
a few chapters' conclusion I sent the stuff on to Scribner's in New York. I knew no one at Scribner's. All I
knew was that this company at that time had no introductory text in philosophy while some of the other
major competing publishing houses did. Then began a
long, long story.

Mr. W. D. Howe was the editor-in-command and

he wrote me to send on more chapters. This I did as the work progressed. Finally, I asked for and received a publishing contract. Then began a long period of frustration. Mr. Howe liked my opening chapters but not the sister chapters that were coming to him. He asked for continual revision—no matter what I sent. And then he suggested I take a long rest from writing. I didn't want therapy from anyone—not even from Scribner's. But I had a solemn contract. I got his message. He, Mr. Howe, had cooled on the initial romance with my work and he was trying to find a way to dump it and me.

On and on I worked—through the fall and winter (between teaching assignments) and on to another academic year. I consulted certain academic people who knew the ways of publishers and they were quite flabbergasted that such a publishing house as Scribner's could be so unreliable with their contracts. It was a case plainly of Mr. Howe's change of heart.

I think now that he had a point—a big point. My work was carrying me away from its original purpose. It got too big and cumbersome. The reason, I suppose, is a sin common to many authors: they tend to put into one book all they then know, not realizing that readers are not interested in an encyclopedia, as such, except for reference. (This is one major criticism of present-day anthologies and the way of many unsuccessful books: the academic author is writing for other professors rather than for students.) But the day came when the book did get born and I was exceedingly happy. But it was born twins!

How could a book be born twins? It is very simple. When you have more than enough material for one book, you make two out of what you have (if you can). This is exactly what happened. I sliced the writing in two and what Scribner's did not get, I offered to another company: not as volume two but with a new title and with material that seemed to have its own unity. The first (Scribner) book came out with the title *First Adventures in Philosophy* (1936); the second book came out (1937) and carried the imprint of The Round Table Press, *First Chapters in Religious Philosophy* and a London edition by Putnam Publishers (an introductory text in the Philosophy of Religion). Confusion did arise, since both books coming out almost simultaneously contained in the title the same word "First." One of the publishers' patience was strained by the mix-up in orders which came in. I was dressed down by this and deserved it mildly. But I had two books and each one was introductory and the word "First" was the only one I could think of as suitable for both. Thus I became father of twins. (Both books went easily through their first editions and soon became unavailable. I had hoped for better; but I settled for my more modest hope: I would contact the world out-there beyond my little campus and its trivial politics.)

One proud thing I may say about both of these projects: they were carefully done and wore well since I checked and rechecked my expositions of the views of many philosophers about whom I wrote to be certain that I was not playing fast and loose with questionable interpretations. To this day I feel safe in consulting them when my memory fails me. And I know of no reviewer who called the twins fat and slobby.

It was along about this time that a new figure came

up over the horizon and entered into my professional life. I had not heard of him. His entrance came one day by mail and my reply closed the circuit of a new contact which was of tremendous influence in the course of my future literary explorations.

Dagobert D. Runes, born in Rumania, had fled to America in the Nazi persecution to seek refuge and to pick up the pieces of his battered life. His family had been dispersed cruelly and he himself was a scarred young man. At the University of Vienna he had achieved an earned Ph.D. degree, his thesis in German dealing with the Ethics of Plato and Spinoza. A well-informed man and academically trained, he sought entré into American philosophical circles which was none too easy. He ended up as a combination of businessman and scholar. With good sense he plunged into a business deal (buying a magazine which had lost the interest of its owner, a Digest in the area of the sciences) which increased his capital of much less than a thousand dollars by geometric proportions by reselling and entered into his own publishing business. It seems he never received a pinch of recognition by those in the profession in America who might have helped him. He was a foreigner without contacts. His firm of which he was owner, editor, publisher and policy-maker set itself to specialize in the philosophical field and continues to this day as The Philosophical Library (New York).

It was from him the letter came. Would I help him with his projected *Dictionary of Philosophy*, go over some of the contributors' definitions and take on a few myself? This was my chance! An outside contact and I grabbed it hungrily. Thus began an almost life-long professional association with a friend, a publisher and constant prodder to my own ambitions. We were about the same age, (I older) and both had had some ambitions and a lot of frustrations—of different backgrounds but of similar drives. Neither one really knew the other. I have no idea why he wrote me—an unknown "x." But the picture comes together something like this.

Already my own publishing career had begun—very modestly and without flair. I belonged to no establishment. My stakes were not deep in the ground. My concerns with my church's theological controversies receded quietly and quickly into the background of my interests and the open field of religious philosophy, theology and philosophy proper took over. In the midst of turning toward other publishing projects, I found myself writing definitions and a silent partner (along with others) in the Runes' project. It was pure fun to do these assignments and they kept coming as fast as I could turn them out. (I followed the apparent rule of Professor D. C. Macintosh [my Yale professor]: to turn out sentences carefully, using terms as precisely as possible—all of which must be observed for dictionary writing. In other words: no rhetoric.) I did not know then why Dr. Runes had turned to me. I still am not sure.

It appears that certain members of the American Philosophical Association (eastern division) had ganged up on him. They complained that they had been taken in by an arbitrary editor who editorialized unduly on their offerings. Moreover, such a work as a philosophical dictionary should be a mutually controlled affair rather than the affair of one man. I do not know the full story of the mess nor how many rebelled and withdrew their literary contributions. I seemed to have been singled out by him as one who could finish unfinished articles, correct some, comment on others, and write my own. And thus the Runes-Ferm relationship began which lasted through some decades. The *Dictionary of Philosophy* was published in 1941 and went through a number of editions, including paperback.

For many years I would have an annual conference with Dr. Runes at his New York office. This was a part of my annual and exciting trip to Union Theological Seminary in connection with the meeting of the Eastern Division of the American Theological Society. I had been elected a member in the days when the old-guard were in power: such as D. C. Macintosh, W. A. Brown, J. B. Pratt, John Bennett, Henry Sloan Coffin, M. Enslin, J. S. Bixler, E. S. Brightman, A. C. Knudson, Eugene Lyman, the two Niebuhrs, R. Calhoun, A. G. Widgery, Paul Tillich, D. Steere, H. Schneider, Rufus Jones, A. C. McGiffert, Sr., W. K. Wright, W. M. Horton and others. Runes was exceedingly well-informed on current philosophy trends (here and abroad) and knew who was teaching what and where in this country and thus could map out publishing plans years ahead of their fulfillment. As fast as I could do the work, he had planned another job for me and I never really caught up with him—since I was making a living as a teacher and had other work cut out for me. After we had shaken hands in his New York City office on a project over which we agreed, very soon a written contract came to hold himself and me in line. Never once did he interfere with my work nor edit

or change a single word of my manuscripts. There was
no superior editor to deal with. The galleys just kept
coming and the books soon after.

A PUBLISHING CAREER—EARLIER PERIOD II

To settle a controversy in the field of the psychology of religion—the claims of pioneer work in the "scientific" approach, or who published first—and to bring this field to a kind of togetherness I hit upon the notion that a book would be in order, especially an autobiographical account by certain well-known scholars in the field. Major leaders then were Edwin D. Starbuck (my own professor), James H. Leuba and George A. Coe. I added three other names, outside of the particular field of scientific psychology, those of S. Radhakrishnan, Alfred Loisy and C. F. Andrews, all of whom were extremely well-known at that time, particularly in England. Their autobiographies—especially their philosophical, psychological and religious pilgrimages—were, it seemed to me, worthy of permanent recording.

To this task, in the mid-thirties I gave myself, hoping also to include Dean Inge of London. The latter wrote me a gracious note to the effect that he had finished all he had to say and that he now was waiting the grand summons. I was unsuccessful in successive letters of persuasion. It griped me no end that the "gloomy dean" (title given him by non-scholarly writers) continued to write after turning me down—giving out a kind of essay I wanted and calling it *Vale, Vale* (Farewell, Farewell). This was one of his last books. He continued to live on and on, perhaps by then impatient with the last summons.

Having no publisher and possessing these valuable manuscripts I began to search for one. England seemed to be the best bet. And George Allen and Unwin (publishers in London) was synonymous with England. So one fine day, my wife wrapped up the manuscripts in heavy butcher-shop paper and I addressed the package to the British publisher—without prior notice of any kind and without any introduction of the editor. It went first class by ship—airmailing in those days was not the custom. I waited. In something less than a month I not only received word of receipt of the manuscripts but also a contract for their publication. The title agreed upon was *Religion in Transition* and the book came out in Great Britain in 1937. This book had class and I was very proud of it. Not too many of the book-public came across it but I know it circulated well abroad. One major obstacle came in the way: World War. And the book came to be a casualty: the publishers were bombed out and it took many years to recover.

One day I received a note from the London publisher to the effect that no royalties could be paid on this volume because of the war and I accepted this "as an act of God" (which legally it was). The book died an early death. Only recently, I received from a large bank in Chicago a generous check which George Allen and Unwin had covered and asked that it be forwarded to me. This was evidence enough, first, that the book still had life in England and, second, that some publishing firms are honest and trustworthy with their authors and editors, and thirdly, that this British company lives up to its reputation as being among the very best in the world. Their stamp upon an author's or editor's work is a gold seal of recognition. (Macmillan of New York issued an American edition in the same year.)

In the midst of all this there was another project in the offing. I do not recall what brought it about. But it turned out to be the *magnum opus* of all my endeavors. I would tackle a one-volume *encyclopedia of religion!* It dawned on me that the standard one-volume encyclopedia widely used in this field—and an excellent one— needed updating. Why not a new and fresh one, with so much new information easily available and written by experts in the particular fields?

So—where does one turn? I did the natural thing: wrote around to some leading figures in the field of comparative religion (as it was then called), church theologians, biblical experts, philosophers of religion, sociologists, psychologists, historians in Christian beginnings and in church history, denominational representatives, scholars in religious traditions other than "Christian" theology, philosophers—not too many but to get samplings. Yes, indeed, the views expressed agreement: there was such a need. But I ran into a few hard-fisted reactions. One was from Professor Calhoun of Yale. It went like this: certainly, there's a place; but it must be done through some responsible organization and through an editorial committee of competent people and properly supervised. (Since I never was a committeeman but a lone wolf, I scratched this one off, interpreting it as a mistrust of my competence for such a big adventure. I knew him to be a kind of perfectionist anyway and such a criterion only makes publications forever impossible.)

So I went at it alone. For four straight years I carried on correspondence and succeeded in enlisting one hundred and ninety contributors. I typed every letter myself and kept carbon copies. I outlined the type of thing I expected. I got a fair share of refusals but an astonishing response from many enthusiasts. I cross-referenced and indexed the material, editing bibliographies and formats to make for uniformity; suggesting revisions (never changing a word without permission); taking suggestions of names and of article-entries; limiting space assignments; et cetera, et cetera. No secretarial help. No Xerox then, only thin, worn carbon sheets. At my residence a mailman continued daily to deliver from his bulging sack a huge pile of correspondence concerning manuscripts, questions, recommendations—much like a small-town factory which of a sudden became national and even international. My postage bill mounted. One long drawer of my four-drawer files marked "Encyclopedia of Religion" gobbled up the stuff for future reference. My correspondence held me captive, since a few days postponement meant only chaos for me and the project. My wife, again, was at my side, checking this and checking that. I had a pool table in the basement of the house where alphabetization was carried on and assorting of such and such a manuscript with its progress (whether checked for errors of spelling, grammar, uniformity of format with others, bibliography, etc.).

Thus a one-man show turned out to be a circus with headaches, scheduled life, social monasticism—but as exciting as if one were contemplating a trip to the moon.

There were not enough hours in the day. I had full teaching schedules—and other projects.

But I had no publisher! It was a project as risky as canoeing down the Niagara River—with some miraculous escape as the only solution or else tragedy. What could I tell all my company of the best scholars if the whole thing fell flat? Only papers arranged and my attic their home? Unthinkable! And so, my search began. It would be costly for any publisher and I was still a Freshman professionally. Such a project should have the backing of the academically elite. Professor Calhoun was right. I was simply reckless and I would have to learn the hard way: by disgrace.

I was in the process of dealing with a lady literary agent (whom I had told very frankly of the rejection slips of some of the larger New York publishers) when Dr. Runes expressed an interest in the project. We came to terms largely through this agent who seemed willing to abdicate and I was in no mood for technical negotiations.

The Philosophical Library profited by this decision and this risk. Already the expenses had been heavy on me and certainly I was less interested in a good contract than in a plain one. So it was. The book moved slowly at first but gained momentum through the years. I became a "fair-haired boy" to my publisher. (I can only know, by his action of confidence, if not by sharing of the fruits of the crop.) After then, contract after contract for projected publications came and to this day I am not caught up. I became a consulting editor without portfolio. I wrote introductory prefaces for unknown authors. I was let in on publishing secrets of manuscripts.

I became a busy contributor to the magazine *Philosophic Abstracts* (Philosophical Library) which brought me many new books to review and own. The payoff was not financial but it was rewarding to my ambition: to make contact outside the small campus where I earned my living and the chance to be on the very inside of the publication game.

It is always amusing to me to hear my sons—and others —talk about "getting rich" off books. They simply do not know what goes on in secret chambers. Academic books are non-competitive with books on sex and the drugstore variety. Nor do they fully realize that a person like myself who loves his literary efforts finds his full satisfaction in seeing book-children being born and finding their way to a destined life on library shelves (rather than stillborn in attics) and even on college and university campuses where they have seemed useful. Money is, indeed, wonderful, wonderful, wonderful. But there are other compensations. This may be a form of rationalization and any regrets seem to dim by such rationalizations.

Dr. Runes told me later that his firm had sunk an initial twenty-five thousand dollars in the book (which in today's finances would sound to me, at least, fantastic). He gambled and won and more power to him! So did I —in the pleasure of knowing that just about every well-informed clergyman (not to speak of libraries and campuses) possesses a copy of this book (hard cover or paperback) and to this day of writing it appears to be a useful reference on study-desks rather than merely a place on a shelf. When they compliment me I can truthfully say: Yes, indeed, it is a fine book. Take a look at the list of contributors. They made it so: well informed, literate and to the point in their contributions.

I proofread the book myself, 844pp., double columns, four times. I trusted no one else with it. Toward the Catholic contributors who had their *Nihil Obstat* on the manuscripts (permission of their censors) I felt especially obligated that no errors or changes would creep in. And there were many Catholics in the project. The correspondence (and copies thereof) which never saw the light of print is more lengthy than the book itself.

The day the manuscript was ready, we gently laid the sheets carefully and in proper order filling two suitcases and I wheeled them in an old wooden wheelbarrow (dating back to a previous generation) to the little old railroad station, the Chicago, Northwestern, in Mercer, Wisconsin, insured it all for two thousand dollars and then waited until the seven-thirty train came in, which was the night train to Chicago. The suitcases were placed on the baggage truck and wheeled to the place along the track where the baggage car would stop. The train's whistle was heard long before it appeared around the north bend of the track. I almost cried seeing this precious cargo leave me—wondering if it would get damaged or lost or if I would ever see or hear from it again. It was, indeed, our "baby" if ever there was one: toward whom much love and sacrifice had been poured and from which we received only the thanks we could speak to ourselves. The train stopped and the baggage man pushed open the heavy doors.

"What's this?" he enquired of the station agent? "Whew—two-thousand dollars insurance! Why, I didn't know there was that much money in this little burg."

All I said (and I remember it well): "Please, please, take good care of them (the suitcases). They are all I have now. Not worth anything to anyone else—but to me—please take good care."

The man looked at me wistfully and said nothing. I suppose he thought I was a queer when the station agent said: "It's just a book."

I now relate in a few sentences about the most marvelous thing about the whole episode. *I had no copies of the book whatsoever!* The book as it was, comprised of hundreds of precious manuscripts carefully edited and properly sorted: the collective work of many of America's best scholars. No one had heard of Xerox in those days. Had it been lost or stolen (who would steal an unborn book? answer: no one if they knew) it would have been a complete loss! I, for one, would never have the heart to try to revive it. I was tired to the bone. All I did was to pray to a God of miracles that I be included as a favorite son when miracles needed to be performed. And this is the unbelievable part of it all: Not a sheet was lost although many hundreds of them came back to me for proofreading four times and generally as fourth-class mail—not to mention the returning of them for repeated corrections—and sometimes I found some of the sheets hanging outside the envelopes which contained them. And they came from strangers in Brooklyn where the publication-action then lay.

As I write this I say: "Thanks, dear Yahweh, for your interference with human frailty by performing this miracle." And after this I say: "Thanks, Uncle Sam" for wonderful and dependable postmen and an efficient post office department for their dedication.

(The latter may sound strange but when I think of and count my blessings I forget my own gripes about the postal service.)

1945 was a peak year for me. *The Encyclopedia of Religion* was published that year. In April my formal paper as president of the American Theological Society (Eastern Division) was presented at the annual dinner meeting at Union Theological Seminary in New York—an assignment which is not to be taken lightly. The following year it was circulated as a pamphlet under the title of "Oceanic Christianity" appearing first in the then disturbingly interesting *Journal* edited by Dr. Morton Enslin, first-rate scholar of Christian beginnings. The thesis of the paper was a defense of the view that pristine Christianity (essential) was an expansive religion rather than a contracting religious phenomenon (prophetic rather than priestly), that the ocean rather than the rivers of tradition is the best analogy. An ocean just is. Truths and values have a status of just being whether uttered by a Hindu or a Jew or a Mohammedan or by a Zoroastrian. Men are everywhere psychologically the same. The divisions are at best tributaries or limited expressions. Nature is our best teacher since the laws of Nature are expansive and need not be revised or updated. Such were the great prophets of all major religions. Denominationalism is name giving. Quality itself needs no names or authentic tradition or orthodoxy or even a normative theology (which always is dated and open for revision). Evil is not an entity which needs to be wiped out by some organized form of salvation "from" somewhere. Evil is a relationship always inherent in the possibility of the good. Its forms may change.

But essentially it is a part of the structure of our world (nature, cosmos, human relationships). We live with it as do the animals. We move from level to level, receding and going forward. But we never eradicate it. To do so would mean at the same breath to eradicate good. For what would good be unless there be an evil? This thought is nothing new: as old as thinking philosophers. But Christianity historically became linked with doctrines of salvation "from" and an institutional church which administered the necessary means. Other religions did the same—for the most part.

And, the other emphasis in the paper was that of the figure of horizontal religion rather than vertical—it is the man who is religious and the direction he should face is that of interpersonal relationships rather than appeasing some tyrannical deity. This horizontal figure was not a capitulation to a radical religious humanism but was emphasized to fit in with the growing disappearance of a two-world structure: the supernatural as over against the natural. To me, it is one world and Divinity is in this world, not outside and altogether transcendent. This is historic Christianity revised from its immediate ancestry, namely a structured Judaism which was wildly vertical and into which the priests moved and took over.

The paper was not too well received, I thought. Already the neo-orthodox were taking over in the American Theological Society. Karl Barth and his transcendental God emphasis was the yardstick and there were Barthians of one kind or another all over the place. All this made me uncomfortable for the simple reason that I had been raised on it in seminary days and had been weaned from that theological bottle. Many of the new adherents had never been through the crisis of a change of theological thought to the degree I had moved. And as the years passed we had a new crowd taking over, men such as the two Niebuhrs, Mackay (Princeton) and less dramatic figures of the conservative party. Those of us who resisted were becoming fewer each year.

Finally, it wound up with Professors Enslin and Widgery probably being the most effective polemicists against the rising tide of conservatism in the Society with others more neutral or less vocative. My enthusiasm for the Society waned and I finally resigned my membership after many happy years with the greater theological gods in America who had stood for the integrity of human reason, philosophy, philosophical psychology and critical Biblicism. The new breed talked much about the Word of God, the church, the impossible possibility, man's sinfulness, the utter incompetence of man before the Lord of Lords, the Bible saying this and that, the leap of faith (Kierkegaardian), supernatural revelation confined to one book which included only two historic religions (Hebrew-Judaistic and Christian) and so on and on. Pessimism had set in and it went along with the tired-blood spirit of two World Wars and the Germans again taking the lead for the new orthodoxy. Numbers of expatriated German theologians moved into the scene and there followed a Tillich era in which theology was interpreted as based upon a Christian revelation and the similar traditional premises dished out into modern terms. (I knew Paul Tillich soon after he came to this country. I tried to capture him for one of my books but

found him then too verbose and ponderous for understanding. I returned to him his long manuscript as un-
suitable and it appeared elsewhere under a different con-
text. We remained professional friends although I felt
that as a philosopher he had abdicated his freedom for a
traditional set of norms [Biblicism]. When in debate he
appeared cornered he seemed to find an escape by quoting the Psalms or some other Scripture. He rode two
horses when in my opinion he should have ridden one.
He pleased the church crowd with his Scriptural refer-
ences but this was [to me] only another case of au-
thoritarianism if not church politics when, on the contrary, a philosophical position demands of a philosopher
reasoning to the bitter end.)

To serve as a text for my classes in philosophy of religion and hopefully to reach a wider audience I worked
on a small book which took the name of *What Can We
Believe?* Dr. Runes (Philosophical Library) took this
one for publication (1948). I thought it was time for me
to take stock with myself and the writing of it helped
to crystalize my scattered thinking. I took the conven-
tional topics such as the church, prayer, immortality,
freedom, God, nature of religion, nature of a good religion, essential Christianity and other topics and gave
them a once-over in terms which I thought college students would find realistic. This book went through its
edition and created no stir. It was never seen on the
counters of denominational book stores nor generally reviewed by denominational journals. I was not only the
bad boy among Lutherans but I had revealed my true
colors to others: I was a bad boy in current American
theological circles. Moreover, the new orthodoxy was

not ripe for critical revaluation. I was dubbed—by those who paid any attention—as skeptic, naturalistic materialist, secularist, nonconformist, destructive critic, and in general professional *persona non grata*. College students, by and large, who have used the book in classes have responded as the kind of treatment which has saved whatever faith was left in them after listening to undisciplined sermons and dogmatic pronouncements of religious elders and a kind of positive pill to a reasonable appraisal of their religious inheritance. This has been the real payoff and it has given me infinite pleasure.

The same year (1948) a major symposium which I had edited saw the publication light. Dr. Runes had asked me to work on it as a part of a series of contemporary studies. Such a series already had included such titles as "Twentieth Century Sociology," "Twentieth Century Psychology," "Twentieth Century English," "Twentieth Century Political Thought," "Twentieth Century Philosophy" and now this one to be entitled *Religion in the Twentieth Century*. I enlisted twenty-three essays by as many contributors who wrote from within of their religious faith or from special studies. As I look back on this volume I am amazed at the good luck I had with my contributors. The reader may judge this statement by a sampling: Swami Nikhilananda (a personal friend of mine, whose services I attended once a year for many years while in New York City) wrote on Hinduism (he himself of the Ramakrishna Order), J. S. Taraporewala on Zoroastrianism, N. H. Knorr on Jehovah's Witnesses, S. K. Saksena (now at the University of Hawaii) on Jainism, Ananda Coomaraswamy on Buddhism, Conrad Moehlman on Liberal Protestantism,

James Hail (my colleague at Wooster) on Taoism, Chan Wing-tsit on Confucianism, D. C. Holtom (world authority) on Shinto, Salma Bishlawy (Egyptian emigrant and a former student of mine who majored in philosophy at Wooster) on Islam—and so on down the list. Other articles consisted of such topics as Sikhism, Conservative Protestantism, Society of Friends, Church of the New Jerusalem, Anglo-Catholicism, Church of Jesus Christ of Latter-Day Saints, Bahaism, Reform Judaism, Conservative Judaism, Reconstructionism (Jewish), Ethical Culture, Salvation Army, Christian Science, Ramakrishna Movement (Hindu) and Naturalistic Humanism. The book helped me to see into the future when men will quit their vertical gaze through some one particular ecclesiastical telescope and find a common Divinity horizontally in the experiences of men of all religious faiths, each expressing some worthy facet of that Divinity which is involved in the fate of all sons of men.

As I write these lines I wonder how I had the time just before 1948 with all sorts of commitments to do these two books simultaneously. I found the answer to this query on the floor of my kitchen in my summer home. I had painted the years of my research sabbaticals in white on the red linoleum and I saw the years 1946-47 which were the years of my first sabbatical. I was supposed to do research. The College of Wooster granted me their first appointment to the new leave plan wherein the recipient would be granted full salary on condition he would devote himself to academic improvement. I took this as a sacred trust and stayed the whole cold winter firing a hungry kitchen range, loading a huge fireplace with logs of birches and maples and cedars and pouring kerosene into the tank of a kerosene stove to counter the wintry blasts. It was no period of martyrdom. It was heaven on earth. The mailman was just as close to me at Mercer versus New York as it was Wooster versus New York. And the galleys kept coming and we (my wife and I) worked the sheets and the correspondence and that was that. I was a privileged person and I was aware of it. Not many academic people have been as lucky as I, to have had four such full-salaried sabbaticals (one each fifth year) when the plan began. I guess I was reappointed because there was evidence that I had tried to fulfill that trust.

From 1950 through 1953 saw another rash of Ferm books and I now wonder what I was doing just previous to this time. My kitchen floor (which has the dates) reminds me that I had another research sabbatical 1952-53. My memory is not clear of the order. This is understandable since more than one book was going at the same time—and I am much older! *Forgotten Religions* (1950) belongs here about which I have heaps of conscious pride. The anthropologists seized on this book and to this day I receive requests for an extra copy lying around the house. It is the kind of book that does not soon outdate itself. It has since appeared under another title, as *Ancient Religions*. Philosophical Library was behind this one. I found no difficulty in gathering the material as editor since experts in certain restricted areas of ancient history and even pre-recorded history are anxious to have their material made public and there is little opportunity so to do, outside of a scholarly article in a scholarly journal. Topics here were: The Dawn of Religions; The Religion of Ancient Egypt; Sumerian Religion; Assyro-Babylonian Religion; Hittite Religion; The Religions of the Canaanites; Religion of Prehistoric Greece; Mystery Religions of Greece; Hellenism and Alexander the Great; Mithraism; Manichaeism; Mazdakism; Old Norse Religion; Tibetan Religion; The Religion of the Australian Aborigines; South American Indian Religions; Shamanism; The Religion of the Eskimos; The Religion of the Navaho Indians; The Religion of the Hopi Indians. All of which made a fairly good cross section which the book title carried.

It took a lot of detective work to find key and top scholars. But I found them—each a super-specialist in his area. I recall that I tried many doors to find a Celtic expert and in vain: researchers in this field were no longer among the living and, moreover, what is now said to be known is no longer reliable. Much of the excitement of an editor of this kind of project is the correspondence with great scholars who are really among the unknown of the day and who as a class are cautious, disciplined and humble people. Which reminds me: most of history will never appear in print because most of the heroes remain unknown. Their selves lie behind their works. Their causes are greater than themselves. I refrain from repeating here the names of the scholars who contributed to this book. Any interested reader will find that the editor tells something of their professional status in a page preceding each contributor's offering. I am proud to have been a part of this company, even though only a master of ceremonies.

A History of Philosophical Systems came out the same year (1950). I need not dwell on this one since happily it is fairly well known among contemporary students of philosophy. It is a long and heavy work and written especially for professors of philosophy. When I was at Wake Forest University as a visiting professor a few years ago, graduate students came over from Duke University to pick up copies at the Salem (N.C.) book shop which had some special entree with publishers of hard-to-get books. They told me that this one book was their savior in helping them pass the written prelims for the doctorate. I am not surprised since a Ph.D. in philosophy should have his material systematized sufficiently under the leadership of qualified exponents such as appear in this book of some forty representatives to qualify for a preliminary examination of his general knowledge of historical philosophy, both East and West. (More on this book later.)

My own class notes over many years as a student in graduate school and as a teacher of the course in "History of Christian Thought" suggested to myself and approved by The Philosophical Library the possibility of a modest dictionary of Protestantism and church origins. Such a book appeared in 1951 under the title of *A Protestant Dictionary* (a paperback of the same appeared later with the title *Concise Dictionary of Religion*). At that date, I could find it a word of truth that I had had some seven thousand students in my courses on the Wooster campus—almost a quarter of a century —to whom I could dedicate the volume. I have no way of knowing how it was received—other than the prodding of the publisher to keep going.

Three new volumes came out two years later, that is, 1953. Against the rising onslaught of non-tempered resurgence of a conservative Protestant theology—a kind of neo-fundamentalism without the hopelessly non-progressive type of initial fundamentalism—it became clear that a volume was in order to express the essentials of a liberal (though not radical) Protestant plurality (variety) of expressions. The participants in this book —which I planned, edited and titled *The Protestant Credo*—were names known to be non neo-orthodox, some, however, liberal to the left and some liberal to the right. No one could be classified as a religious humanist or a cultist. Gaius Glenn Atkins, one of America's outstanding men of the Protestant pulpit, led the list and then followed John Bennett, Francis Buckler, Morton Enslin, Senior Bishop Francis McConnell, John McNeill, Conrad Moehlman, Floyd Ross and Henry Wieman. The editor poked his nose into this family by suggesting his own frame of mind, in effect: suggesting that Protestantism has in its own spirit the seeds of its own dissolution. The fully emancipated mind is essential to Protestantism and the full implications are not in the bag of any foreseeable prophet. This stance itself was a declaration of my own emancipation — and I did not then hold, nor do I now, that it meant a kind of iconoclasm. As my own studies and self-reflection had developed, much of the tradition of Protestantism itself needed to stir beyond Protestantism (the title of the essay) in whatever values need or can claim survival in the best experiences of men. As I now see it my mind had taken wings which leaves even the present-day ecumenical movement as one tied to the mother's apron strings and not yet taking independent steps toward a maturer Christian theology. Frankly, this leads to a

kind of revaluation of the Christian religion itself—
Protestantism being only a single chapter—something
after the pattern of "Oceanic Christianity" (already discussed). We, in our time, are faced to exchange experiences with other religions of whatever the name and
capitulate on the long standing platform that religious
truths are the copyrights of only one religion—there
being a Divinity that casts its influence among all the
sons of men. Thus there is a "beyond Protestantism," a
liberal interpretation which this generation is not ready
to acknowledge.

The second of these volumes published in 1953 was
The American Church. This was a composite historical
account of the several denominations of Protestantism
presented by exponents informed from *within* their
respective groups. Fresh appraisals were asked for from
the score of contributors. The topics consisted of: The
Moravian Church, The Lutheran Church in America
(the editor appointing himself to this task—since no
one else would conceivably appoint him!), the Men-
nonites, The Presbyterian Church in America, The
Protestant Episcopal Church in the U.S.A., The Reformed Church in America, Unitarianism, The Congregational Christian Churches, Baptist Churches in
America, The United Presbyterian Church, The Society
of Friends in America (Quakers), The Evangelical
Mission Covenant Church and the Free Churches of
Swedish Background, The Church of the Brethren, The
Evangelical and Reformed Church, Methodism, The
Universalist Church of America, The Evangelical Unit-
ed Brethren Church, Seventh-Day Adventists, Disciples
of Christ and The Church of God (Anderson, Indiana).

Some of these works (as listed in this chapter) came out under different titles; some came out dressed in new outer garb and in paperback. The ways of publishers are mysterious and not fully comprehensible to authors and/or editors.

The third in the group of books published at this time (1953) was an editorial task—and it was not easy—assigned by the new publishing firm calling itself Library Publishers entitled *Puritan Sage, Collected Writings of Jonathan Edwards,* an appointment which took me back to the Yale Library where there is found an Edwards' depository (his handwriting at places almost illegible). 1953 marked the 250th anniversary of Edwards' birth and this volume was a modest recognition of the extremely influential American theologian and philosopher—certainly of the colonial period. He remains an interesting character: a dedicated student amidst an environment not too conducive for scholarship and a time not too opportune. Some hitherto unpublished writings of his were included along with rare memorabilia reproduced in his hand. I pretended to be no authority on the man. I was only fulfilling an assignment and wished to invade a territory which had lain outside my professional career.

I recall my first encounter with the name of Edwards many years ago while on the Yale campus: it was strongly urged on me to do a doctoral thesis on him by a responsible man on the faculty. I spent some weeks in the Yale Library pouring over his penmanship and decided then and there that my degree would be, if successful, postponed perhaps a decade: 1) because it would take months on end to decipher some of the material and I was not that kind of a literary scholar and 2) because my interests were elsewhere and 3) because time was running out: I had a family already making too many years of sacrifice for human comforts and needed soon a decent breadwinner, or, in other words, a job that promised at least a living wage. This volume thus was for me a kind of easing a rather undisturbing conscience and a fulfillment of some curiosity of what I may have missed earlier in my academic life. So be it. The book got around and I was only mildly pleased.

Jonathan Edwards' works (following the path of John Calvin) may make different and profitable reading for our present generation which has strayed far to the left from the paths of self-discipline!

A PUBLISHING CAREER—MIDDLE YEARS—
AND SOME INTERLUDES

Some books do not get born. They die at various stages. Attics may be their earthly-eternal home. They may be executed by some political censors. Some disappear by mysterious decisions of publishers or committees. I had one such experience with a book that was to be called *Polarity* and destined for public life in 1951. I still do not know what caused its death but here is the brief account of what I do know, mysterious as it remains.

One day a letter came asking if I would complete a book unfinished by a designated author. His name: Hugo Bieber. I took a look at the typescript and found myself at that time quite sympathetic with its thesis, especially after having studied under Professor Sheldon at Yale and had come to know his wholehearted support of a philosophy which at heart was dualistic. I did not then know what was back of the projected book. All I did was to accept the assignment and proceeded to spend hours on it, with supplementary material stating the case for a polarity (dualism) — a title I gave the book — at work in the world of reality.

The book died without any obituary. I wrote around to find out what the sickness had been and when and where the funeral had taken place. This led me to the

175

name of Mr. Franklin J. Matchette and The Franklin J. Matchette Foundation (New York).

It seems that Mr. Matchette was a very wealthy man whose chief interests lay in the area of inventions and patents and business. But he had a hobby. It was that of reading the philosophers. There was no pretense of professionalism. He just liked what the philosophers are supposed to do: speculate about the Universe. And then he had come to the conclusion that this is a Duoverse rather than a Universe. The number "two" is everywhere. It seems that he had a book published on the subject of Metaphysics with his name as author and this doctrine was the thesis. Somehow the book did not make any "break through" other than to be bound copies (perhaps limited in number). Meanwhile, he died and left a substantial estate which his nephew administered from his home in upper New York City.

My name seems to have been suggested to someone and I recall visiting the nephew one spring in the early fifties at his New York home—(was it 63d St. near Fifth Avenue?). I recall ringing the doorbell and a butler responding. I had no card other than my name. I was asked to wait at the doorstep and it was quite some wait (as I recall). Then, the butler reappeared and escorted me ceremoniously to the inner chambers. My first impression was that of affluence everywhere. Soon a distinguished-looking gentleman appeared and greeted me profusely. I remarked about the attractiveness of the home and especially about the ceiling-to-floor bookcases filled with books.

"All, more or less on philosophy," he said, in effect.

"And there are other rooms. In the vault there are philosophy manuscripts and special editions."

(I could only wish he would have invited me to stay there—for months!) He then told me something about The Matchette Foundation of which he was an executive and its plans. He knew about my assignment and to the enquiry of "What had happened?" he said in effect that the publication had been held up pending some current projects of the Foundation. I asked if there might be another office than this one. And he said modestly: "No, this *is* the home."

I thought it idealistic: money, manuscripts, potential books, books, money, beauty, quiet residential area of New York City, money, projects,—heaven.

Such was my contact with The Matchette Foundation at its heart in New York City—and it was extremely brief. I had received a fully adequate check for my part of the contract on the projected book. I had no further claim. I only had the concern that the child would sometime be born in the fullness of time and be acceptable to the reading public.

Mr. Matchette (I learned) had ownership in the Pennsylvania Hotel in New York City opposite the Pennsylvania Railroad Station and later called Hotel Statler; that he pioneered in agricultural bacteriology; that he was an inventor of some kind of door-within-a-door through which laundry could be collected from carriers in the outside hall (of hotels) without gaining access to the hotel suites. (I myself have stayed at the Pennsylvania-Statler Hotel many times and saw the unique thing—which I never understood but knew to be functionally operative.) He had many other inventions and investments (real estate, for example). (When the tunnel was constructed into New York by the Pennsylvania Railroad, Mr. Matchette saw the great prospect for a hotel at the terminal—which under him turned out to be the largest hotel ever constructed.)

It was he (I have been told) who financially sponsored Bertrand Russell's tour and lectureships (at least in part) in America. He also sponsored some significant agricultural research center at Madison, Wisconsin (perhaps connected with the University?). And his Foundation had sponsored the Bieber-Ferm volume on Polarity which (as far as I know) never appeared— probably still in the vaults somewhere unless destroyed and sent on into eternal oblivion. I have no Xerox copy of the book (years before Xerox or "the B. X. era") and I am not sure I could find carbon copies of my own chapters hidden away in a present-time cluttered attic in Wooster, Ohio. Thus is my tale: sad to me and there are probably no other mourners, not even Bieber who had died and thus spared such curiosity and mystery and sudden death of an unborn book! And that was that.

Authors, I suppose, whether they admit it or not, some time or another, toy with the idea of writing a novel. I had my case of novelitis—with a fever to go with it— about the year of 1953. And I set myself madly to ridding myself of the plague. The only way to do it was to write.

This I did one summer—sitting in a small bedroom in Mercer, Wisconsin with the door shut and without anyone knowing about my dedication except my faithful wife. When company came she shut the door and could cover up no more for my unhospitality than to admit the noise of typewriter keys came from the bedroom to which I had quarantined myself for the duration.

I really had a story to tell (so I thought). How to do it I had no idea. I had been intrigued by Sinclair Lewis' *Arrowsmith* (which Pearl Buck recently calls one of the greatest novels of our time). I had asked for an interview with Louis Bromfield at Malabar Farm (Lucas, Ohio) only some thirty miles from Wooster and had an appointment approved. I wanted to ask him how he went to work in writing and especially novels.

I was warmly received. Four huge dogs kept nagging me, two in my lap and others pushing at my legs—fearful at any moment that I would meet an untimely death. He sat at his huge crescent-shaped desk, explaining to me that the worktable for a writer should serve ample space at a moment's notice. When he wanted something all he did was to slide his chair on rollers to that part of the table where such papers would normally be found. His typewriter had its place. It was the comfortable swivel chair that took him places. (I understand that his table and other paraphernalia are still in his workroom at Malabar Farm for tourists to look at for a "donation" as it is now called.

He then told me of Sinclair Lewis' writing habits. Lewis would draw maps of the theoretical farm or place of his projected story so that he could keep his detailed descriptions accurately throughout the plot. (He was, I guess, spatially minded.) He told me also that there must be a story not just an essay. (And then and there I recalled my reading that great tale of the South by Margaret Mitchell *Gone With the Wind* and how deftly she ended each chapter in the midst of some sort of reader-suspense to whet the appetite for that to follow: a number one secret which I carried in the back of my head hopefully some day to emulate.) And as other authors have said, he reminded me that authors have to get used to "pantsitis": which is an ache that begins at the top of the spine attaching the head to the torso and concentrating with full force at the bottom where two half-moons rest unevenly on the more or less hard seat of a chair, with human legs dangling here and there and sending aching signals to the brain to remind the human animal that all this is abnormal and an abhorence to the son of an ape. Bromfield gave me his blessing and the dogs spared my life by losing interest in me as the conversation had entered into a dull stage of interest.

The story of my novel is about a young fellow who had been raised in a very conservative tradition and had gone on to college where brainwashing continued and then had gone on to Yale for something he sought but did not have clearly in mind. And there is romance and all the rest. His encounter in a small denominational college as a teacher reveals the temper of the times: hypocrisy, dictatorship, Christian-oriented—and then a tragic fire which rearranges the order. There is plenty of sin in the book—without being sexy or vulgar. And the character of Harland comes out with a kind of victory no one really knows (except that of vindication). When I am asked, "What became of Harland?" I have answered that I have not yet read the sequel and thus do not know. I sometimes wonder myself what became of my hero: John Harland.

This book was written in secret and when it came out in 1954, it came out as news to the campus at Wooster with a bang. The *Cleveland Plain Dealer* had a bit about it (which I did not know): something to the effect that the small "Christian" college had finally been exposed and that the author was a professor at Wooster. The yellow jacket had the sub-scription (an announcement prepared by the publisher) "A Novel of Campus Politics and Intrigue."

Soon after, at the end of a Monday night faculty meeting, I noticed the new president of Wooster College (Howard Lowry) stalking hurriedly in my direction (my seat usually being close to the rear and to the exit—in case of fire!) and he looked me in the eye:

"Vergilius, so you have a new book out! Saw it announced in the *Plain Dealer*. Remember, *you have to live with it*." (Evidently, he was afraid that I had brought a bad image to the college.)

And I remember what I said in reply.

"Howard, I'll live with anything I write."

Thus, and after, campus whispers came to me: His (the author's) character-So-and-So is So-and-So on the campus! When asked, my standard answer was: all the characters are fictitious. If anyone would press me further I would have to answer further: fictional characters are composite characters, some qualities of real people mixed with other reals into fictional composites. It is difficult to keep these characters the same throughout—the task for any writer of fiction (I think).

The novel was published under the title *Their Day*

Was Yesterday (438 pages). It was, indeed, a beautiful book in terms of its physical appearance: fine paper, clear type, beautifully-bound, striking yellow jacket and generally impressive. Among all my book-off-springs I think this one takes the prize for looks: in my judgment, this is how a good-looking book should appear!

The story of this project is still not finished. I visited the publisher (Library Publishers, New York, who had already done my Jonathan Edwards book) in his small but plush office on East 40th Street, in New York City, during the days of negotiation. This was to be his banner book and he gave everything to it. After its birth, I waited for my correspondence to be answered. The mailman continued to respond with just nothing. Nothing, I repeat. I tried to contact the publisher-editor. Nothing, I repeat. It was months later that the word came: my publisher had had a nervous breakdown and was a committed patient. No address.

Thus, except for enterprising friends of his who had distributed the book as calls came for copies I heard nothing further—except "status quo." As I write these lines, I still do not know and I still wait for the mail to bring me the good news of his full recovery. Bless him: he was my monitor and both he and I deserved better treatment from Mother Nature. I guess it is not easy to be a new publisher. And I guess it is worse if a publisher's first major effort had the bad luck of taking on a work by an unseasoned novelist! Thus ends this tale except for the haunting aspiration that someday the Hollywood people will seek me out for permission and a contract to make John Harland, my main character, a leading star. Had it been possible earlier, my choice would have been Clark Gable. Now that he is gone I have none.

The fate of my book, I suppose, was the same as that shared by Deems Taylor, Louis Untermeyer, the biographer of Valentino (Alan Arnold), the biographer of David Belasco (Craig Timberlake), and others in the early fifties. So I was not alone in my memories.

I make a dead stop at this point. And turn back. Why, I ask myself now, did I undertake such a venture as a novel when really I had no such literary background nor a good "rational" reason to do so. There was other work to be done; I still had unfulfilled promises to work on, other projected books by a publisher who found somehow he had use for me. As I reason this query to some rational conclusion I find myself recounting a tale which I have not yet told in this autobiography. It goes like this.

The summer of 1937 gives the answer to myself at least for the course of my own literary career. It was the summer of a lectureship which was offered me and which I accepted at Auburn Theological Seminary, Auburn, New York. The invitation came from Professor John Bennett, long a colleague in the American Theological Society. He wrote to ask me to take his place at a summer conference of clergymen to give a series of lectures on the philosophy of religion.

I was very young professionally and this seemed to me to be a large order. There were some hundred or so clergymen who took my lecture course and I was surprised that they all stayed with me throughout the whole period listening attentively and taking notes each morning. It was a lift I badly needed. Certainly in this respect they gave me much more than I gave them. I recall one morning a tall middle-aged man strolled in late as I was lecturing. He looked much like Ichabod Crane or Abraham Lincoln. He took a chair in the back of the room with his legs sprawled out in front of him. I kept wondering who he was as he seemed somehow to be an unusual person. After the lecture I made a point to pass through the crowded aisle and headed toward him. I was introduced. I now recall vividly his name since it is the same name as our family piano: McPhail. As the conversation turned, I soon found out that here was a well-informed Presbyterian clergyman who really knew his way around in philosophy.

"You seem to have studied in this field . . . Have you?" I asked.

"Well, yes," he drolled . . . "Pretty much my life."

"And did you do graduate work in philosophy?" I asked.

"Well, yes," he replied.

I waited for more but I hadn't succeeded in priming the pump.

Soon some philosophical ghosts appeared. To my amazement he had studied with William James, Josiah Royce, George H. Palmer, George Santayana, and with other of the then Harvard gods.

"Did you stay on . . . for a degree?" I asked, hesitatingly.

"Well, yes."

"You mean," I gasped, "you worked on your Ph.D.?" Pause.

"Yes, of course."

"So," I said in surprise, "you are a Harvard Ph.D. in the day when Harvard was at its peak? You are Dr. McPhail?" He remained silent.

I then said the only thing I could think of:

"Dr. McPhail, you should be standing up there where I stood this morning and I invite you to take over tomorrow morning."

And he said politely: "Well, you are doing all right."

This was an expression of good manners or it was sarcasm or it was a compliment. I took it positively (positive thinking) and I experienced a lift which I never forgot.

Before he left the lecture room I bombarded him with more questions—interrupting the greetings he received from my Presbyterian clergymen students, many of whom recognized him.

"Dr. McPhail, what was your thesis?" I continued.

"Oh, it had something to do with the belief or disbelief in God and immortality on the part of men of the sciences."

"You mean," I said, "the thing that Leuba did years ago in his book on *Belief in God and Immortality?*"

"Yes, yes," he said.

"Did you come to the same conclusion as he?"

"Yes."

"And was it not that the greater the men of the sciences (physics, biology, psychology, and the like) the less positive the belief?"

And he said, "Yes."

(Both of us understood the why of this: God had been made small by the clergy who had proclaimed Him; and such men of the critical sciences were agnostics if not atheists in mood [if not in expression] as they contemplated the orthodox.)

So it must have been William James who was McPhail's sponsor—so I deduced. And it was psychology of religion: his doctorate. I thought to myself: I had psychology of religion a-going at Iowa and I had Starbuck who helped James! Brother . . . here is a brother.

"Did you publish your thesis?" I asked.

"Nope," he replied.

"How come?"

"Never got around to it."

"Was this about the time of Leuba's famous book?"

"Yes, it was."

"So he moved in on you?" I said bluntly.

"Yes, he did."

And this is the tale of many a person who procrastinates, I thought. Delayed publication is no publication. How stupid or how unlucky or how indolent can a person be! And so, then and there I learned something: if you have something to say, say it publicly and get going. Why wait around and let someone else say it? Is waiting selflessness? Or is the other, egocentricity? I thought these thoughts all the way back to my room and I made a decision then and there. "I'll be like Dr. McPhail?"; and again "I won't be like Dr. McPhail?" And this is why I introduce him at this point. Unwittingly, he gave me something which I carried away that morning: *Don't let things just happen. Make the happening yourself—at least try!*

Two more items about the man—my Ichabod Crane, my hero.

"Did you ever think of going into college or university teaching?" I asked him.

"Well, yes, I did—once."

"How come that you didn't?" I prodded him.

"Well, there were no offerings. I just kept on with the parish I had and hoped. Then, one day, a telegram came from a college president out in the mid-west: Illinois, somewhere. He asked if I would come out for an interview. So I thought it over and talked with my wife and she said I ought to go out. So I did. It was a long train-ride. The country out in Indiana and Illinois is awfully flat. I changed trains in Chicago and took another down south and west to the little college town. The country was flat. He offered me a job and I told him that I would think it over. My, the country is flat out there! When I got home I said to my wife: 'Would you like to move out into a country that is flat all over?' And she said: 'Not particularly.' Well, that's how I felt and I wrote him I wasn't interested."

I stood there in amazement. Compared with the beautiful countryside in and around Auburn and the Finger Lakes region, he was dead right. But one doesn't go into teaching merely on the basis of geography or scenery! One has to take what comes and go from there —or one stays in a beautiful surrounding and settles for some kind of stalemate. This was another lesson: "I would like to be like Dr. McPhail?"; and again, "I don't want to be like Dr. McPhail." Must one not launch out into some unpromising land if one has the chance to do what one may want to do? So, I felt better to realize that I was living in a small town in Ohio where the traffic at that time was negligible but I did have a job I grew to love with all my heart and to encounter young minds searching for some decent way of thinking about the world—*even as I was searching*.

Sunday morning I chose Dr. McPhail's church for the place of worship. Very few were in the large, old building: The First Presbyterian Church. The organ was powerful and stately and hid in the rear upstairs choir loft. There were none of my young student-clergy-men in the pews. (They had gone to a go-go church—they told me later—to see the wonderful equipment of Sunday-school rooms, kitchen, lounges, etc. etc.) I came to worship with my young family and to hear Dr. McPhail.

His topic: "By the Waters of Babylon." His voice was deep and Hebrew in character. His long gown draped about him and gave him the picture of an ancient Hebrew prophet. Things went along smoothly and monotonously until he climbed the stairs of the wine-glass pulpit and then read the Scripture. I heard him read one of the Psalms. He read the chapter with rever-ence and with a kind of dramatic quality. Suddenly, in the midst of the reading of "sacred scripture" he stopped —he looked up and out at the pews and at us and then said quietly but firmly: "And the rest of this chapter is not fit to be read in a Christian Church." My eldest son got the message. I looked at my wife and she looked at me. My son whispered "Dad, where is this Scripture?" And I said "Psalms"—not remembering which.

Our family still talks about the early days when our

kids hurried back to the dormitory rooms reserved for our use and looked for a Bible. What Psalm? They got a good dose of heresy in church that morning. And it was Dr. McPhail—an honest preacher, a scholar, forthright, dedicated—but not ambitious about the things of this world that others (like ourselves) get concerned about. It was a memorable sermon and a memorable occasion and a memorable man—whose life (I learned later) ended somewhat young in years.

There were other experiences during that summer in Auburn that touched my life with a kind of an impression that never quite left me as things get themselves recalled in memory.

My clergymen students told me not to miss the Auburn Penitentiary. They would (some of them) arrange that I be permitted (!) to enter on Sunday morning for the service. But I would not be allowed to take the Mrs. nor the children. It was so arranged. I had to be on the dot at the gates at 8:30 a.m. I was very eager about attending a prison church service. How would it be conducted? Who would be there? What would the minister say? Would they sing? What?

Six of us—mixed company—were at the gate on that Sunday morning. (The penitentiary was in the downtown area—I seem to recall.) A guard took us through a series of locked gates after initial identification. Finally, we arrived at the huge auditorium where a program was in progress. There must have been some two thousand men—captive audience! Dressed in prison garb and with uniformed guards standing here and there and military-like, we had a situation unusual indeed. We were ushered on to the platform where a band was in the process of playing some loud swingy march. Six straight-back chairs were reserved for us. Whispers reached me to the effect that So-and-So playing the tuba was a murderer in for life and So-and-So is the famous So-and-So who a few years ago made the newspapers in such and such a crime—all the while my fears being aroused that I myself may never see freedom again—even if my life may be spared. "In-ter-es-ting—very in-ter-es-ting," said I to me. But—what will the chaplain have to say? The sermon? "Very in-ter-es-ting."

Suddenly, the music stopped. I was glad. I had the tuba long enough in my ear blasting umppa, umppa—umppapa with only a change of key. "Onward Christian Soldiers" was the grand finale of the prelude-concert and then the musicians removed themselves and their instruments and we were left alone on the large platform facing a huge throng waiting for the next number on the program.

The chaplain was a Methodist minister whom I had never seen or met. He made no announcements of coming committee meetings, nor ladies aid, nor coffee hour, nor deacons or trustees nor anything consequential—until he came to introduce the guests. We had "orders" to write our names and where we were from on a small piece of prison paper and these were handed to the chaplain just before his appearance.

I was expecting some Scripture reading or some preamble of meditation. Of a sudden our names and where we were from were read at the rostrum in the order of our seating, left to right. My name came second—as I was assigned the second from the left. When I heard

"Vergilius Ferm" I shuddered at the thought. "What is Vergilius Ferm doing here?" said I to me. (The minister chaplain stumbled over my first name.) Another case where sheer curiosity gets one into an unpredictable mess. And an unpredictable mess it was! Even we were captive prisoners, without any chance of freelance escape—until we were properly paroled!

And then the awful words came. The chaplain, after reading the last name on the guest list, announced gleefully:

"And these people will now speak to you."

"My Gawd," said the young Presbyterian minister who sat at my left.

It was at best a prayer but the tone sounded like swearing. And he was first on the list. My mind went blank!

This first fellow was an Italian Presbyterian minister from somewhere in New York. He stalked to the platform—a little fellow—and yelled: "How many of you men speak Italian?" Hands went up all over the place. And the clapping was thunderous. (By the way, every new thing announced and concluded received loud hand clapping—even before and after the Lord's Prayer.)

"This guy has it made," said I enviously, when he began to harangue the audience in Italian which neither I and a good many others understood. After about twelve minutes he finished with his audience in an uproar of clapping all over the place.

And then the inevitable happened "Wergi*lus* Feerme [the chaplain gave the pronouncement a new version] will now speak."

Meanwhile, I tried my best to think of something to

say. All I could think of was the verse from Scripture which was "Go ye out into all the nations," etc. and I couldn't think of a single place where these men could go. Every new thought was crowded out by this one passage and I arose on my feet a washed-out invalid, a college professor who had lost his tickets and afraid for his life. I couldn't even think of "My Gawd."

I have promised myself that if anyone asks me what I said on this public occasion I would refuse to answer. I now remember the same oath and will not make an exception to anyone who reads these lines—*except* for those who bought and paid for a copy of this book I shall reveal a part of the secret right here. Borrowers of this book will now stop reading farther in this paragraph. ((SHHH—I said something about *gghitz wldpog norqthuz philosophy zumdix tetrak philosophy agtlible peyhlamto karishtayo prag ooggala.*)) What prisoner would be interested in a professor of philosophy on such an occasion and at this stage of some life sentence? I was properly brief. And when I got through I was given the same round of applause—the Auburn prison liturgical applause—and I sank into my seat a first-class villain, sinner like all the rest. A brother meeting brother. (If the reader doesn't understand my account of the gist of my speech, I suggest either he or I consult a psychiatrist. I did reveal something if he missed it!)

The next speaker was an American Indian, Presbyterian minister from (I believe) Oklahoma! He got up and smiled and asked: "How many of you men would like to hear an Indian love song?" Here the applause approached the magnitude of a first-class thunder. And so he sang. He didn't have much of a voice nor do I know (nor does anyone else) what the love part was. All I know he had more than two or three lengthy verses. "Now here's a guy," said I to myself, "who is taking advantage of the rest of us. He is like the Italian. Both getting away with a mode of murder. Smart men? Yes, indeed. Diplomatic? Yes, indeed. Sinners? Yes, indeed (I said to me, enviously of all the speakers).

The service was not yet over. Three more to go. It seemed to me that I had experienced Eternity and I wanted no more. "No more, O Jehovah, No More." But the Yahweh heard me not.

The next person was the one woman—on the platform. I know not how she got there. Probably a special edict from the governor. I didn't worry about her. Not a prisoner (thought I) would go for her. She had whatever is the opposite of pulchritude and now I can't think of a single word that begins to size her up. Her technique: just as corny as the others (including myself).

"How would you men like to hear a song?" she shouted. They clapped again. The fifth person on the platform suddenly got up. He was her accompanist and this would pass for his performance!

"The Chisler," said I to me. "Playing the piano is getting by with murder—and here we had to make impromptu spiritual and inspirational speeches or sermonettes. The piano was a half-block (it seemed) away from the stage. The man had his music with him. I noticed as he passed by that he wore earphones. This certainly meant something. To me this meant impending tragedy. And so it went. She began to sing "Where is My Wandering Boy Tonight?" She was off key. Her voice was like an old-fashioned gramaphone with a worn-out needle and an antique record. Moreover her voice was a trembling vibratto not settling on any one note for long. The accompanist evidently couldn't hear her, he was too far away. And the piano hadn't been tuned for years. And I sat and answered each line of her song "Where . . ." by muttering to me: "He's right here—there's no other place to go."

So that leaves one more victim. He was a fundamentalist Presbyterian minister who began by asking the large audience: "How many of you men believe in Gawd?"

Hands here and there—scattered hands—easily countable were raised. "How many of you men are saved?" he yelled.

The speaker noticed the mild response of hands and then madly said, "So the rest of you are going to hell, are you?"

We got an interesting hell-fire sermon which even scared me! When this was over I felt like a dead duck.

The chaplain went to the platform after the final applause and said "Thank you" to us (the villain!) and then took some papers from his outside pocket and, as he folded them, he placed them inside his coat pocket and said: "Well, I have my next Sunday morning's sermon ready!" (The villain!)

Ever since that day I maintain an unsanctified feeling toward Methodist ministers—this man a trickster, if ever there was one. I hope he reads these lines before he leaves this transitory life. If not, I hope St. Peter stops him along the way somewhere and recites these pages which concern a major sin, brother against brother, especially those of the cloth who can be so mean.

I was told later that the attendance at Sunday service was optional. Any prisoners not electing to go to "church" on Sunday (such as this one) were to remain in their cells for the duration of the meeting. This was supposed to be punishment—so I guessed. I knew better. It was the others who came who were punished. The ways of Jehovah's admirers are mysterious!

Before finishing the Auburn episode I must write about a few other matters.

My clergymen-students asked me collectively (next day) how I liked the service. And I said: "You villains. You weren't there yourselves—except a few of you who got caught with me. You have the Lord to answer for this."

They howled. The sinners had passed the word around about the Methodist chaplain and had kept only a few sinners unaware of the deep secret. Had I given grades for the course, I would have flunked every one who failed to attend the Auburn Prison service on that Sunday!

Two other men came into my life (other than Dr. McPhail) at this time. A few words about each since both came to live in my memory as a kind of special blessing from that summer's experience.

On the teaching staff in Auburn was one of America's leading pulpit men, Gaius Glenn Atkins, of Detroit, then in his full prime. I audited his course on homiletics or the art of preaching. He and Charles Reynolds Brown (mentioned earlier) together with Harry Emerson Fosdick and E. F. Tittle (Evanston) belong to the golden age of American preachers—an age which has not been duplicated since. In my estimation, we just do not have great preachers any more: either ministers are Liturgists, social reformers stuck on one theme, contemporaneous rather than in-depth interpreters or else merely light and homiletical or what is worse: buyers of canned sermons!

Atkins lectured from the overflow—as do all great teachers: not student-oriented (as now so glibly popular and called "dialogue") but from a fund of knowledge with method and style personal rather than professional. He would come into the classroom having no idea of what was to happen (not particularly virtuous, I am sure); but what evolved by some student-clergyman's first question there flowed a systematic lecture of the greatest art. Dialogue was for him a jumping-off board and then there was a swim into the deep. His reading was wide and voracious and he could tap his subconscious mind for the most appropriate information and analogy. He always carried books and he was eminently unaware of himself. If that was his style he must have had it in the pulpit for I could hardly imagine his preaching without teaching and his audience-touch without inspiring. Somehow we became more than casual friends. I dimly recall a movie we took of him at some park where he held my youngest son on a merry-go-round—which always fascinated us since he had not impressed us as being so personal. I had a happy correspondence with him after that. He gave me a norm by which to work: anything really good comes from an overflow rather than by conscious intent. This goes for scholarship, teaching, morals, for professionalism, for what is called "class." An achievement, an art, rather than a preparation or an end.

Then there was the incomparable Shailer Mathews, dean of the Chicago Divinity School, also then in his prime. I had heard of him at my theological seminary years ago as the epitome of heresy: preacher of the awful "social gospel," heretic along with Rauschenbusch of earlier time—both liberal Baptists. Somehow, he took an interest in me and I invited him to join me in Professor Bennett's private study on the campus (occupied by me for the duration). I recall his geniality and his pipe-smoking. He treated me "to the best," taking out a pack of old Granger tobacco (which from that time forward I called "Mathews' tobacco" of academic memory and reverence). It was coarse and strong but I learned to like it. I asked him about this and that. He was an unordained head of a theological school of heresy and a scholar in the particular field of history. His *The Spiritual Interpretation of History* was on every liberal preacher's bookshelf—including conservatives like myself (?). I told him of my notion that all concepts are symbols and especially concepts of God. Then he let me have it.

"And do you not know that Thomas Aquinas taught that? It's old Roman Catholicism."

And he reached for the proper volume from the Aquinas' set on Dogmatic Theology on Bennett's shelf and then, after a pause, began reading sections to me. The Catholics had adopted Aquinas (I knew) but I did not sufficiently realize that the orthodox position held that reason may be trusted to give symbols but symbols must be treated as symbols. Of course, I knew that

Catholics argued for revelation of even the symbols of God. But it was brought home to me that Aquinas was not a heretic as a philosopher so long as he remained faithful to the tradition that the philosopher deals with the *That* (God) and the church proclaimed the revelation *What* (God).

We had quite a discussion from which I learned to stretch my mind some more and to take my thoughts as not so much personal discoveries as thinking for myself and coming to know that few ideas, indeed, are original.

Then, my question:

"Dr. Mathews, I have a manuscript ready on the philosophy of religion. This is what I am doing with my class this summer. I am not sure that I should publish at this early stage of my life. Should I not wait until I mature?"

His eyes pierced mine and he said authoritatively:

"Publish it now, don't wait."

"But," I said, "I may change my opinions."

"Sure, you will change—you will always change. You must change. Publish now and when you change and you are ready with another book, then publish it."

This sank in, deep down into my literary aspirations. I later thought of the many writers who have changed opinions, especially Bertrand Russell (who always is quoted with a year-date).

I made up my mind then and there: I shall not strive to expect perfectionism. I shall speak and say and write under a specific date and not worry about changes. Not to change is to pontificate and to pontificate is a mortal sin (somehow not recognized as such by the church fathers *ex cathedra*).

This is how I came to let manuscripts go from my typewriter. No one belongs to the category of perfection. Publication is a dated expression and that is that. If it is immature, it is immature. At least, I was led by the spirit of Shailer Mathews to be free from a tender conscience which would say "wait" until you really know and are sure. *You* take the step from where *you* are . . . and then you go on. These two men: McPhail and Shailer Mathews along with the resourceful Gaius Glenn Atkins were the three wise men who came into my life for a very brief spell and gave me the good sense of being unafraid of the printed page with my name attached—any printed page will haunt an author forever but he can always say as a member of the human race: Well, now, that's how I felt *then. So what?*

And that is how I came to write and publish a novel (and a rash of other books)—a writer without portfolio in this field but one unafraid to make mistakes. Quoting Mr. Lowry (earlier in this book) "Remember you have to live with it," he said about my novel. And I now say: "Sure, that's right . . . I'll have to live with it. Be it so! —*even this book* upon which I am now working."

A PUBLISHING CAREER—MIDDLE YEARS—
MORE INTERLUDES

1956-57 was a big academic year for us: a third sabbatical with plans for study abroad. Just previous to this
another book appeared (1955) which I called *A Dictionary of Pastoral Psychology*—a manuscript which I
had given attention to over many months and culminating a long interest in psychology (as previously recount-
ed). Psychology is psychology; pastoral has reference
only to the application of this psychology to the work
of the parish minister, as pastor and counselor. It was
not a difficult work; it just took time to write out the
definitions and short articles. I had the help of six contributors, otherwise the definitions were of my own
responsibility. The work turned out well enough, the
publishers (Philosophical Library) doing their usual
cooperation in a fast moving printing and binding
process. Again, the proofreading was mine as well as the
alphabetization. I have no idea how many of the clergy
saw this book nor how it was received by critics. I was
then too busy to search the magazines. I was in the
midst of other assignments.

One day in the spring of 1956 a package came to the
house—a modest thing. I was not particularly interested in opening it as I thought it was some advertising
material which would see the waste-basket. Imagine my
surprise when later I opened it up to find a two-volume

work with foreign characters on it which I did not understand. Some far-off foreigner, I said, wants me to review his book! I fingered through it and noticed I had to go backwards to get my continuity. The title struck me almost dead. It had my name on it and there were two volumes. It did not take me long before I got a genuine interest in it! It quickly dawned on me. This is a translation of my previous *A History of Philosophical Systems*. Who sent it, why it came, how it ever got itself over into a foreign country and translated—I do not even now know. I took it to a Japanese lady in East Union (near Wooster) and she started to read some difficult philosophical terms and I had to admit that this, too, belonged to me. It was a pleasant surprise and I never found out whom to thank. The ways of publishers —like the ways of God—are mysterious, indeed.

I had planned to settle down for a spell at Uppsala where the ancient university is located in Sweden and if this did not work out, I would choose Cambridge, England. This is a story in itself and I must here forego the telling of it. My intentions were honorable and the trustees of the college trusted me to use the privilege of a year with full salary in a way profitable. During the summer we toured abroad but after that things got complicated beyond belief.

On the boat at 55th Street in New York, just as we entered our cabin, a messenger came with a special delivery package from the Philosophical Library. I signed for it and laid it on the table. After preliminary inspection of the ship and after the excitement of shipping out and viewing the grand scene of the New York harbor and the Statue of Liberty and the fading land-line of dear old America and after an excellent dinner called "the captain's" we went to our cabin and I saw the package. I thought it was a kind of farewell bon-voyage-thing from Dr. Runes who knew of my leaving.

To my consternation on opening the bundle I saw a mess of galley sheets. Another book! Good Jehovah, what now! A message inside said in effect: We want these galleys corrected and sent back immediately after you land—airmail. Of course, I recognized the stuff. It was a book I had worked on for someone else for whom I was the ghost writer.

Sinners know no rest. There was nothing else to do but to comply. What would I do carrying that thing on a European tour? For five solid days—time off for sleep, meals, bouillon or coffee on a deck chair at stated intervals—I read proof on this book called *In the Last Analysis*. At our first landing, I had the book properly wrapped, insured, air-stamped and receipted. I gave it to a uniformed stranger at the dock in Cork, Ireland and said a prayer that Jehovah once more take care of all this work. The whole trip across was spent reading proof (I had promised to do it and there was no way to beg leave in mid-ocean). I did not miss the scenery for water is water and the horizon is the horizon. But I did need rest.

Our tour was lengthened beyond Stockholm—another story which does not belong here. I found the philosophy people at Uppsala University were engrossed in the analytic movement and this I shied away from and by the time we hit Cambridge, England in October, we were both so dead tired from travel that we decided that

Mercer, Wisconsin was our only haven to health and sanity.

It was the month of October in that summer that we flew west-bound over the Atlantic, stopped in New Haven to pick up our car and headed directly to our summer hideout. It was a beautiful fall season with the leaves all painted up (it seemed *for us*) in every shade and color. The winding paved roads through the Iron County forests seemed to promise nature's healing balm and we were looking forward to a plain old-fashioned recuperation. Then one day the telephone rang.

It was Dr. Runes calling from New York. "I want you to do an important book and I'll write and explain the proposition and send on a contract. Oh yes, I'll be mailing a large box of books immediately and they are yours and more to come for the project. There's only one hitch: we must get on to it right away and anything you need, you need only ask for. I have in mind this manuscript by next spring. I'll be writing you details. Just wanted to be sure you are back in this country." This, of course, is not a quote but it is the gist of the slam-bang request.

When it comes to books I am "chicken." To turn down another project was rationally unthinkable. To meet such a short deadline was rationally ridiculous. To receive complimentary books was like fat worms wiggling near a school of trout.

Before I could count a week (and it was still October) I was head and heels on another major project—which held me captive throughout the short fall period and into the heavy winter. Winters in this north country are beautiful beyond word description. The snow begins to fall about the middle of October and the ice on the lake below us is not completely unfrozen until the beginning of May. Winter is god hereabouts. Summer is but a teaser courting the tourists' raves. Nowadays with snow-mobiles and ski-jumps and weekend frolics this area takes on the spirit of a carnival—after the deer season in November. The snow drifts mount to hills whereever shoveled. The town tractor comes in as far as the garage. We sweep a path that far and sweep the snow all around the house to "package" it against long winter blasts. Kerosene stove, fireplace and kitchen range have to be tended to, ashes removed, wood carried—it's all part of the fun and work (these go together for us). The storm windows are in place and the cracks in the window casings must be plugged up with tape strips. Only at thirty below does one begin to question the wisdom of such a place for a sabbatical. Otherwise, zero weather and even ten below are manageable and not too uncomfortable. One wears heavy winter underwear unashamedly and two pairs of socks besides heavy laced-up boots. To dress (and undress) for the outdoors and indoors is quite a chore and one learns to exit and enter prepared for a habitual ritual. (One doesn't just "go out.") Meanwhile, one prays that the pump will keep going, the water doesn't freeze, that the train keeps running (bringing daily products), that the ice doesn't bog down the telephone wires and that the mail keeps coming and going.

With more modern conveniences which we have nowadays it is not as bad as it sounds. The latest fashion —believe it or not—is for retired people to come far north (rather than south) where the air is fresh and clean and invigorating. With the roads plowed with monster machines and gasoline-operated snowplows blowing it all aside for travel—all adds up to comfort. Lake property is now at premium demands—and the buyers are the two-week tourists who exchange their workaday world to twelve-month retirement, winterizing their homes (as we did) and coaxing their friends to forget Florida. (The additive argument always is: then too, you escape the heat of the deep south and the awful humidity that stifles the senile breathing process. Moreover to Arizonians the argument is: why substitute sand and cacti for the evergreens, the tall pines, the Christmas trees, the blue or the white snow-covered lakes, the cool air and all the rest? Where is the moon more beautiful than coming up full sized over the tree-lined horizon of a quiet lake!) And so on and on—presenting not only my own personal thoughts but the opinion of the local Chamber of Commerce, for which one year I wrote their brochure which was distributed to Chicagoans and Clevelanders at their annual Winter Sports Show. (I doubt that it increased the tourist trade.) You have to experience it to understand that my own emotions have not altogether called for the bankruptcy of reason.

The book about which Dr. Runes had written me and which was to slow me down completely for this sabbatical winter was eventually to be entitled *A Pictorial History of Protestantism*. This was the day of *Pictorials* (of circuses, negroes, baseball, philosophy, American history, etc., etc.). Foreign volumes came into my mail, volumes extremely valuable even for their ancient printing. And I was asked to clip out pictures—some going back to plates during Reformation days—and paste them on the proper sheets with running commentaries. I protested the clipping business. How can one with integrity perform surgery on an out-of-print and scarce volume? But the pressure was on. I did as few as I could get away with. I still have some mutilated corpses from this weird action.

Meanwhile, into all this chaos, two new books came for my library carrying my name as editor (the one) and someone else's name (the other). One came to Mercer on November 27th and the other November 28th—same year—books on which I had been working immediately prior to 1956. To see manuscripts in book clothing is a thrill—especially when you have been correcting typing and galleys and sorting and suffering the pangs of literary childbirth. And here are two more of my children. It was just the spurt I needed to nurse another book—and I was in the very process with the pictorial book. November gave me a lift over late October. (More about these two volumes shortly.)

During the winter months of early 1957, I developed psychological and physiological tension and had to go up to Ironwood, Michigan, for help. I sought an elderly statesman physician. After listening to my heart, he told me to jump up and down fifty times on one leg, rest, and then repeat with the other. (I have two legs, and thankfully, no more. Lucky to belong to my species rather than to that of a centipede!)

"I'll die," I said to him after about eight jumps.

"Keep going," he demanded.

"I'll drop dead," I warned.

He waved the command. I just couldn't comply. I felt my heart pumping like our crazy pump in Mercer.

Then he said: "Don't worry, I'll pick you up if you fall."

I was pronounced, after this awful examination, as fairly normal but I had a bad case of nerves. I must quit doing "whatever" I was now doing—he commanded. (I didn't dare tell him about the pictorial book and the deadline coming up in the spring and how both my wife and I were typing and pasting and recording and arranging the material for our potential monstrosity of an offspring.)

Spring came and I began getting reminders of the due-date. I had written letters of requests for pictures to practically all available denominational librarians, public relation officers of churches, officials and wherever there were historical files; I consulted personally the New York City Library, the Yale University Library, Boston University—from some of which places I got photostatic copies of wanted pictures. The staff at The Philosophical Library served my every request. When it was finally done, I had (I thought) a respectable panoramic book on Protestantism both in terms of the printed word and by representative illustrations. They had called me from New York promising a special gift of an engraved wristwatch if only I would hurry and even beat the due-date. (I still carry this watch on my left wrist which in an engraving carries with it the reminder of my fulfillment of their assignment: "Presented to Dr. Vergilius Ferm, Wooster, Ohio—The Philosophical Library— N. Y. Publishers, 1957.")

And so another potential baby boarded the Chicago,

Northwestern Railroad baggage car one night and we stood and watched it carry our precious cargo (which had no duplicate copy anywhere and if lost would never be replaced!). I don't remember the insurance but that was a minor factor; what insurance money could recompense me for "Blood, sweat and tears" and a nervous constitution about to break but happy in the outcome. Again, Jehovah answered favorably my anxious prayer for the safe journey of this manuscript.

I am proud when I go into city libraries across the country to find this Pictorial History (published in 1957) still displayed in their foyers and I smile and take a deep breath of thankfulness for the health given me to have survived the hectic year and to see the baby very much alive at a maturer age surviving the hazards of extinction. It is a beautiful book, the handiwork of skilled printers and binders and jacket-makers.

A few pages back I mentioned two books of mine which were published in the fall of 1956—the period about which my narration now covers. These two books carry their own story and to this writing I now turn.

The one was an edited volume called *Encyclopedia of Morals* and the other is the ghost-written *In The Last Analysis*.

Concerning the first. Again, it was Dr. Runes who had appointed me to this task. I found it fun, fun, fun. We did not want a Dictionary with short listings; nor did we want to try a kind of complete work. Our hope was to find something in between for the general reader and also for scholars. Summary essays and expositions by competent people. I turned to Professor Melville Herskovits and his colleagues at Northwestern University

(Evanston), scholars in the anthropological field and from them I received valuable guidance in the selection of topics and men in their field. For the theological, religious and philosophical aspects of the project my way was much easier—since, naturally, I had already some modicum of experience.

To me "morals" meant anthropology, sociology, social psychology, folklore, primitive peoples and the like; not just theological and philosophical theories. (These latter being, of course, proper in such a book.) And so, the topics were assigned and experts responded gladly and before I knew it the thing came to being. It was one of my easiest projects. As I now dip into the book I find my impression of it altogether satisfactory: it is attractive as to type, paper, two-columned setting,—quite comprehensive and certainly authoritative. Over fifty contributors attest their reputation to the writing of these specially assigned articles. It is generally cross-indexed (the chore work of an editor) and each person has his signature to his article.

To sample the type of book (which, I think, is somewhat unique for a one-cover affair) I list only a few of the entries (essays with bibliographies): "Rio Grande Pueblo Indians" by Edward Dozier (Northwestern University); "Moral Philosophy in America" by William Frankena (University of Michigan); "The Stoics" by Nathaniel Roe (Wellesley College); "Aboriginals of Yirkalla" by Richard Waterman (Wayne University); "Navaho Morals" by Clyde Kluckhohn (Center for Advanced Study of Behavioral Sciences, California and Harvard University); "Muslim Morals" by Kermit Schoonover (The American University of Cairo);

"Soren Kierkegaard" and "French Existentialism" by Ria Stavrides (Vassar College); "Current Soviet Morality" by George Kline (Columbia University); "Leo Tolstoy" and "Fyodor Dostoyevsky" by Helene Iswolsky (Fordham Institute of Russian Studies); "T. H. Green" by George Sabine (Cornell University); "Code of Hammurapi," "Sigmund Freud" and "Friedrich Nietzsche" by Walter Kaufmann (Princeton University); "Puritan Morals" by C. Covey (Amherst College); "The Morality of Classical Quakerism" by Howard Brinton (Pendle Hill); "Immanuel Kant" by Herman Brautigam (Colgate University); "Christian Moral Philosophy" by John Krumm (Columbia University); "Alighieri Dante" by Archibald MacAllister (Princeton University); "John Dewey" by Rubin Gotesky (University of Georgia); "Hindu Ethics" by Swami Nikhilananda (Ramakrishna—Vivekananda Center, New York); "Moral Philosophies of China" by Yi-Pao-Mei (University of Iowa); and so on.

Now, concerning the second volume *In the Last Analysis* (a few pages back). Back of this is a somewhat fantastic story dating back to August 18, 1955. (This date is an entry in our Mercer Journal showing the signatures of two new friends from Three Rivers and Gould City, Michigan—visitors for the first time at our home in Mercer.)

At the front of my *Pictorial History of Protestantism* there is a dedication page to the name of "Adam Elliott Armstrong, D.Sc."—small token of appreciation of a warm friendship with a man who up to 1955 was unknown to me. He and his wife "Bonnie" (until his death a few years ago) exchanged visits with us regularly each year at our respective homes either in Ohio and lower Michigan or at our summer homes in northern Wisconsin and upper Michigan. The book about which I now write concerns this relationship.

Adam Armstrong sought me out in Mercer—late summer of 1955. The backstage story is to the effect that a vice-president of The College of Wooster (Joe Harris) had sent Mr. Armstrong my name in connection with an enquiry about the college's professor of philosophy. Mr. Harris on his part was one of Mr. Armstrong's many friends and, frankly, hoped to claim him as a likely generous donor to the college; Mr. Armstrong's part of the story was his interest in finding someone to finish a projected book dealing with his own philosophy. The two points met at one spot: my front porch on a hot August day.

I demurred at the request for our meeting. My reason? I was in a cast, neck down to the end of my spine. I was in pain. It was hot. I had just come from a hospital stay in northern Michigan where I had injured my back (crushed vertebrae) in a fall down some stairs carrying an armful of books! (It was a hot July 1955. Along with rabbi Victor Reichert of Cincinnati, Ohio—a great Old Testament scholar and a brilliant lecturer—I had been invited to speak at a ministers' conclave in Michigamme where the accident befell me—necessitating a long ambulance ride back to an Ironwood, Michigan hospital with the prospect of a long span toward recovery.) Mr. Armstrong insisted on the visit and assured us that he and Bonnie would find a motel and visit briefly over the period of two days.

Bonnie will recall my saying to her at our dining

table: "Your ring sparkles so—it hurts my eyes." It was her only suggestion of affluence which we mutually understood would be the only reference.

Adam Armstrong, I soon learned, had two major interests: securing patents for his many inventions and then manufacturing the possibilities and secondly, an avid interest in the field of philosophy as an avocation which took up his leisure hours in reading and pondering and wondering. Many years ago he and his brother opened up a bicycle shop at the spot in Chicago which later came to be the site of a major railway station near the heart of the city—next to the river. He had some patent on wheel spokes which caught his business fancy and took him from a farm in Illinois where he was born. This business was transferred to Three Rivers, Michigan (a curious story indeed) and he remained there until his death. He headed the Armstrong Machine Works which made steam traps (his patent and distributed over the globe) with subsidiary offices still operating in many major countries. He was a generous citizen, taking part in civic enterprises, donor of a park, a community house, charitable endeavors, colleges (a chapel at Alma College in Michigan) and instituting profit sharing in his own business and so on and on. A modest person, indeed, but strictly a businessman and an explorer of ideas.

He once told me—in my very yard—that his biggest problem was the distribution of money since he had more than he knew what to do with. Requests for his donations were continous and even pestering. But wherever there was (he said) a genuine need he would give loans to help. He had come up the hard way and he despised the hangers-on who wanted something for nothing—unless poverty or ill-luck struck. I had his confidence in helping him make a few decisions of financial gifts (this, of course, developed later in our friendship).

What was on his mind in this first interview? I soon found out! He had "hired" someone to work out a book for him on his philosophy and had gotten no place with it. I believe there was a second person who was to take up the task—a woman, this time. (I am not sure of the story here.) Would *I* help him? His philosophy? He outlined it to me: everything in the world is determined; there is no freedom whatsoever. We are all caught in the vise of cause-effect relationships and we might as well admit it. Our choices are really no choices but the results of previous situations. (He was a rabid Calvinist without knowing that he was and fittingly, a good Presbyterian!) This was the essence of the Armstrong philosophy.

So we argued back and forth. He pleaded with me to show him if he was wrong. And if he was right, was it not time that this philosophy be spread abroad and sons of men be guided by it? He said (in effect): "I want nothing more—now in life—than to spread this truth and do away with man's illusions of freedom. As a man sows he reaps—this is the law of life. We are the products of a thousand and one circumstances: parents, chromosomes, geography, climate, pocketbook, culture, education or lack of it, weather, temperature, earth-planet,— all chugging away like a machine. Our place in all this is to accept it. This is the way the men of the sciences operate and when they learned this simple lesson that there is a cause for everything and to search for it—

look—how rapid has been man's progress: in technology, in medicine, in exploration, in inventing time-consuming and labor-saving devices, in the setting up and the directing of computers—where do you stop? And there is no philosophy that goes along with all this modern insight! Can you not see: philosophers themselves are blind to the very world they live in!"

We argued during the whole time he was at our home.

I told him about Bergson and Bergson's answer to determinism. I admitted to him how the scientists, indeed, had been successful in their methods in so many areas but how precarious it is to say that the whole Universe necessarily is amenable to this same approach. Maybe the human mind transcends the rigid sequences of the cause-effect relationships of the physical world. Maybe all of the Universe cannot be caught in one set of traps: cause-effect. Elephants are not caught in the same traps as mice nor vice versa. Perhaps there is spontaneity in nature which one misses by the rigid methods of scientific investigation. Had he heard of Whitehead? Had he heard of William James? And all the rest.

We got no place fast with each other. The arguments went round and round. Then, finally, he asked:

"Will you help me with the book?"

My answer:

"Yes, I will help you when I feel better but I cannot add my name to the job publicly since it is not my philosophy."

Then we had another round: Would I co-author it? It would perhaps help distribute the message. My answer was adamant: It would have to carry his name for it was Armstrong's philosophy.

He was sad because I was not yet his disciple. I kept telling him determinism is not something new. It runs its course all the way through the history of philosophy, both East and West, and the issue of man's freedom and nature's creative spontaneity as over a machine-precision-world is as old as the hills of human thought. Moreover, here was a dedicated and successful laboratory scientist who had tasted the juicy fruits of his method in his life of invention and discovery. Of course, it would affect his philosophy. And yet, he could not consider the fact that a method successful in some areas (large areas indeed) does not necessarily argue for the same method in all areas. More power to the inventors and scientists! But again, there may be such phenomena as spontaneous mutations in nature, (little ones like Darwin maintained) or big ones ("leaps" as DeVries maintained) or little tiny choices (freedom) which face all of us which evenly balanced alternatives present and we must "decide" or "choose" and thus set up another chain reaction of cause-effects.

Before he left (he would take no "no" from me), I assured him—and at his suggestion that there would be some contractual agreement I would try the job: muster all his arguments and those of some others in the history of philosophy about which I had some knowledge and present the case *for* determinism, knocking down the alternatives. It would be *his* book. I would be a ghost-writer. It would carry his name. I would write an introduction and give a brief biography. And so we parted.

A few days later (at his insistence) I wrote my terms. I made them cautiously and conservatively. I needed two years. If I died, meanwhile, my inheritors would not be responsible. The length of the manuscript must be agreed upon. The compensation would be mutually agreeable. I was not too anxious and yet—again my weakness—here is a chance to do another book and really try to make myself believe in a philosophy to which I was and still am not committed!

And so the contract came and it was generous and more than satisfactory. And in my pain I began to outline the attack. The college administrators had written me (after they had heard of my physical incapacity) not to hurry back but to stay on until the physicians gave me the go-light. It was not until sometime in October that we left Mercer for Wooster and I took up part-time teaching during the fall term. All this gave me time to work on the Armstrong book. By Christmas I had finished it—a short book, indeed, but it contained the case for determinism in a setting of Western thought.

Meanwhile, I asked him to tape-record answers to my questions (which I kept piling up on my own tape-recordings). Thus we communicated at length without secretaries and writing. It had to be Armstrong's views—otherwise there was no point to having an Armstrong book. I insisted that he approve any imputed view (beyond the plain historical views of others). He would call me long distance frequently and if necessary speak forty-five to sixty minutes. The toll charges either way were high (I never knew how high).

I mailed the manuscript neatly typewritten, introduction, biography and all. The book might be about one hundred printed pages. I promised to proofread it and work out an index. I would recommend some publishers but he would have to worry about the terms and settle them. The package arrived just before Christmas (the same year!) at Three Rivers. I received a telephone call. He was shocked to learn it was done. I told him that there was no more to say! He was surprised, glad and concerned. I told him I thought he needed a Christmas present (and I knew, too, that the span of his years gave no promise of too much time left—as it does for all of us—and he should see his philosophy summed up). All through the month and after there would be a call such as: On page 47 don't you think there should be a comma? Don't you think there should be a new paragraph after such and such a line? Don't you think you ought to use this word rather than that? If ever a manuscript got the personal treatment this one had it. I kept a copy of it at the telephone to be ready with my reply when he called. It was a clean copy (proofread for errors) and minor changes were approved. As time wore on, he became more and more pleased. It was the short time it took the ghost-writer that seemed to bother him. And there, indeed, was hardly more to say: unless one padded the thing with unnecessary decorations. And he contacted the publishers (whom I had recommended) from his home office. All I did in this matter was to recommend the book as "an excellent book." Could I say less?

And so the year following his visit to Mercer, on our trip abroad I read proof of *In The Last Analysis* all the way across the Atlantic (already mentioned in a previous section) and in the fall of 1956 the baby was born. (The Philosophical Library of New York published it.) Bonnie and others told us of his utter pleasure in distributing gratis copies of this book, taking a supply on his trips to Hawaii and other vacation excursions. And our friendship deepened. (I am certain that Mr. Armstrong was the kind of person who would approve of my telling this story in my autobiography.)

We visited him often at his summer place near Gould City in northern Michigan, a large log house on a large lake with a trout stream beside the kitchen door. We sat at his fireplace and discussed determinism interminably never resolving our points of view, going over and over the same arguments. A few years before his death I invited him to Wooster to lecture to my students. It was a very happy hour for him. He had never been a college student. He was proud to speak of his philosophy and especially to sit on the platform in a college lecture room. He did extremely well and the students promised to write out their criticisms (which I later mailed him). I sent word to the president of the college to attend the lecture if at all convenient. He sent his vice-president. (A vice-president although a worthy person is not a substitute for a president—especially when so important a guest as mine was on that day on campus.) I took Mr. Armstrong to call on President Howard Lowry at his home. But he was not there. He was in town and on campus but somehow muffed an opportunity to present the college to a man now somewhat emotionally attracted to the place. I knew very well that Adam Armstrong was not only in a position to do something perhaps in a grand manner for the college but his mood was favorable. I repeat: Wooster lost an opportunity. Mr. Armstrong remarked to me that he was disappointed not to meet the president and I gave no alibi for there was none I could honestly give.

One day I received a large-sized envelope containing what seemed to be extremely important papers. There was a note from Mr. Armstrong. Would I take a look and express an opinion? In a few words: here was a copy of a contract which an educational institution in southern California had drawn up by its president, to wit: for a handsome sum of money (I shall not here repeat the figure) from the hand of Mr. Armstrong he would be invited to give a series of lectures on philosophy and so would I, my name plainly included in the contract. (Do not ask my connections. I don't know myself.) And other details. I contacted my son in California and it turned out (as I suspected) to be an academically questionable institute dealing with Far Eastern religions and what not; so I quickly notified Armstrong to lay off. This he did. And the family privately gave their expression of appreciation to me.

A rich man about to leave this planet has problems I never dreamed could be so significant. With whom do you share your wealth? To unappreciative relatives whose claims are tenuous, to causes which dissipate the funds in nonessentials or "administrative costs" which include percentage rake-offs by incompetents or social leeches who would beg or play politics rather than work their own way through the trials and frustrations of life, to philanthropies loaded with expensive overheads (such as churches with all the paraphernalia of secretaries and swivel-chair clergy in ecclesiastical offices), to missionaries off on safaris (not all of them, of course), to children's children who are taught the unrealistic lessons of Santa Claus who "takes care" of their every want and know little of what it means to earn a penny? Such is the plight of the rich. Mr. Armstrong and I discussed this more than once and I knew it bothered him. He wanted much to share his fortune (self-made); but where can the needy be reached, those who deserve help, and where are the deserved causes without percentage losses along the way? Even a person of modest accumulation understands what this all means. One can give gifts which may damage the receivers into not only further ungratefulness but even to the loss of their own dignity and their own *personal* contribution to life.

There was a question about my fourth sabbatical coming up at the college in 1961-1962. Was it legal to give one a sabbatical so close to retirement? There were pros and cons and the cons seemed to outweigh the pros. I was caught in this one. (After my case, the issue was settled for those who followed.) My petition for another sabbatical was sent in and though Howard Lowry (president) said he hoped it might go through he would bring it to some committee. (This, I knew, was a possible case of "passing the buck.") I told Mr. Armstrong about the situation not expecting him to enter into it but mostly about my ambition to complete some other work before retirement.

Unknown to me, he picked up his telephone and asked to talk to the president of the college. What would it take to give Ferm another sabbatical before his retirement impending two years hence? The answer: at least a good portion of his salary. Question: How much? Answer: say, about ten thousand dollars. (This is the version told me much later.) The new vice-president of the college (Winslow Drummond, a good friend of mine) had interceded with Mr. Armstrong in my behalf and the college had an immediate gift of ten-thousand earmarked. And so it was that I went on in the fall of 1961 to my last research sabbatical. I remembered Mr. Armstrong once saying to me in effect: any academic organization without *research* leaves is in a state of dissolution—running down. Education like scientific pursuits is a quest for more knowledge and faculty as well as students need to prime their pumps continuously. Both Wooster and the Armstrong Machine Works had research budgets (his own firm constantly seeking to improve its products) and so I again called myself lucky to have time off to work on and to enquire into some fresh projects which were in the offing of my mind.

A PUBLISHING CAREER—LATER YEARS—
AN AUTHOR'S WORLD

At number 15 on East 40th Street, we continued to have our annual meetings in conjunction with my attendance at the spring meetings of the American Theological Society in New York. I would come in earlier in the week and spend at least a good morning with Dr. Runes who was already brimful of new ideas for books. I then learned who was teaching where and who was an authority on this and that and what was going on in the world of books.

Two further projects emerged at this point. One was a book on *Classics of Protestantism* (which was finished in publication form in 1959), an anthology, and the other was *A Brief Dictionary of American Superstitions* (published in the same year)—both attractively-bound books but, as all books go, each having its own story.

In looking through the *Classics* book at this stage of life, I find that my selections among the classics in the Protestant field were not too far afield of what by any reasonable standard would be called classics: books which had an imprint on their time (some, indeed, dull and, almost all, not in the popular class) or which represent a trend of the time. Any editor will, of course, betray his own judgment or slant. But I still think for a one-volume job, this book at least represents what a person interested in Protestantism ought to know something about if he is aspiring to some modicum of literacy in the field.

Editing is not a sophomoric job. It requires a lot of dull reading before the scissors are applied: what to omit and what to include to make for "selections." It is a kind of labor of love since one sacrifices the time spent on what otherwise may be more interesting and useful work on one's own professional interests. For the general reader there must be an editorial comment on the work and the author so as to make the classic understandable as a classic. My choices are here set down— not necessarily classics to me but classics in the literature of the subject of the book.

"Theologia Germanica" (author unknown), a medieval work, ranks top place before the Protestantism of the 16th century came into full bloom. And the book opens with it. Then, Luther's "A Treatise on Christian Liberty" a kind of *magna charta* for Protestantism. Then, a taste of Calvin in his "Institute"; then, Samuel Clarke, philosophical theologian, challenging the firmly entrenched Trinitarian doctrine; then, William Law who influenced John Wesley and a spiritual awakening with his call to holy living; then, John Wesley, the founder of Methodism with his Essay on "Free Grace."

"Sinners in the Hands of an Angry God" and "Freedom of Will" are Jonathan Edwards and vice versa and included next in this book. William Ellery Channing who launched the Unitarian controversy with his famous Baltimore sermon (1819) is here; and also Friedrich Schleiermacher for whom religious experience is the ground of all Christian theology, the father of empirical theology; Soren Kierkegaard, a father (among many) of the existentialist theology and philosophy with the work which represents the turning point of his theological thinking (his admission); Horace Bushnell (a favorite of Dean Weigle at Yale), spokesman for the idea of normal fruition in religious growth ("Christian Nurture" as over against convulsive conversions as normative); Theodore Parker, a typical philosophical theologian, a voice in Protestant liberalism which blew fresh breezes upon the Protestant scene; Albrecht Ritschl who inaugurated the most celebrated school of Protestant theology in the nineteenth century, a school known as Ritschlianism in a reinterpretation of the Christian religion as an independent value-judgment (not metaphysics nor mysticism) which launched controversy and schools: then, Dean Inge (mentioned earlier in this volume) who would revive Platonism and mysticism in Christian thinking; and, then, Walter Rauschenbusch of "social gospel" fame (who was rated in my earlier seminary days as an arch-heretic), an earlier prophet of our own time of the 1960's which is social-reform conscious; and, finally, Karl Barth whose reign as theologian-king among the conservative church theologians (conservative as to theology if not in other areas) has lasted *until very recent times.* He is the theologian who emphasized Deity as the wholly-Other. (Some of his students at Basel, Switzerland, revealed to me that he seldom participated in church religious exercises and seemingly preferred his study to the established sanctuary. Nevertheless, the church heralded him as their theological saint, both abroad and in America, casting a spell that is almost unbelievable in an age as critical of tradition as ours.)

The book has seemed useful for students in the History of Christian Thought—one of my fields of special study and interest. But it is confined, as the title suggests, to the post-Reformation period. Since then, of course, new movements have sprung up—so, church theologians come and go in influence, each having their "appointed" time.

The second book on superstitions came out also in 1959, and it is a book about which I am least proud. I should never have undertaken it. It amuses me no end when quotations from it with my name attached appear in the press here and there. It seems to be assumed that an author because of a "hard cover" publication is some kind of authority. My only apology for attempting it was: 1) my weakness for the smell of printer's ink and 2) my love for books, *of any kind*. The publisher showered me with books on superstitions: folklore, witchcraft, aphorisms, American and the like. My library suddenly became swollen with material. To sort out and to alphabetize and to edit (the mechanics of it) did not sit down well as my heart was not in it. But the publisher did another beautiful book (printing, binding, etc.) and I look at it with reserved admiration, stepchild among my manuscript-children.

I have only a few words more on American superstitions. Superstitions are the enemy of the rational mind, whipping up false fears and false hopes, therapeutic for some but eminently dangerous. A superstition can make a fool out of anyone more easily than jesting. I introduced this definition of a superstition: It is "any belief or practice whose trusted efficacy is independent of and contrary to the foundations of critical truth and objective fact." It feeds on the non- or irrational mind, a cousin to any faith that plays fast and loose with intelligence. Back of some superstitions, of course, may be some folklore twisting a pragmatic and once workable theory or notion. It may sound silly to anyone (including its adherent) but silly it was never meant to be. It promises delivery but the risk is appalling. And what is more: among the religious this human characteristic runs rampant intruding in expressions of theology and faith and entering into cult practices. Dipping one's fingers in oil or water or wine or drinking fermented or unfermented grapejuice can easily drift into a first-class superstition. As for example, a boy came to my house this month as I now write and said: he goes to communion to get his sins forgiven and that is the only time he goes into his church. There is something here of the beginnings of a religious superstiton with this lad—which, of course, he would not recognize. Theories of the Lord's Supper which have divided the churches in antagonistic camps have elements of superstitions which only good sense and critical reason can control. Superstitions feed on emotions; emotions curtail reason. Superstitions stimulate miracle explanations and faith in fantastic explanations (e. g., the change of material into supernatural elements—such as the transubstantiation doctrine holds). It is almost impossible to uncover the sources of superstitions. I found myself giving up the search. I also found myself avoiding doing a book on *religious* superstitions since 1) this was not the aim of the plan of my book and 2) I saw wholesale condemnation of the book by religious people everywhere in whatever religion and this book was not dedicated to fire the fur-

nace of hatred but to collect casually some of the everyday expressions common to Americans.

1961-1962, my last research sabbatical before retirement, was another academic year in the woods of northern Wisconsin. Between desk-work and yard-puttering
and wood-piling and the like, the days passed quickly,
all too quickly. After the beautiful scenic Christmas
when Santa Claus-land was in full glory we took a vacation of about two months in midwinter, January to
March. We did it up pink. This time no car—just the
luxury of the train and leisure of the then railroad service. From Chicago the Santa Fe's "El Capitan" offered
comfort beyond compare even though we did not go
first class. Many people of our own age-group were
heading west in search of something—as did we. There
was the memorable stop at Grand Canyon and then on
to Los Angeles. We made headquarters at Claremont
where we lived in a rented apartment close by our son
who was then stationed at Pomona College and we met
some academic people known professionally to me and
indulged in my favorite pastime of gossip about the academics. A rented Corvair took us to the usual spots
where tourists like to go, to Mexico's Tijuana, San Diego
and north on the beautiful coast-drive to the redwoods
south of Frisco with a memorable stopover at the Hearst
Castle to admire the striking collection of Grecian and
other art that bedecked the hillside far from their origin.

My one sentimental journey was Point Loma where
the theosophists held forth. In my student days, I visited this spot on a summer's assignment for the Lutherans and came to be interested in Mme. Blavatsky's version of the philosophy of the Far East. To my amaze-

ment, this Point was now taken over by some conservative church group. I recall that I was introduced to some secretary and was asked, after she learned that I had had certain ecclesiastical connections, if I would pray into the microphone! Well, I wasn't in the mood and furthermore, when she told me it would be broadcast all over the area, I shuddered at the thought. When I told her I didn't like "canned prayers" she said: "We won't use it until next week." This ended our visit except to stay and admire the new campus of one of California's beautiful state universities snugging the hazardous shores of the Pacific. On our return we did get to do Disneyland (which Nikita Khrushchev missed to his regret); and then on to the hot spot of America's oasis where entertainment is dispensed in the grand style: Las Vegas.

When we returned north we found that King Winter was in full sway. Our driveway was impassible. The snowdrifts hid the house from the road. There was no use at all to try to enter. What would be the point? Mercer people are a tribe of God's people and they help when you need it. Within a few days the big snowplow had made the path for the car and the little snowplow made a walk from the garage and wood-house to the main cabin. We soon moved in. The pump had to be primed and coaxed. And we went through our usual pump prayers. The water had to be turned on and the tanks slowly filled; the stoves lit, all of them, each and every one with tender care and more prayers. In three days we were back in operation and tired and satisfied and happy.

And so the research-sabbatical was resumed. A fresh spirit renewed is worth all that it costs in time and money. I had not lost time; I had regained myself which was worth more to me than time. And when I say "I" I mean "we." Just the two of us.

And thus back to the desk. Out of the year came two books, both of which I am proud. Not big tomes. Rather, books more personal than all the others. It was a time of life when you begin to take stock of yourself rather than worry about the thoughts of others. There is much more freedom in being yourself than in touring and trying to invade the thoughts of others—which was my life pretty much up to now. In 1964, the year of my retirement from The College of Wooster, the two books appeared almost simultaneously: the one called *Inside Ivy Walls* and the other *Toward an Expansive Christian Theology*.

Inside Ivy Walls is an informal book in which an author speaks freely of this and that. This one is about the college campus. I included in it some of my infamous chapel speeches through the years. (Included was the one in which I reported one of my research-sabbaticals in a manner which offended the dignity of the dean who presided. The students seemed to approve my address and disapprove the dean's "behavior" causing (unknown to me) a campus uproar. It ended with the dean calling me, asking my presence the next day to receive a public apology by him for his alleged demeanor and my refusal to appear and hear any public apology by anyone!

There were, in the spring of that year (with only a couple of months away from retirement), loud campus whisperings "who was getting what" in the book *Inside Ivy Walls* and although I mentioned few names I was noticeably being avoided by some of the campus profes-

sors who were certain I was digging near their basements. It proved to be a fun book. And I promised myself (somewhere set down in that book) that since I
hadn't touched bottom with campus matters I would
do so after the freedom which is supposed to come on
the day of retirement. That promise is partially fulfilled
in the present book—with more to come if there is such
a thing as "more grace" to live out a longer time span.

I was unhappy about the publishers of this book although they did produce a fine-appearing volume.

The other slim volume I rate as my best. An author
has a right to be his own critic and if he thinks the book
is good enough (to him) he has the right to say so. It
is the kind of book I wanted to write for years—and I
felt that enough maturity had been earned for me to
sum up my own personal views in matters which had
concerned me over a rather full life in assessing the
views of others.

Toward an Expansive Christian Theology (Philosophical Library) is a brief systematic theology and/or
philosophy of the Christian religion. I dedicated it to
my three sons who were close to me at the period of life
when sons are beginning their own professional lives
and quite on their own: all three with earned Ph.D.'s
and one with an extra Doctor of medicine. When one
recommends something, he ought to be thinking of his
children's generation and thus I thought.

The book is heresy in that it upholds naturalism rather than supernaturalism, Christ is an oceanic figure
rather than a Jewish rabbi become Son of God according to Greek Platonists (Trinity), evil as being not an
insoluble problem but soluble by admitting it in the
structure of things and therefore never overcome (my

grandson sees this going on in his aquarium when little muskie fish devour their cousins all over the place, asserting their mastery of power even before they become kings in northern Wisconsin) and that evil is transmuted (like good) into something else but never eradicated (thus "peace on earth" is a cosmic matter rather than a mere human adventure of interpersonal relationships of hope and thus reaches into the creative processes themselves).

Heresy, again, in the view that good is impossible without evil, success without frustrations, love without suffering, day without night, happiness without unhappiness, state of well-being without illness, hope without despair, visions without myopia, heaven without hell, freedom without necessity—and a host of other built-in opposites. Heresy, again, in the view that the resurrection story is not the basic position of a belief in life going on (there are too many precarious ingredients in the accounts) but that belief in immortality rests on man's insatiable hope for more and more of life, believing that the positive somehow is superior to the negative and noticing that all people at their best believe in some form of after-life; heresy in the belief that the atonement theories are in need of revision, in the admission that religious institutions with their frigidity belong primarily to the priests and that the genuinely religious responses belong to those of the prophetic order; heresy in the view that sacraments and liturgies and the status of bishops and popes and creeds and all the rest are secondary to *ongoing* insights and philosophies of men as they go on into some kind of maturity; that faith unattached to sweet reasonableness has the seeds of its own dissolution, that God is not a wholly Other but that there is Divinity in the world of nature (not pantheism but panentheism which means the kind of transcendence of the ego in experience amidst the pluralities of life's experiences), a world of the supernatural apart from the mundane as no longer tenable in the face af a naturalism or a cosmos or a *Universe;* that loves do not spell the elimination of dislikes and likes, that the good outweighs the evil since the Universe is fundamentally positive (creative) rather than negative; and on and on.

The highest good seems not to be pleasure, nor fitting in with everything indiscriminately, nor personal salvation nor therapy, nor successful adjustment (which may spell out only "a fitting in") but rather the bringing to some measure of fruition of what a person is meant to be and this is to approach to some effective point that stature that makes a human proud to be human, not aspiring to be a god nor a spineless saint nor a neutral entity. This is salvation and essential Christianity approaches the other greater religions of the world not as a competitor but a fraternity under the same Divine indwelling world of experience and fulfillment. This is more than ethics. Any religion worth its salt is more than a company of do-gooders, or a chorus of dedicated saints trying to achieve an impossible possibility, but the expression of adventurers moving toward that which appears in the long run to be more fundamental in life.

Such is the *expansive* view and I could hardly expect many to agree with it. It is beyond ecumenics which is only a patchwork of a plurality of institutional churches each staking out a claim and planting its own

flag alongside others. It is beyond ecumenics by looking
for a *rapprochement* with other insights and experiences
of men be they from the East or from the West, tan or
white, ancient or modern, not all co-equal but children
of the same household of the Divine. This or that prophet is a part of it and to the pantheon of prophets Yes-
hu'a of Nazareth may be counted and evaluated by anyone as to his essential stature without the paraphernalia
of some house-of-bishops' pronouncement or some creed
or some church.

At the heart of the whole matter there is to be sought
a good way of looking at life (which is normative philosophy) in an expansive manner rather than from the
observatory of some one religion tied to some century
or to some written authority or to some prison-house of
orthodoxy.

I may add a footnote to this volume: *Toward an
Expansive Christian Theology* contains the essence of
the lectures I gave in Boston on invitation (during a
week in March, 1957) of the Faculty of the Boston
School of Theology of Boston University.

As I write, I await the publication of my next book
which is to be born (September, 1969) before this present work is finished. It will be a return to my first major and mature love: the love of philosophy. Everyone
has some kind of philosophy, good or bad or mixture.
Most people—by far the great majority—have a bad philosophy and what makes it worse: do not know it. And
this is what they live by, and it therefore becomes their
real religion. It is the attempt to show this: which is a
part of the purpose of the new book: What is religion
and what is a good one? What is philosophy and a good

one? What is a theology and a good one? How does philosophy stack up with all the other human disciplines (sciences, history, art and all the rest)? And what major problems have haunted professional philosophers, especially in the West, from the Greeks down to the Existentialists? And how and what can we know? What is the world like: spiritual, material, or a dull neutral entity or perhaps a mere dynamic series of events like a wind that blows and blows without any end or purpose other than that of sheer pointless energy?

These are questions campus students today are asking—the same as yesteryear. And the answers given by their elders seem to many to be too artificial. So . . . let us praise philosophy by bringing it to the college student level rather than by bringing students to the traditional level of incomprehension. They are hungry for it perhaps as never before. The world is getting smaller and larger, more simple and more complex and our inherited norms go crashing. Must we not think together again and seek out some compass of understanding of the things wise man of all ages and climes have sought —but in terms of today's fast changing world?

This is the task set out for the new book—especially for open-minded laymen and certainly for college and university students. The book's title is *Basic Philosophy for Beginners*.

The Christopher Publishing House (North Quincy, Massachusetts) has taken over the publication of this last book. I may say that what led me to this small (but old) publication house with this new child is an advertisement that came during the year announcing that one of my most revered professors at Yale had entrusted his most recent publications to this firm and if it is good enough for Professor Sheldon it is good enough for me. (The big publishing houses nowadays frown on introductory texts; they are committed to anthologies [which most beginning students do not comprehend] which appear to play upon the status of one compiler as over against another; an anthology offering a sales' pitch with greater mass production over less financially promising projects.)

I have never taken inventory of my writing and publishing. I do know that I was lucky enough early and through the years to be included by some professional magazine editors to review current books. These assignments I cherished since the recompense was excellent; a "free book" and it kept me current. A look at my library where I have kept these books together as a kind of special family will show that they number in the hundreds. My articles in professional journals were much less frequent. I had too many assignments elsewhere. Contributions to volumes edited by others were more than a few besides introductions to books by new authors. Encyclopedic articles have had a modest share of my time and effort as well as confidential appraisal of manuscripts sent me by publishers.

Dr. Runes never quite got everything from me which he assigned. One contract to do a book—an anthology —on current theologies took a lot of reading and preparation. But I never finished it since my heart was not in it. I recall I worked on Teilhard de Chardin, the current Roman Catholic rage, and on Dietrich Bonhoeffer, the now popular German theologian who suffered martyrdom. Neither impressed me: the former was writing about cosmic evolution as if it were a new idea and did not seem to have much more to say than had been said: the other was, in my judgment, far from a "Christian" martyr in his plotting the death of Der Führer (not that I am partial to the latter) and seemed to have earned his kind of martyrdom and moreover his conception of Christianity seemed too far out to be significant. And there were others included in the project. The "God is Dead" movement did not seem to deserve the immortality it seemed to wish to achieve and I came to think that it would soon backfire (which it did). Another book for which I had a contract is still much alive in my hopes to do some time. But there was just not enough time to get at it although my notes have piled up on it. So it remains stillborn.

And, like all authors (I suppose), I have manuscripts ready for the press; to be specific: for two more which may see the light after my second retirement (my first in 1964) from teaching (which in 1970 continues).

Some people have the affront to ask me: aren't you in the money by all this effort? My answer is the same as I give to those who ask my age: I say I never speak of my age to anyone. (Some questions even from friends have to be turned aside quickly before any further involvement.) One never asks anyone to confess his salary. (To do so should embarrass the questioner rather than the responder.) But I gladly admit that over the years when the Wooster College salaries were much less than apprentice bricklayers any extra income was not a luxury but a necessity. (We lived in a time when one was expected to earn his way and to remember that Santa Claus comes but once a year.)

A writer's world is physically a restricted world. Pearl Buck has said more than once that her life was a lonely one. But it is that *physically*. Spiritually (which here means just the plain realm of spirit) it is a rich world, full of surprises, excitement, anticipation, new insights (and hindsights) and far from lonely.

What becomes telling to me (as I write these lines) is what many of our young people lack (and do not know it): a sense of history, a perspective beyond the present. If they did they would not just march and protest and burn and destroy and block offices on the campuses and throw books and precious things around and explode and have sit-ins and love-ins and all the rest of insane behavior: they will find that wars are as much a part of nature as is man and that Vietnam as bad as it is and Korea and all such are the awful characteristics of life which will not be wiped away by a few prayers nor by peace commitments. Rather, as we move along in social evolution there continues to be strife, levelings, progress, regression, plateaus and new evils and regenerated evils, and new goods—life as it is and has been and will be. Amen. This is not pessimism. This is realism. And the optimism is still there: for example, the lust for life and well-being that comes out of the experiences of frustrations and difficulties. To have our own way makes for insipid characters. Permissive parents breed problem-children. When *their* (the children's) storms break (as they surely will) they will be swept under. They haven't yet known what the essential ingredients are that go into making character: a lot of frustration and blocks and the doing of a full proportion of what we do not like to do but what we have to do to get going.

Brooding, reading, thinking—bring all such things to focus and furnish rewarding perspectives to life.

While the subject of publishing and writing is at hand in these pages—and in the previous sections of this book —something might be said about the manner of one's writing.

There is no stock formula and I am certain "summer schools for potential authors" ("literary retreats" under self-styled authorities) can only be the testimonies of men and women who expose their own personal peculiarities. Only a few norms exist: such as spelling, grammar, punctuation (most disputable) and precision of fact and description.

What I have to say (very briefly) is certainly not normative to others. I was lucky in my grade-school days and in high school to have teachers of English who were strict grammarians and who taught and disciplined us to spell. I recollect how important it was to diagram sentences (independent clauses, dependent, adverbs modifying only certain words—certainly not prepositions)—and all that. I write about this now because it seems deplorable to me that students today besides being poor in spelling have never heard of diagramming sentences. The current theories with phonographs and free-styling and rhetoric all seem to me like houses built on sand. My experience with college students over many decades is that they had pussycat teachers of English in the grades and high school and will never be able to repair the loss of acquaintances with strict fundamentals. I had my hand slapped in my day when, before the class standing in line, I misspelled a word publicly. It was good therapy then and it still is. (Although we hear that children must not be frustrated either mentally or at the seat of their pants!) There is no substitute for discipline in fundamentals in any language and English is no exception. (And this goes for any academic subject.)

I have some peculiar quirks in writing. For example, I type my material letting the thoughts get expressed as they come without worrying about spelling, punctuation, mistakes in grammar or any detail of performance—but to get the lilt of expression going with whatever words seem to fall loosely and spontaneously. Later, the corrections. In this way, I feel free to let the subconscious take over rather than the critical consciousness stand in the way. (This is much like the phenomenologists who insist that ideas or patterns or even consciousness must not stand in the way but stand aside for the pure consciousness to flow—and for them reality is best apprehended *in the flow.*)

I learned to use all my fingers on a typewriter, even though having had no lessons. I write double-spaced so as to insert corrections (if I choose to stop along the way). I have no exact pattern or outline—other than a sheet of loose paper on which sometimes (but not always) I note down reminders of things along the way at this juncture which might be considered.

When I wrote my novel many years ago my characters had idiosyncracies and I pictured them as to weight and sizes—so as to keep them intact. But the plot (if any) developed as I went—not knowing what was to happen except as my "sciousness" (William James' word) directed. I wondered after each chapter where we would land next—and I wondered about it all with the author (myself) at the table. Sheets of blank paper should always be handy for quick replacement so as not to disturb the flow. And I had one rule which I respected.

This rule was never to leave the typewriter when I was stuck in my thinking. This would leave a block and it would be difficult to pick up the threads again. I would wait to stop only when I was ready to begin a new paragraph or a new chapter and excited enough to go on. Stopping in that kind of middle (or mood) made me anxious to come back to work and the story could go on where I left off with a kind of self-propelled momentum.

In this book (which I am now writing) I followed the pattern of the writing of *Basic Philosophy for Beginners* while in Winston Salem, North Carolina. I set so many pages for each day—except Sunday. The schedule for this present book began July first (1969) and the date was entered on the sheet of page 1. I wrote a scheduled number of pages a day as a minimum or a *must* (double-spaced regular typewriting paper), numbering the sheets as I went. I marked the big calendar each day plainly so that it stared me in the face. Some days I did seven, some days ten. If no pages, I had to make up my work. If I planned to be away from the desk on a given day I saw to it that I would not get behind, by keeping on the plus side continuously.

As I write this line, it is August twelfth and I have one hundred and fifty pages completed (full pages), limiting chapters or sections to about fifteen pages plus. In a book of this type where reminiscing goes on according to topic I do not set limits since I have no idea ahead of time how the flow will come. If it is an editorial piece of work, the approach is different, one's book-size is determined by the number of topics and contributors and in consultation with publishers.

Dr. Henry Nelson Wieman of Chicago University told me how he and Mrs. Wieman operated on their books. He took me to the third floor of his apartment near the university after a dinner and an evening of interesting conversation (he and I, independently, had been coming to similar philosophical views, namely naturalism) and showed me their desks adjacent to each other. Each had an understanding that, while at work, the other would not speak. When conversation was sought one of them would so indicate by placing an object at a certain spot on the desk and, at the convenience of the other, conversation resumed. Whether or not this may be helpful, the point is: you simply cannot concentrate with too many distractions.

I recall when I was a small boy I was never allowed to go into my father's study while he was there (and without permission). In our home the study was a kind of holy of holies. I continued the custom and still recall my children sometimes waiting at the open door hoping to talk to me but respecting the dividing line. At my home in Wooster (and I would never think of having an office on the campus as a study since there are too many distractions—such a place [on campus] is for counselors only who are supposed to counsel) my study is the best room in the house. My wife always favored me with this privilege. A door could be shut in case of unexpected callers. Never a phone on my desk—the most irreverent rascal of all. At our summer place, I have the favored room of the big house, overlooking the lake with book dividers setting the study apart from the living room and now a sign is posted marked "Study." In case of emergencies I have a cabin to myself where I may retire. This, too, is a reservation.

I take lines to tell all this since I feel sorry for professional people who have no place of privacy in their homes. I have seen wives usurp the privileged places for everything under the sun but a study. It may be that there is a spot reserved in the damp basement somewhere or by precarious stairways into a reserved room in a hot attic. This treatment shows a lack of appreciation of that which is associated with a professional life.

Such are some of the antics of one person and one family. I can come into my room at any time of the day or night and find my papers just as I have left them. Now and then, I am reminded of my awful housekeeping but there never has been a quarrel about one privileged room where books some times have to be stepped over when a piece of writing demands their proximity. Moreover, books are my close friends and my professional aides.

"Have you read all these books?" ask the uninitiated when they take a look at my library. My answer is "No!" And they (the uninitiated) wonder if I decorate with books! If they asked "why so many?"' I would tell them these are the tools of the trade such as a carpenter has near his worktable: a saw, hammer, screwdriver and augur-bits of every conceivable size and so on. (He may be sane even if he never has used all his purchased tools more than once!)

As for proofreading and index-making. No secretary on earth should be blamed for errors if an author has delegated such responsibility. Such tasks can never be delegated. You just have to follow your writing through, using your own wits and eyes and pencil. Only a printer or typesetter can be blamed if he drops a line in Brooklyn and the line is either lost or put back in the wrong place. He may justly be cursed and you will just have to say to yourself to such errors: I am unlucky. This happens and happens and happens. So be it.

WE BOUGHT A SUMMER HOME

We did one thing in our earlier days which many people would perhaps think foolish. We bought our summer home before we settled on a substantial permanent residence. This gamble paid off in many ways and changed the whole pattern of our family life. Actually, we lived during the fall-winter-spring seasons in anticipation of the summer—the peak of the year. After each summer, we felt we had to start over again submitting to the long months ahead. It gave a peak time to our family life. And as the clock has turned and as I now sit in a comfortable room which opens up to a wide expanse of trees and a Wisconsin lake, I feel a strange sense of satisfaction and happiness of being here—now for the fortieth year.

It was not planned. It was a happening. The north country is the parental home of my partner in life. We have memories of being together in this area for over fifty years. She came to college in Illinois and I was already there and time and circumstance brought us together which meant a sojourn on my part to her home in northern Michigan.

One summer, when our children were small, we rented a cottage on Mercer Lake, an old, old cottage. For my partner there was some sentiment. Her family had more than once rented the same cottage for a week or ten days' vacation years ago, their family migrating by train from Ironwood to the little town twenty-four miles south in northern Wisconsin. They followed the one path from the station to Mercer Lake, bearing baskets of homemade bread and the supply of delectables commonly seen on a bountiful table in typical Scandinavian homes. She felt herself at one with this cottage since it held memories sustained through the earlier years.

And here we were for two weeks with *our* family: same cottage, now noticeably venerable, same yard, same trees (now stalwart Norway pines), same lake, same view, same distance from the little Northwestern depot of modest appearance.

It was during the depression in the early thirties. All I had of the world's goods which could be called "assets" was an insurance policy to which I was pledged to donate premiums for the rest of my life. It was a shock to us when the owners asked us to buy their cottage. They had grown tired as most older people are wont. The thought was a shock to us since, at this stage in life, the purchase of a summer home was unthinkable and we could foresee only the continued rental of a winter residence for years to come, lacking capital. And these were depression days—no time for saddling ourselves with a mortgage. What is a mortgage? I had only the remotest conception of what it meant then. Nor had I heard of such a thing as an abstract of title, nor of land surveying (other than in a geometry course).

People were losing their properties; the banks were circumscribing their depositors; money was tight, there was hoarding of cash in tin boxes; people looked suspiciously at each other; charge accounts were bulging. Who would buy a summer home at such a time? Answer: we did!

The owner of the property suggested that I borrow on my insurance policy, pay him a modest down-payment and string the annual payments with a modest interest along through the years. No hurry about it. Moreover, who knows but maybe the insurance companies would go broke and the crash would be complete?—I asked myself. I was surprised to learn that I had already some cash-value on my life insurance policy which would more than satisfy a down-payment and that the company would only demand of me my own signature and a modest interest payment each year as long as I kept my premiums paid. When the decision had been made and the down-payment given to the party acting in eskrow (my father-in-law) and the deal signed, I made my first pilgrimage to the place of our dream. The day stands out as a kind of sanctified memory: I went into the property, knelt down, and picked up a handful of the moist soil (pine needles and all) and then stood up, looked up at the stately pines and said in a voice which I myself could hear (though no one else surely could have heard) "This is my dirt. This is mine . . . at least, *this much* is mine" and I am reminded of Rolvaag's novel where the hero of the story did the same when he grabbed a fist full of earth (could it have been dung?) and said, "This is mine, this is the good earth" (or some such words).

I didn't worry about the future payments. I had health, a good wife, a small family, a job, a salary, ambition, an insurance policy which traded credit with debit and a heart full of hope and enthusiasm; and what is more, the feeling of a capitalist whose joy is in personal integrity and responsibility and ownership.

It took many years to pay off this decision. Many years. But I asked for no credit and I was beholden to no creditor nor benefactor. That life was kind to me to make possible earnings on my own, I can, of course, take no credit. I was just plain lucky. Though I had no idea of an investment, I can honestly say as I now view the same scene: this investment paid off in money five times over and for health it brought us to the out-of-doors each summer through the many years when we badly needed the out-of-doors, family togetherness, fun and what is more: a change of pace each year and an acquaintance with mother nature in the rough, an immediate contact with nature's cool breezes, storms, one tornado, the sport of fishing, acquaintance with pumps and boats, outdoor toilets, snowstorms and not the least of any I might name: the acquaintance with the most wonderful people in the world: unsophisticated and sturdy German, Norwegian, Swedish, Finnish and Italian and Irish settlers, people of the most modest means who know the good earth and work with it and relax with it and take things in stride, good people who may swear and get drunk at times and who know the art of loafing and yet will come in and pitch for you if ever you need them.

I am proud of my many friends in these parts. They respectfully call me by my titles when they should call me by my first name. (One could not say "Verg" but called me "Bert.") I am proud to be an elder citizen now, somewhat of a pioneer to the present generation-

gap. And I love them all for their idiosyncracies, mixing
their own with mine.

One thing, I think, we have learned about content-
ment and happiness in the experiences of a summer
home is the value of a commitment to some one major
project each summer into which all are somehow involved. (Speaking about a project reminds one of the
Swede whose brogue bothered a friend. Said the friend:
"Ole, you must practice the word 'job' and not say
'yob.' " Some time later Ole reported to his friend:
"I have practiced and practiced. I have learned another
vord. I now say 'proyect' instead of 'yob.' ")

We learned to have major "proyects" each summer;
one year it was building a fireplace for the living room;
another, painting the house; and then it went on: a
"Hund-Hus" (Dog House) for tools; a wood-house
for slab-wood and logs for the fireplace; a cabin for a
hideout (when company came to interfere with study
and writing); a brick patio; underbrushing the bank to
the lake; building a gate to the driveway; and so on.
Each year the chores were consistently repetitive: rake
needles, reseed the small lawn, rake leaves, paint screens,
calk the boat, rearrange the garage, pile wood, repaint
the outdoor furniture, fix the dock, haul garbage to
the city dump and so forth.

Not to have a "proyect" is to invite boredom. So
many people come north to the lake region and after
a few days' fishing, haunt the bars or the newsstands
hoping somehow to be entertained. The happy ones are
busy, busy, busy. Ownership of a place is the spark-
incentive or motivation to busyness. We have found the
summer in our area too short to fill all the demands.

Thus, a vacation is a rest, not in the sense of doing nothing but doing what you are not accustomed to be doing in the routine months of the year.

People (or as Carl Sandburg would say: "Peeeepel")! They have been the most intriguing of our summer experiences. People different from those with whom we associate in our professional life. Real people—they!

Take the case of Julius, a neighbor over many years. A self-made carpenter, a strong German character, stubborn, independent.

One day I asked him:

"Julius, I notice each Sunday you and your wife go out in your car just about three o'clock. I am sort of curious: where do you go?"

Said he curtly: "Well, I take the woman out for an airing."

(This was the only time I ever saw them together. Some of the townsfolk claim they have seen them together, he walking about five feet ahead of her.)

More about Julius. The story goes something like this: Some Chicago tourists stopped at Julius' home when they saw the homemade sign in his front yard: CABINTS FOR SALE (Cabinets for Sale). The two tourists knocked on his door hoping to buy cabinets. Julius appeared, newspaper in hand.

"You have cabinets for sale?" they asked.

"Nope." answered Julius.

"How come you don't have cabinets for sale?" they asked. "We saw your sign."

Julius answered promptly and finally: "None of your damn business."

They tell me (and I know this to be true) that Julius

worked on a wooden cross in his carpenter shop. (He was not a churchgoer.) One day he went out to the little village cemetery (near the city dump) and set the cross in the ground in a spot selected by himself. He asked no one if it were permissible. It happened that when the village authorities came to survey the lots in the area they found the grave of his wife smack in the middle of the main driveway, appearing on the plot. Since she was already buried, they had no alternative but to make the roadway conform to Julius' arbitrary decision. I have seen the wooden cross, which now indicates the place of his own burial beside his wife. The cross at least was something sacred to him although he gave no evidence in his life of any recognizable religion.

It was Julius who supervised me and my young son, Bob, when we took on the job of laying a brick patio alongside the front of our house. We were amateurs of the first order. Each morning he would come and say to us: Now you dig down, level off and lay a thick layer of gravel, smooth it all out—and later on place the bricks alternating their positions, etc., etc. And each evening—no matter what we had done during the day—he would come in the yard, take one look at our accomplishments and say: "It's all wrong, boys,—you've got to tear it up, do it over."

This we did with due respect—until one day my son announced his retirement from the "proyect"—throwing in the one and only alternative: "unless Julius disappears from the scene altogether." It finally ended up somehow.

We both to this day proudly view the brick patio, look at each other and smile—and anyone watching would understand if he knew that our smile was the sign of satisfaction over a brick patio which has lasted some thirty years. (It has withstood years of storm, rain, hail and Wisconsin blizzards.) Julius was right, after all. He must have somehow taught us something which to this day we don't understand. (I guess the foundation was laid right—that is, after his critical supervision.)

No matter how hard I tried to be an outdoor man, a rugged Wisconsin native—I never did succeed. In one thing, I became an expert: I was a good errand boy. The men I hired bossed me completely. I submitted easily not by my having a good nature but by learning that if you wanted a native to work for you, you had to humor him always within the edge of praise. I ran every errand. My marches to the local hardware store were innumerable: perhaps for six-penny nails, size three screws, sandpaper number three and what not. (I learned, however, not to ask for a "sky hook" which was the usual examination of one's IQ.)

It was a cold October day when Julius (whom I had hired as carpenter) ordered me to ascend the ladder and help him put on the tarpaper roof on the woodshed.

"It's a going to snow," he commandeered me, "and if you want the roof on, come up here right away."

I obeyed as a hired man. The height of the place made me dizzy although the roof was hardly ten feet up. I tacked in roofing nails one by one as he swore at me and then—suddenly the hammer connected with my finger. I saw the red blood ooze out on the green roofing paper and I knew it had been severely injured. I started down the ladder for help.

He yelled at me: "Where are you going?"

I showed him my finger and showed him my face writhing in pain.

"It's blood," I said.

Then the familiar Julius voice was lifted in an impolite rage: "Come back up here. It's a going to snow. We haven't much time. Besides, the blood won't hurt the roof anyway."

This was his manner of condolence for those who were sick or in pain or in the abyss of utter frustration.

He was my boss. They all have been. My ignorance in their opinion and my own was enormous. Maybe I was a college professor. But what is that in terms of the world of cruel nature that operates with calloused hands and issues rugged commands. You never cross a native. Your criticisms had to be veiled with diplomatic questions such as: "Are you going to do this such a way or such a way?" "Do you think it would be better if . . . ?" And so on in the whole gamut of diplomacy. And this brings me to another character (still very much alive at this writing) who is another Mr. Mercer of pioneer days.

His name: August Peter. The one and only man in the area who could get water out of the ground with a guarantee. He used the birch branch to seek out the underground stream and would stop at the spot where the branch bent itself toward the good earth. His face became tense as if to say: "It's strong here, I can't hold the stick; it wants to go down." And down it went. I have seen it unbelievably many, many times in his hand. (And I remember the skeptic, the trained geologist, who stands there in ghostly presence deriding the "superstition.") August would never be told anything.

To suggest deftly any idea to him was an open target for ridicule. There was only one way, one opinion: *his*. And what is more: he performed and you stood aghast at his words of wisdom. They were words of experience and there was an authority which only comes by way of rugged outdoor life.

My oldest son one day made a casual remark to him while he was working at the well. August dropped his tools and announced briefly and plainly that if the boy knows so much, let him do it. He went home. It took days of persuasion to get him to return. I found him berry-picking although I knew he badly needed the coins that come with hired labor. To this day, my son remembers the day when his father looked at him in utter dismay that one so young should speak so carelessly in the presence of an adult. My son never uttered a word of suggestion to a hired man again. He, too, joined the ranks of the humble errand boys.

The character of the man was revealed to me in a major business negotiation I had with him. It concerned the necessity to draw water out of the good earth as bounded within the limits of my property. Formerly, neighbors had shared a well which furnished adequate and clear water. But neighbors are better neighbors (it is my experience and also that of Robert Frost who once said in a poem that fences keep the peace) if each is on his own ground. So August promised me a contract which was altogether verbal. He would guarantee water supply on my own property at one dollar per foot (I furnishing the point and the pipes and, of course, the pump).

"August," I said, "suppose you don't get water? What then?"

His answer: "You owe me 'notin'."

His faith in the magic stick knew no bounds. So was the agreement. He and his son (handicapped by the loss of one arm in an accident) worked at a spot near the property fence along the road. It was a long way to the house; but water was there. He and his son worked with a homemade pipedriver: pull the rope, let the weight fall; pull again, drop weight, pull, drop, pull, drop—in an unbelievable monotony. And slowly inch by inch the pipe with its point disappeared into the bowels of the earth. It took hours and hours. Each time he tested, the answer was negative. Finally, at about sixty-four feet he hit rock—the big boulder that underlay the property—and, of course, the point broke. He pulled up as much pipe as he could. He looked at me and smiled and said:

"Dere's water dere but can't drive de rock."

I said nothing but commiserated with them in my own disappointment. He picked up his tools and went home. A few days later I went to his house.

"August," I said, "what do I owe you?"

Answer: "Notin'."

Well, I asked, "Are you willing to try again at some other spot?"

He smiled but gave no promise.

One day he and his son walked into the yard with their paraphernalia, including the birch stick and he singled out another spot nearer the house but still quite far away.

"Here we find water," he said with reassurance in experienced defeats.

And so it went again. Pull, drop; pull, drop; on and on. One arm was the only power applied and it was the arm of his son who continued in absolute silence. An end of the day came as do all days. And the end came with nothing accomplished. He looked at me and he still had a smile, not a big one, just an ordinary smile of confidence in defeat.

"Dere's water here; but dere's de rock," he said.

So next day the salvaging of the pipe began and the two picked up their paraphernalia and threw it all in the truck and went home. I waited a few days. Then I went over to his house again.

"August, what do I owe you?"

Answer: "Notin'."

"Come now," I said, "I surely owe you for your day's work."

He turned on me and with a voice sharp and clear and final said: "Didn't I say: no water, no pay?"

This was not poetry. This was prose, hard and cold with an unmistakable finality. In my desperation and with a feeling of utter shame that I no longer could communicate with him, I found myself saying:

"August, I know you are a man of your word—'no water, no pay.' Why not let *me* take the chance? You have done the gambling. Why not come over and try again: this time we'll set up a pay-by-the-hour basis with no guarantee of water. *I'll* take the risk—*this time the whole risk.*"

He looked at me and smiled and said, "I'll tink it over."

Another day—much later—came. And here were August and his son with their paraphernalia. And the stick. And he looked at me and announced: "This time —dollar and hour."

"Agreed."

And he said: "No guarantee. Dere's water here, right here, a few feet from the cottage; but dere's rock, too."

I said with my conscience growing softer: "August, it is agreed. No water, pay anyway $1.00 per hour."

It is a kind of fairy-tale to relate the end of this encounter. The two began work at 8 a.m. Pull, drop; pull, drop. And the point (this time with another new point—a third one) sank quietly but slowly into the same good earth. We watched and waited with nothing to watch except to catch the expression on August's face. He knew the meaning of hard defeat and it was part and parcel of his style of life: to meet such defeats by going fishing, picking berries or perhaps a trip to the town bar.

I remember that it was 4 p.m. that same day when I heard him say to his son: "Well, put the pitcher pump on; we have struck water. Don't know how much; but we have water."

His words spread to the house. My family gathered around the sacred spot—which to us was to become a major shrine on the property. Yes, we had water. It was unbelievable to see clear and clean spring water issue from that rusty pitcher-pump and flow lustily into the sod by the push of the hand lever. Such waste, I thought.

"Dere's water, here. Dere's plenty of water here. Don't think the flow is too good. Maybe it'll pick up if the gravel down dere is a-plenty." These were August Peter's words of victory.

By nightfall we had drinking water: cold, cold—much like the refrigerated water we now have except that it was fresh, fresh. It took about eight hours at one dollar; the pay for labor $8.00. The depth of the well twenty-two feet.

And would anyone believe it if I say: August refused with that German stubbornness of his to take a cent more than the agreement? I had to find some other way to square matters up with my conscience. (I can report to the reader's uneasiness that I found a way which did not break the oral agreement.) There's always a way. But August came out victor and August lived peacefully with his own conscience. A word is a word and nothing need be written down to guarantee that word. This was his character. And with it: the philosophy that a promise is not only a promise but a promise tied in with the labor of sweat and frustration is still a promise.

Another town character whom I hired to do some work for me was the town's unlicensed plumber. He plumbed without knowing any theory of plumbing. His son was helping in the kitchen one day installing an oil hot-water heater. In the process the son—a strapping fellow of 5' 8"— got himself locked in back of the heater next to the wall and the father was turning the big wrenches under the heater. Neither one presumably saw the other. When the operation was finished, the father crawled up from the floor, stood up, and looked on with quite some surprise to see his boy behind the heater. Only high heaven in a miracle or a quick unscrewing of the pipes could save the fellow.

The curious thing about it all—the son didn't complain but seemed to accept the inevitable performances of his dad. I stood there and witnessed the Big Boy Scout save the life of the Son of the Big Boy Scout wondering all the time if in my kitchen there was to occur a major human casualty.

The same plumber was looking at some connections he had made in the little basement of our cottage. He had reached an impasse and was looking and looking at the connections he had made. He knew something was wrong—could it have been the connections with the wrong pipes? I stood there and watched (as usual, I was the errand boy to those whom I had hired).

Suddenly, he turned toward me, holding two huge wrenches, one in each hand. His eyes were not altogether parallel. It was a strange, ghastly look.

Said he (and these are accurate quotes which I seem to recall when I forget anything else): "Jeeeeeeshush Kweisst—what do I do now?"

Well, I wasn't "Jeeeeeeshush Kweisst" and I hadn't the slightest idea to offer him. Moreover, those piercing eyes which did not focus together upon me scared me out of my wits. I was alone with him in the basement and I did the only thing that a true human instinct can offer: I ran up the stairs and disappeared outside.

We had a first-class tornado one sultry August afternoon. I was home alone in the house. The wind seemed to sweep in without warning. Leaves and branches and needles were tossed with terrific force horizontally following the surface of the ground. I have never witnessed nature in a more violent mood. The house shook and I grabbed the kitchen cupboard (which was the only solid thing next to me and which was actually of little promise in such a situation). I bent over hugging the floor. Huge limbs swung against the house. The battle of Armageddon was on and here alone I knew my Maker had come to avenge me of all my sins. I had no time to be penitent. I was so scared that I was numb from the eyes down. What passed my window I do not remember but I knew that part of Mercer, not of my property, all of a sudden had arrived pell-mell. It was over in a couple of minutes—not the rain, nor the sickening darkness—but the wind. "Gone with the Wind" a phrase that to this day has experiential meaning. It is no longer a poetic phrase. It is Mr. Tornado.

When it seemed safe, I unlocked the door and took a look outside. Wires were down—I knew them to be live. Trees were sprawled helter-skelter on the lawn. The roadway into the place was blocked as if in preparation for another attack. Pine needles stuck to the house as if they were long hairs attached to the body. The white paint was discolored reminding me of a healthy vomit. I surveyed the forlorn landscape and decided that I must be careful where I stepped. It was at least fifteen minutes before I ventured beyond the little porch. Chaos everywhere. I later learned that I had lost some thirty sturdy tall maples, pines and birches on the property which took years to saw into firewood. To this day numbers of trees are still bowed as if to say: we pray this will never happen again.

A strange man came into the place. I had not seen him before.

"Is anybody hurt?" he asked.

I assured him I was the only inhabitant. He left as

quickly as he had come. The town had sent out its
volunteer firemen (I learned later). With power lines
down, I walked cautiously out to the main highway.
Nature, I found, had not singled me out as the only
sinner. The town itself on the southwest side looked
as if it might be a place in some scarred forest of Belgium.

When my wife heard about it in Ironwood, Michigan, she managed to find friends to take her to her
husband—alone in the Wisconsin woods. She told me
that the radio had announced a major tragedy in our
area. The trees for miles north of us were like naked
skeletons bereft of skin—miles of them. The beautiful
forests had been scarred. Men stood along the road
warning cars of debris ahead. When she came through
to the place, she could find no husband.

In a crisis, there is only one place to go: to the village
grocery store. So the search for her husband and father
of her children began. The town was filling with people
curious and seemingly happy that some excitement had
finally struck.

"Where is my husband? Have you seen him?"

And the answer came from someone coming into
the store: "Well, he's across the street in the restaurant
eating his supper."

Well, now, what would you say to that? I only had
my own answer: I was hungry and there really was
no other place to go than a place to eat. Just that simple.
I believe I was scolded for my nonchalance. But nonchalance I did not have when I began to realize that
somehow I had been spared from sudden demise.

People have a way of enjoying fires, tornadoes,

calamities. The tourists had their hey-dey for the next week or so. They drove past our little place—bumper to bumper—peering in to see if they might see havoc. I suddenly got the idea that I should contribute something to their enjoyment. I put on an old, old hat which was oversized and my oldest clothes (which are not hard to find at a summer home) and then placed myself along the barbed-wire fence and just stood there at the roadside. I bent over and held a crooked cane (a glorified branch). I put on my saddest look which at any contest would at least have been a runner-up to some prize. And I stood there as long as I could endure it. And I heard the kids in the cars say to their parents: "Poor old man, poor old man." I wouldn't look up at them for fear I would destroy their illusion. I enjoyed them as much as I believe they enjoyed me.

Nature heals many scars. Many of them, however, are still here even though covered over by fresh vegetation. This is true, of course, of sorrow. One may feel a deep hurt inside but time seems to offer the therapy to pose and take the freshness off of memory—even though one knows inside that a pose is a pose and that memories are never fully erased—ever.

MORE ABOUT MERCER AND THE
NORTHWOODS

The most vulnerable section of a building in the north country is, of course, the roof. The weight of heavy snow which "perdures" through the long winters (there is little springtime and a beautiful though tricky fall season) works havoc on flat roofs. Our summer cottage has a long flat-roofed porch which has been enclosed and turned into a dining-sitting room at one end and a study at the other and another flat roof over the kitchen (probably the oldest section but now one of the most attractive rooms with its genuine pineboard walls). Each year when we leave, there is a full Episcopalian ritual consisting of a major operation: long poles are put up, each in its proper place (all clearly marked), which give the roof at each spot a sufficient heave so the support will stay where it is appointed and thus prepare the roof for the onslaught of snow (beginning in October and then on and on). Our garage is flat-roofed and so the woodshed. So the ritual is prolonged. But it pays off. It would have paid off better had the roofs been constructed other than flat—but one doesn't change ancient architecture easily and cheaply. Hardly a house escapes the snow damages unless properly constructed.

After the tornado (about which an account has just been given) the roofs had been badly damaged. Tough tarpaper is the common type of roofing and north Wisconsin hail storms can ruin the best of such protection. So, again, you have to go out and look for some strong native who can lay heavy roofing paper.

As the years fly by, this kind of fellow is hard to find. You still have to humor your man and even persuade him to come, perhaps by a long conversation at some local bar. Many such fellows whose labor is precious in any line from masonry or tree cutting or to just ordinary repairs use the word "Yes" for "I don't intend to." And thus the word of mouth becomes a kind of friendly and vacuous spout.

My man for the repairs of the roof after the tornado was an unforgettable character. He was husky and rude, opinionated (many of them had harsh words for Washington, D.C., until after social security was instituted and then the political saints came to be almost altogether those of the Democratic party). He swore continuously much as the rest of us use prepositions, adverbs and split infinitives. He came and conquered not only the job but all of us involved as simple human beings. He was king for over two weeks and we bowed before him at every turn. We had coffee ready at his beck and call. I even climbed ladders to serve him. I kidded with him when I thought he might perhaps laugh (seldom, seldom, once more: seldom). His boys were afraid of him. When he didn't swear one knew that something was wrong and the explosion would soon follow.

I'll give him credit. He did a good job except when one day it rained and a few leaks showed up. One major leak was on the front porch. The water just trickled

down. He came one day after I kept pestering him
about the leak. He surveyed the scene from the inside
up and, seeing no light coming through, announced
pontifically: "That's from your dog."

Now, please tell me (says I to myself): how can a
dog with its usual ritual whether male or female ever
make such untidy relations with the ceiling? I asked
myself: might he or she jump up on the table, lie down
and take aim? Such questions are those of a nitwit, said
I to myself. Well, I just couldn't believe this one, even
though I turned on the faucet of my best faith. I consulted others. And they were of the unanimous opinion
a dog could not possibly be responsible for a leak in the
ceiling. Moreover, we had no dog and as far as we
could recall, there had been no recent visitors with a
canine nor (to add to it) even cats.

Thus was the character of this rude brute—my repair
man—whom I began to dislike while fighting off hatred.
And yet sandwiched between my better and my worse
moods, I felt thankful, almost prayerful, for his kind-
ness in coming and working on my sick roof. On top
of it all (as if to drive me to distraction), he sent me
an enormous bill. On it he had working days which
any meteorologist could verify in court were rainy and
cold and impossible for the laying of heavy and stiff
tarpaper. Even his son made the mistake of telling his
dad that on that such and such a Friday they had gone
up "to the city." The father almost killed him with his
threatening stare.

"If you don't pay by tomorrow," he snorted, "I'll
go to Hurley to my lawyer and bring suit."

Thus the job was concluded in an atmosphere of

legal threats and I even feared for my life if I met him
on the village street. His theory was (and he had said it
earlier): "If you've got insurance get all you can and
more. That's what premiums are for!"

To this day when I see Mr. X on the village street,
I lose my Christian religion completely and become a
member of John Calvin's hordes of infidels, disbelievers,
hypocrites and all the other eternally "damned" before
the foundations of the world!

Our little town of Mercer (and immediate area) has
a population of about six hundred in the winter and
about six thousand in the summer. You can tell which
season it is very easily. The barometer is the number of
cars on Sunday parked around the small but attractive
Roman Catholic Church in the village and also by the
number of masses. The great wonder of our disturbed
and permissive day is the deep loyalty of Roman Catholics to their mother church. Lately, of course, is the
new dispensation whereby Saturday church attendance
is permissive for the Sunday mass, a concession to
tourists, fishermen and sleepers. Nevertheless, tradition
is stronger than new edicts. The barometer still holds.
The village is noticeably deserted during the winter
months and there is more leisure at the post office to
get caught up on the latest gossip. The oral news at the
newsstand is more current than the Chicago and Milwaukee papers and it is, by the same token, more exciting.

A famous bar stands at the corner of Highway 51
and the boulevard leading to the lake (and in the direction of our cottage). Here notorious characters have
come and gone—and the not so notorious: the village

constituency. In our earlier days, one could there (if one chose) meet Al Capone and his fratres. And to this day, his brother Ralph may rub shoulders with anyone who happens on the street, especially at his own bar. Ralph (they say) is a generous Santa Claus to the Mercer kids. His summer home, until recently, was less than three miles away: there being no sign or gate, just two wooden wagon wheels. A sign says "private" and this is for keeps. Some signs one respects. Those who know are very respectful when they look at this one.

Eight miles from our cottage is Little Bohemia—of Dillinger fame. To this day there is the little cabin where for a modest fee (it used to be ten cents—many years ago) one may enter and see blood-spotted clothes, underwear belonging to certain celebrities, copies of the *Chicago Tribune* with appropriate dates and other personal effects. At the main lodge bullet holes are in evidence if one looks for them. (A carpenter friend of mine said he worked at the lodge doing repairs and helped to give it atmosphere by shooting holes in the log walls which tourists enjoyed to give them a conversation piece when they returned home.) The escape cars of that period were on display in our village and for a long time we heard many versions (like the New Testament) of what actually happened. Little Bohemia is a beautiful lodge in a beautiful setting and the thicket of trees in the area offered a beautiful haven for escape should the FBI move in. The bar is dark and (some say!) very attractive. I met Dillinger, Sr. and heard his lecture to my three sons (forty cents for all of us). It went like this:

"My son was a good boy until he met older boys who were bad. He went to the little Methodist Sunday School. I tell you boys: stay away from older boys who may be bad company."

It was a sincere lecture (I am certain) and it made an overwhelming impression on small boys. (He outdid Sunday school teachers in effectiveness—this is my honest judgment and certainly was worth forty cents.)

Hurley, Wisconsin, is (or was) as renowned a town as Reno, Nevada—in earlier days. (It still is of renown.) The druggist once told me of a couple touring the area who had stopped for an ice-cream soda. The waitress obliged. Just as they began sipping from their straws they happened to ask: "What town is this?"

When they heard the name "Hurley" the couple looked at each other in consternation and fright and then one said: "Let's go." And without another word and leaving the soda (and the money) hurried out to their car and drove away.

"Hurley" is the county seat of Iron County, Wisconsin. Here I pay my county taxes. I have each year (until lately—when many reforms have taken effect) counted the number of bars on Silver Street (the main thoroughfare). It added to about ninety plus. (Not too many years ago.) The woodsmen frequented this town through the many pioneer years. And the merchants responded with their wares: wine, women and song. To this day "Lovely Girls" is the conspicuous electric sign on Silver Street. During prohibition the town was wide open. The FBI had "raids"; then there would be a lull; and then the papers (especially Milwaukee papers) would announce another series of raids with arrests and fines and the exodus of franchised girls from somewhere.

Many of my best friends in northern Wisconsin are Hurley residents. I may hasten to add: they are solid citizens, Roman Catholics, Presbyterians and agnostics (or non-identifiable). The sign (until this year) which appears at the south entrance to Hurley on highway marked "51" (which runs north-south from Hurley to New Orleans) reads: "THE END OF 51 WHERE THE FUN BEGINS." Strong supporters of Hurley are Ironwood, Michigan customers who need only to cross a creek from one state and city to the other. (We used to count the Gogebic County [Michigan] cars and wonder what Roman Catholic, Presbyterian, Lutheran or Holiness Mission Friend was out celebrating the onrush of dusk.)

I still do my banking in Hurley among the best of my friends: helpful, efficient and outgoing. Not too many years ago this same (the one and only) bank had barbed wire strung over the tellers' windows, the visible sign of defense from sudden attack of highwaymen. (I suppose now some kind of electric signal has superceded the former defense lines.)

The Presbyterian minister of many years and the town judge (also a Presbyterian) were both friends of mine. And though they said nothing about it, I knew from hundreds of sources that they worked in cahoots to save from ignominy many boys and girls (shall I say young men and women?) the cruel chains of the law. In the land where the redeemed are to make their presence there will be among the friends in heavenly welcome such young people shaking the heavenly hands of their pastors and lawyers, while those who filled their moneybags will look on from afar. Questionable legal deals? Perhaps. But certainly questionable places that made questionable legal deals—all over the place. Name one. I cannot. It is a part of the folklore of the place and where there is folklore there are the wind and the weather that keep fanning the embers of such folklore.

One never runs out of telling of "characters" all over the place. One need not go to northern Wisconsin to find characters. We find them everywhere—including, no doubt, the chronicler of these lines. The previous section of this book has its generous list of some of them. Let's add a few more.

There was the fellow who tended bar in one of the village restaurants. He was one of Mercer's early residents but still in his forties (I believe). His wife was a wonderful soul who had worked hard and was one of the world's best cooks. We frequented the place often and were always entertained by Mr. B whose stomach outdid the rest of his body and who found the easiest way to tend bar: to ceremoniously lift his stomach and place it on the bar (at stomach level). It eased the strain he was under. (Today we have another way of talking about such a misfortune: we have a *good* four-letter word which we now dare print and advertise: the word is "diet".) It no doubt would have helped him had the tap not been so close by. A friendly guy— if there ever was one. His body was laid aside forever at what we now regard as an early age.

His former competitor "at the bar" was an old-timer of many years ago. I still can see him in front of his desolate-looking place on main street: a man of enormous weight with a stomach that could not be embraced, sitting there tilted on a slender little chair with thin spindly legs, the back resting against the outside wall—watching, watching, watching, the cars that went by and enjoying every minute of it even while he dozed. The first letter of his name was Mr. E. Oldtimers will recognize it and know that neither the initial nor the descripton I have set down is fictitious.

Creed Boyer (died, 1970) was Mr. Mercer. Living alone as a widower for many years on a farm across our lake, he represented one of our closest contacts with the American Indians, although a typical Virginian. How he ever came this far north is still a conundrum. He just came and staked out his log cabin and his acres.

His stories are a part of the folklore of both Virginia and West Virginia—outposts of the later 19th century and he still could sing many of the popular songs of his earlier days. I visited his southern parental home and saw the country church and the cemetery where lay buried the clan of the Boyers. I brought back pictures and stories about his living cousins and he cried all the while I described them. (He told me he looked at the pictures during the winter months and enjoyed his tears of recollection.)

When he came to town each morning he stopped and shook hands with everyone—a daily renewal. I suppose he has pumped my hand a thousand times and his friendliness shook through his hard masculine fingers. I sometimes steadied my self when I saw him limping in my direction almost ashamed to admit to myself that I was soon to endure an ordeal of sudden right-hand arthritis.

"Beautiful day"—he would say (rain or shine). Then he would say he had had the usual sunrise walk up and down his road talking to the birds and the porcupines and even the skunks. He loved everything that moved. Deer came to his door. It was not unusual for him to see a bear cross his garden. (We still have the bears coming in from the dark forests to our village dump and enjoy to take our visitors—if they wish—to see one born free and enjoying the freedom of the fields and forests.) He knew the habits of chipmunks, squirrels, skunks, foxes, bucks, and birds of all kinds and colors, even their distinctive chirps and singing. The chicadees were his favorites in the wintertime (as it has been for us at our place—cute little rascals who love to sing and fight, never seemingly at rest but using their little wings nervously throughout the day).

I once recorded Creed's voice as he sat on our porch telling of this and that. He did not know of such a thing as a portable recorder. And when I showed him the hidden machine and turned it on, he couldn't believe that it was he who was speaking and saying the very same words he had just uttered.

"I'll be a darned logobstree," he said, in unexact words.

He never said "damn" (to my knowledge) for he was a converted Methodist from the south where in Virginia the Baptists and Methodists wore their religion on everyday clothes. (Not Sunday best). The modest sign he had made and hung over the front door of his house is descriptive. It just said "Home Plate' and that, indeed, it was for him for perhaps some six decades. He drove an old jalopy, made the rounds of handshakes, did the ritual which all of us performed when we opened our secret post office box and then moved on to the newsstand to listen for gossip. He sat with his rheumatic leg stretched out beside the table and I can still hear him say: "Come, brother, have coffee with me this fine morning." Optimism gone mad was his natural instinct and it oozed all over the place.

Now and then in the morning he would limp over to our place nearby, walk down the long driveway, knock heavily on the door and holler: "Anybody home?" Then we had our second and third rounds of coffee which my wife gladly warmed up for us—the coffeepot always ready to serve. And then the stories poured forth "from way back." And with these came memorized poetry by the reams which the nerve cells of his brain had stored away and needed only a little prodding until they spoke through his mind and eyes and voice, long stanzas of romance, struggle, faith, happiness—sermonettes which out-sermonized any preacher I have ever heard. There was always life when Creed was around. And he was a very lonesome man. We sensed it and hoped that somehow he could share in some of the lightheartedness which he himself gave us so spontaneously and creatively. I shall always remember his praise of the early morning hours, when each day breaks through the blackness of night.

"If you want to feel right," he would say in so many words, "you've got to get up early in the morning and hear all these quaint conversations going on in the woods and the fields which disappear with the rising of the sun. You come alive and you're glad to know that you are a part of God's green acres."

Speaking of nature, I must intrude with a happening of only a few years back. We had come home from a day "in the city" and had washed up and gone to visit at another lake for the evening. When we came home later in the evening, we heard the strangest noises. We singled out the concentration of the noises as coming from the inside of our home. Peering through the windows, we could see life all over the place. We thought then that the bats had made an invasion of the Ferm homestead.

This was a time when one needed expert help. I had been warned of the danger of bats, the carriers of infectious diseases. One respects a bat if one is sufficiently informed. And so help we got. A trip three miles away to get my medical son, a trip to a favorite of ours who is a native professional guide to Chicago and Milwaukee fishermen to help. And then we were prepared to enter.

Leonard Scheels (fisherman guide *par excellence*) led the way. I followed next. The kids were warned to stay out. I followed nervously with a covering of some kind over my head. There were birds, birds, all over the place, flying here, there, at, up, down, toward, away, missing you by millimeters, flying madly without rhyme or reason. When the lights were turned on, Scheels (who knows the whole of the northwoods as a Ph.D. knows some one little segment of knowledge) announced the diagnosis of the happening: not bats. These are chimney swifts!

With this curt announcement in came the rest of the clan who had watched excitedly from the outside places of safety. Then the battle was on. Windows opened. Made no difference. You had to catch them and throw them out. They resented every effort to banishment. As soon as one was thrown out, in he or she came again. So open windows had to be closed. This battle continued for hours and past midnight. The next morning there were the stragglers which had clung to the bedsprings underneath and back of pictures. Birds, birds, birds. Cute little birds. Sad-faced birds with innocent little beak-faces. At the time of dusk they had come down our large fireplace chimney, swooping in to roost as is their custom—free rent for the night. They were beginning their migration from the north country to South America or some such place (according to the accounts in encyclopedias) and in our area this migration began in August. It was August!

Everything had to be taken out of the house the next day: rugs, pictures, books, hangings, chairs, bookcases, —they had left their mark behind and many of their feathers. Mattresses, bed-covers, clothes, sheets, sheet-music, magazines—in all, three days' job by many hands before everything was brought back to shape.

"And do you know something?" I ask the reader of these lines and those who have "listened" to my story. I called my insurance man who took from me a generous premium only months ago. I reported to him the tragedy. He said he was "sorry" to hear about it and would contact insurance headquarters. I called him again in a few days and the word came: "Your Home-ownership policy which has full coverage does not cover 'birds' and you are ineligible for collecting damages. So sorry." Before he hung up, I spontaneously brushed aside his "regrets" by saying to him: "I don't want your commiseration. I want money."

To this day I have never collected a cent. And I consulted my lawyer friends of the faculty at the Law School of the University where I was then teaching and their research ended up something like this: "Birds are not in the footnotes. You may sue. But we advise you that you are hooked. You are dealing with 'an act of God.' " (Poor God gets the blame for everything!) If anyone reading these lines would like the name of the specific Hartford, Connecticut Insurance Company which advertises nationally their much-needed wares, I shall gladly furnish the home address and the name of my "forever-former" Mercer agent who still is trying to sell his all-inclusive insurance to the natives.

There is one member of the family we have retired without pension. He is both hated and loved. When we have hated him we did it in full measure to overflowing; when we loved him we thanked our God for having brought him to us. It is the little rosy-red Sears-Roebuck pump that came to us some decades ago. It is now in our garage waiting final rites. Once in a while I view his little body and now smile. I hardly ever pass him without my memory-box playing some kind of carols. This little rascal was the crux of our cabin-life for years. When it coughed, we all coughed. When it got sick and needed some kind of rest, we got busy *pronto* to help him recover quickly, sending for the best surgeons in the community: pump-knower-hows, Doctors of Pumpology (D.P.). And there have been night calls and early morning calls. I have met more

Mercer people through this little Sears offspring than through any other medium. They used to address me at the post office—not saying "Hello" or "Good morning" but: "How's the pump acting up?" For many years it lay some twelve feet under the surface of the earth in its lonely shelter and sang chug, chug, chug. And like the beat of the heart it went unnoticed until there was a flutter and skip and a jump. When it ceased we knew that something on the place had died: something very central to all our living. Then the ritual of climbing down, turning wheels, priming, and what not, went on and not unusually: a prayer to our Heavenly Father who presides over the Universe, even the universe of pumps.

Sentiment builds up unconsciously and surely and gradually and sentiment attaches itself to no end of things: to certain pictures, to dolls, to an old catcher's mitt, to a tree, to a pet skunk—just about anything. If you have deep emotional attachments which provoke the pleasant in you sentiment is born. Sentiment is the term for this attachment to something. We all in this Ferm generation have had sentiment for the Mercer summer cottage of forty years. And this has caught on to our children. It is an attachment that has paid dividends: one is a kind of family shrine. When our sons grew up and had their families, Mercer was brought with them into their several families' folklore. When privileged to have fairly generous vacations they naturally turned to Mercer as a part of the summer pilgrimage where vacation was sought. It, no doubt, was this kind of thing that prompted all our sons eventually to purchase their own cottages in the area on some quiet and attractive lake. They could have chosen from a million other spots.

Part of the story of this family acquisition was the strong element of fate. There were properties suddenly available—three miles from the old homestead. I was there at the time of the sale to negotiate at their request. I pride myself that the facts will sustain the claim that this was their money, their investment and their choice. There was no pressure on our part since we felt strongly that what is their money determines their choices and responsibilities. If it had been a gift it would have been otherwise. They chose it. We acted as mediating negotiators in the case of two sons. The other had already made the purchase without our knowledge. And the choices were risks like all choices. Without giving a history of the colony at Payment Lake, three miles from us (the elder Ferms), their pilgrimages have continued for some seven years with annual visits and interchange of picnics, ball games and controversial discussions.

Though it has not always been easy for families to stay together, ours has managed on the principle that "each has its own, makes its own rules and develops its own mores." Interference (we were told by inference more than once) breeds difficulties. We four families are not one family. Each has its own peculiar set of habit-patterns—developed through years of separation and the influx of outside parties called "in-laws." Some of them are more out-going; some are more reserved; some favor scheduled visits; some are much more informal. And this goes for the grandparents who know they have had their day with their own families and are now content not to take on another generation of child responsibilities.

It is our opinion that sentiments can change and new ones take over. This is not for us to say. When sentiments have gone, new sets of relations take over perhaps undermining the old in favor of the new. We ask for no patriarchal nor matriarchal loyalty where sentiment has ceased. We ask now that our own sentiments be continued and respected and are content with the amount of privacy which increases with age and a slower pace of life. We all can't play baseball forever nor enter into old-time patterns with new responsibilities. We become more selfish and prefer to walk rather than run. This is respected by the new generation, who, in return, may ask for the same for its own developing habit patterns and ways. Visits are enjoyed so long as sentiments remain.

It is a mistake to try to form a colony or tribe of a parental family. Three miles separating grandparents from their children and their children's children is about the minimum. Two different lakes are better than one lake in the ever-present generation gaps. It is nice to be together and it is nice to honor our distinctiveness. Daughters-in-law and sons-in-law will appreciate these remarks and certainly understand them. This is a lesson marked "first" among the rules. We have made our mistakes of interference and know many of them. We have learned from our mistakes not to let the father-son relationship overshadow the converse; there is the converse side: a son-father relationship which is different and just as important. It is the latter that has to come and develop through the years. The other is not only permanent but tends to be interfering and disciplinary.

When the property of two of our sons was bought, I sought out my banker and lawyer friends in Hurley (the bad city of America). It is a good thing to have a lawyer and a businessman in any major purchase—especially when acting as a negotiator for someone else. I met a hard-fisted real estate dealer who was ready to take us all for a ride (I learned this later). We called him Mr. BIG. He was pompous, authoritative and loud-mouthed. He set his price and I was ready to be sucked into a financial maelstrom. My lawyer and the bankers knew that the price was too high and the command came from them for me to turn in the keys and say squarely to Mr. Big: no sale. This we did ceremoniously. I still recall the scene of surrender (Appomattox?) of my option on the land.

There were three of us in the scene: Mr. Big, the judge (who was my mentor) and I,—with the keys surrendered and laid on the desk in the main cottage of the small resort. I hated to give this option up. Mr. Big grunted and we left. Hardly had we gone out of sight of him, driving toward the main road, when the judge, who was at the wheel of the car said: "By nine tomorrow morning, your telephone will ring and you will have your terms met."

I have never met a prophet although I have heard of many, such as those of the Old Testament. Sure as I breathed: at nine the next morning the phone rang and the voice of Mr. Big heavy with authority asked: "Was that deal we had made 'cash'?"

I said: "It was—the bank had agreed to the loan."

"Oh, I never knew that. I thought I would have to wait for the money. Oh, that's another story. Sure, we can revise our agreement. Come on out by ten and take the keys."

I was told he was a big bluff and now I knew without any doubt. My friends had saved us some five or six thousand dollars—had saved my sons, that is, and had saved me from impending shame and disgrace. Mr. Big is now selling real estate in the next world and the boys have one of their poorest boats named after him: printed white on green "Mr. Big"!

To help make reminiscences easier, on Friday, August the thirteenth, 1937, I bought a cheap "Record Journal" of some hundred pages. The cover is cardboard and the Journal rests on the shelf in my cottage study. It is now marked from page one to page ninety-eight, with the signatures and the records of our visitors: parties at birthdays, anniversaries, drop-ins, relatives both living and dead, picnic committees with signatures and dates—perhaps the most interesting volume in my library—to the elder Ferms, that is. If sentiments need to be revived the provocations come from this book. Each item is dated—which ends all argument about "when" and "who." Even major purchases are listed: when the floor was varnished, when the kitchen had a face-lifting, when the house was painted, the new roofs, boat painted, the patio chairs re-whitened, slab-wood eventually piled, rocks in the yard painted, new refrigerator, electric stove, the dates we were connected with the city water and sewer (what an event!)—you name it and the book has it. Our major item: the big Lake Superior stone-fireplace built by eighty-year-old

Charlie Schroeder, last in line of the royalty of local masons—whose voice I can still hear commanding his errand boys (me and Albert) to serve him quickly with "more mort" (mort for mortar)—stubborn, artistic, plebian aristocrat, homemade bread-maker, town character, who fought me with vicious words and almost quit because I insisted on a huge flue and the new product called "heatilator" which guaranteed the proportions necessary to function smokelessly. There never has been nor will there be the likes of him.

I commend most warmly to my readers: a guest book. It is the meanest thing (asking for signatures) to haul out when company comes but it is the most precious inhabitant of the house when the decades pile up on each other. It is more than a conversation piece. It is sure stimulation of those memories (so easily forgotten) which have added spice and taste to full living.

A Postlude to this chapter. As I scratch the surface of my memory here are other Mercer personalities who come to mind, all of whom have contributed to the complex of memorable experiences of the Ferms through the many years: Bill Flecks (neighbors), the Senior Brandts (pioneers in the area), Gehr (postmaster of yesteryears), the Vaughns and the one and only Leroy Vaughn (who came to help on short notice of the Ferm emergencies), George Craw (genial neighbor, Washington, D.C. critic and helper at odd jobs), Bos (super-jack- of-all-trades with a specialty in repairing electrical breakdowns), Nilsson (carpenter and contractor), "Timmie" Parrett (electrician), Kannenberg (town mayor), the Gaylord Thompsons (representatives of Uncle Sam's world-wide postal service, always cordial),

Earl Barncard and especially the Senior Barncards (ready to help), Peterson (humorist, storyteller, violinist, piano tuner, house painter), Mr. CNR (faithful servant of the Chicago Northwestern Railroad and telegraph dispatcher), "Blackie" Schwartz (jack-of-all-trades and second to none), the Alvey brothers (capitalists in hardware and how-to-fix-it items), Jack Natrop (legionnaire and carpenter), Frank Reinhart (who could tackle any job and come out on top and now master of ceremonies at Mercer's crossroads' News Center), Jug and Darrell Brandt (whose grocery store we partly own as their most ancient customers), the Sutherland brothers, Claude and Russell (painters and lovers of Nature)—where can the list ever end?

CAMPUS SHENANIGANS
AND THE FOIBLES OF THE ACADEMICS

What is a shenanigan? The "inspired" Dictionary (as most people regard Webster) gives such synonyms for this word as: trickery, humbug, fooling and adds that it is United States slang. My use of the word is: maneuvering, goings-on behind the scenes, together with some humbuggery mixed both with humor and much pathos. Wherever there are human beings there are shenanigans. It is only a matter of degree.

There was one major episode at The College of Wooster in my day in which my participation in a shenanigan of major proportion is a part of its unwritten history. It was the occasion of the election or appointment of a new president succeeding the long reign of Charles Wishart. We all were quite aware that he overstayed his presidency. Only he seemed to be unaware of it. A man's cycle does run down and he had reached his nadir years before the fatal day. He retired a lonely man—very lonely. Many of his "friends" on the campus forsook him since he was not in the seat of power any longer and they had other more fertile fields now to sow in their own interest. It is interesting to watch faculty people—frail as human beings—hanging around those close to the moneybag and to decision-making: how friendly they are and how soon the warmth of that friendship disappears when certain powers are suddenly removed.

The administration in Mr. Wishart's day was very closemouthed. Anyone who worked close to his office was beholden to him and their job was secure only in the measure of their "loyalty" to his whims and fancies. So the chorus of praise singers and devotees floated in and out of Galpin Hall—the new administration building. On the second floor was the *sanctus sanctorum* where men and women were hired or fired, promoted or demoted and salaries determined by fiat, who was to be on what important committee, *et al, et al.* Even the Alumni Magazine editor was very much beholden and this was important. This magazine contacts the outside world and the administration's soiled linen (if any) certainly must not be hung out for the world to see. (To this day, I have a kind of dyspepsia or innersick feeling when I take up an alumni bulletin, knowing full well the news is very much censored or properly written up—to keep the powers in power. A good corrective now has come on the scene in the student rebellion on campuses where student-oriented newspapers are appearing without some editorial and administrative okay.)

We were speculating about Mr. Wishart's successor. It was in whispers. The majority of the faculty—if not all—were ready for a change and the mood was for a radical change. But very few knew of the behind-the-scenes operations—and certainly not even most of the trustees. (Trustees in those days knew little of the inner workings of a college except from the slanted report of the president and from the dean beholden to the president.)

And here is where this writer enters the scene—

among those who stood outside and wondered with the rest of us what was going on. And it happened this way—and this is for the record and belongs to a section in this book with this kind of title: shenanigans.

I received a telephone call from Columbus, Ohio. It was my old friend, Dr. Oscar Winfield, with whom I had renewed old friendships when we were students at Yale. I knew he was acting president of a Lutheran College in Minnesota. His phone call dealt mainly with a proposed visit to our home now that he was in this vicinity.

"Would we be home?" And then. . . "I met your president. I overheard him asking a fellow-president to do a favor: to give an honorary degree to someone at Wooster. Then I heard him say that this fellow would be the new president and he lacked a doctor's degree."

(I held my breath.)

"Did you get his name, Oscar?" I asked.

"No," he said—which floored me completely. Then, after hesitation, he said: "It seems he is one of your deans."

Thus—the news broke. I needed only to fit in the pieces: eliminate this and that dean and find the "darling."

One of my closest friends during the many years at Wooster was John R. Williams, minister of the large First Presbyterian Church in the city. We were closer than brothers. How we came to be, I can only explain that between us there was a natural *rapport:* we had kindred spirits, same type of prejudices and convictions and our personalities seemed to just fit in. Our wives, too, found so much in common that their trust and confidences were taken for granted and never abused.

It was to my friend I turned with the news-of-the-hour. Williams was a man of tall stature in the Board of Trustees of the College and fearless. He would be beholden to no one except his own integrity. For years he espoused lost causes; in his church he was criticized for his "social gospel" long before the current outbreak of interracial strife and the demands of the forgotten man toward his government and society.

It was Good Friday. I remember it well. I was a speaker at the community three-hour service for one half-hour. He was the speaker at a later half-hour. When it was over we met at the house—in the kitchen. I was supposed to take care of the ham in the oven—which I forgot. We talked over the situation, agreeing that Wooster College was at the critical cross-roads and that the action that was going on, in the quiet, needed a first-class counter-action—and *now*.

One pope was setting up his successor pope and the cardinals (the trustees) would be easy prey—since they were not in the know. We agreed to divide the alarm call: he to some selected trustees and I to some of the unhappy faculty members: a small group representing each group and that a sounding be made.

I am honest when I say we both had no personal animosity to the "selected" candidate. He was a hale and hearty and well-meant individual. But not only were his qualifications as a college head notoriously limited (in our judgment) but he was a stooge for the president all the way through (in our opinion). I knew that the faculty would go into an uproar and Williams knew that most of his fellow trustees with sufficient information would at least call for a postponement.

So the "Bund" (as we called it at home) met in an office of one of the five or six faculty people—a neutral office. The opinions of these people were not only unanimous that the trustees must be alerted but they pledged to enlarge the circle. My part ceased almost at the beginning since the snowball gained in size and momentum in a very few weeks. A formal petition was sent around for faculty signatures and the list grew to such a size, that when presented to the president of the board, he (the board president) not only was shocked at the unanimity of the opinion but at the lateness of the hour to suspend plans. Already the name of the "selected" candidate had circulated among some of the trustees (confidentially?) and the situation came to such a swift crisis that the faculty had been alerted to stand by on a given Saturday for a faculty meeting at 4 p.m. when the new president would be announced!

Dr. Arthur Compton was president of the board and he was handed the faculty petition at a rather late hour on the Friday before the trustees were to meet the next day. Three people visited him very briefly that night, one of whom was my friend Dr. Versteeg who was exceedingly excited and anxious to participate.

The candidate (I am told) had been partied by some people in-the-know in town; drapes for the president's home had been ordered; the candidate was in Stype's Drugstore on Liberty Street (main street) in the morning dressed immaculately for the big day; the *Daily Record*—so the information passed about—had the news coverage set in type with proper first-page headlines and we, the "voiceless" faculty, sat on our hands waiting for the phone call to summon us to a special meeting with the trustees and the "secret" out.

There was one major phone call at our home that Saturday. It was the announcement about noontime that the faculty meeting had been postponed. The candidate was not seen in town later in the day. And the word was passed to me in my quiet little home on Beall Avenue—before the day ended—that the trustees, in the light of the surprise-package (faculty petition) had decided (not unanimously) to postpone decision and make a "further study." Williams had done his homework conscientiously.

This is the story of how Dr. Howard Lowry came in. He evidently was not a Wishart's choice. Lowry was then a member of the board of trustees and I am told was one who spoke up to say that any trustees' action in such a matter must have the counsel of the faculty (at least from the older members).

The dean-who-almost-became-president had a difficult role assigned to him to finish out the semester. I visited him at his home on Cleveland Road and confessed my own personal position with the explanation that it was my honest opinion that he could never have handled the faculty since he was so tied in with the present president and his dictatorial policies to court any cooperation. He said he knew who were his opposers and said also that he had no intention of being a stooge, that he envisaged a reign unhampered by such pressures; and so on.

The whole thing was a sorry mess. The dean resigned and took a church (where he did unusually well as a clergyman). The mantle fell on Howard Lowry who accepted (after an unusually long span of indecision); some dissident faculty-members were consulted by the trustees and the appointment received unanimous approval.

I do not know if Dr. Lowry knew this story. I meant to tell him—after my day of retirement. But our paths crossed very briefly. His last words to me came at an alumni shindig at Attorney Robert Critchfield's affluent farm-home near Wooster. We met at the barn, Lowry leaving and I just coming in from North Carolina.

Said he: "Vergilius, we just must get together. We have so much to get caught up on."

And I said: "Howard, yes, we have a lot of talking yet to do." And I never heard his voice again since death took him soon after and quite unawares.

Shenanigans to end all shenanigans is the practice of awarding honorary degrees. This has reached the point of scandal. No reputable college or university of stature —that is, the better ones—plays this game any longer. Happily, the zenith has been reached. Only lesser schools go on their merry way.

For many years I was a member of the faculty committee on honorary degrees at Wooster.

So I claim to know something of "the inside" in the matter. The whole thing is incredible by any decent set of standards. It was the rule of Wooster College (statutes) that all honorary degrees must pass through a nominating committee and a vote of the faculty and then on to the trustees. The president who ran the show had to have a committee chairman beholden to himself, with whom he could exchange "confidences." We who were members were always suspicious of the chairman when his voice became enthusiastic for some candidate.

The first committee meeting each academic year saw the chairman coming into the trustee chambers with a huge file (looking like a manuscript of an unabridged encyclopedia), a file always kept in the secret places of the president's office. We would sigh. Here we go again.

There were divisions among the sheets marked as to relative importance: new names, old names, older names, persistents, and then on to almost-dead. There would be names coming up each year and passed up and down the file. Then there were the applicants! Imagine! Applicants!

Correspondence from noted or wealthy alumni with a recommendation or two, a church which just must have a minister with a doctorate, a possible donor to the college whose name on the list must be studied with special care, some celebrities who would give glamour to the commencement program and so on and on—such material had to be gone over. Some names were so far down on the list that the death of the candidate cancelled them out automatically. But then there were the die-hards. Faculty kept pressing the committee to limit the number which was to say: can't this thing be controlled? The president always had his favorites and it was fun watching him maneuver his preferences.

One minister in New York City (Presbyterian) turned in his request for a different kind of a degree since he had the usual assortment. The chairman of the religion department and I were given the assignment of researching the letters this candidate seemed to want. I did no research on it and bluntly took the stand that if he didn't want the standard letters after his name on the church bulletin board or the parish paper, he had better settle for a duplicate or cancel out.

A local minister's name came up each year. He just wanted this honorary degree and had certain confidants in Wooster City to light the candles for him each year. We staved this one off and he finally got one elsewhere. One honorary degree was apparently turned down flat and I have always admired "the guy." The committee voted (nominated) James Stewart, the Hollywood actor, an honorary degree. The president (Mr. Wishart's successor) was behind this one: Stewart was well known, glamorous, wealthy and a Presbyterian! But nothing came of it and the president never reported the negative response to my knowledge. Always candidates each year must be representative: in the sciences, in some church-relations (preferably an official), in literature, Presbyterian clergyman, alumnus, national figure and so on. (And what was never said out loud: he or she must be sympathetic with Wooster's program and have financial contacts.)

The D.D. degree is the bane of all degrees. Oskaloosa, Iowa (some school there) charged a clergyman fifty dollars for this degree and for a Ph.D. the price was seventy-five dollars. (Such shenanigans have been stopped as of recent years. But I knew a minister who bought his sermons and could not read the script well who flashed his Ph.D. around in the district and we never knew from where it came.) Professors of speech are known to seek out honorary degrees. (And I have often wondered how public speaking *as such* qualifies!) Two-year Junior College presidents must have some kind of doctor's degree (even though the name of the institution is not publicized.)

When the D.D.'s were awarded their degree at Wooster commencement, one could hear the muffled groan that went up among the faculty which I often hoped some day would reach the platform and stop the mess. I would prefer to see the name Jesus Christ, D.D. rather than a preacher's name so decorated on an outside church bulletin board and in the parish bulletin. But that would be most inappropriate! If clergymen were fully dedicated spiritually to their high calling they would prefer the title of "pastor" which means "shepherd" as a title of honor in contrast to this hocum-pocum. A "pastor" *is* a high title and to be called by that designation in a parish cannot be topped by any other. The Roman Catholic title "father" is greater than all this D.D. mania.

Honorary degrees are legitimate when they are academically honorable. But the whole thing has reached such a low point that hardly any good seems to be involved. There are phony Ph.D.'s and LL.D.'s and Litt.-D's and all the rest. So hungry are academics and others for degrees that it is now being planned to give the doctor's degree out almost indiscriminately upon graduation of three years post-college training. Such as: D.M. (Doctor of Ministry), three years of theology; Doctor of Jurisprudence, three years of law. So we have a new alphabetical combination D.M. and J.D. and where will it all stop? Even foot-specialists are now doctors. And there are back-specialists who are doctors. And so on and on—in shenanigans gone wild. Dean Brown (Yale) once told us that it was sad that there was no such thing as a Doctor of Goodness (to give self-styled saints).

Mr. Lowry, the president of Wooster College, loved the commencement exercises. He was himself an excellent platform speaker. And when it came to Baccalaureate exercises, he reached his peak and was enjoying himself to the utmost. He and his predecessor reserved Baccalaureate speeches for themselves! Thursdays were reserved for the president (who had a captive audience —required chapel) and then occurred pontifications. Mr. Lowry introduced a special convocation awarding degrees *during the semester* so that students could see such a show. So honorary degrees could come at any time as a part of the academic splendor. Even summer schools with small enrollments now have the thing going. Like the stores you have special sales and attractions for the seasons—and so it goes.

In Europe, traditionally it is different. An earned doctor's degree was earned. Edinburgh University—an exception—had a spell not too long ago (we have their output all over the scene) of awarding Ph.D.'s in a kind of wholesale fashion. The saying was: flunk out at Yale or Harvard and enroll at Edinburgh. (One could even mail in his thesis.) Against Edinburgh stood the ancient tower of strength of Glasgow University which frowned upon its sister Scottish institution.

I recall an incident on a trip up the coast of Norway, stopping in Trondheim to have an aching tooth tended to. It was suggested that I seek out So and So. No Doctor's degree initials on his door and I became frightened. But the thing hurt so badly that I must see the man. In the conversation I called him "Doctor." And he said, "No, no, I am no doctor."

"How come?" I asked trembling, under his care.

"I am only a 'tand-läkare.' " (This translated means: toothfixer or tooth-healer.)

"But you are a graduate of a University?" I asked.

"Certainly," he said.

"Then you have no doctor's degree?"

"That's so. Only those in graduate schools who do theses are doctors. Please. . . . I am not a doctor. I am a technician. Doctors are students who do research and in the vanguard of education."

This was the voice of medieval and modern Europe in that little Norwegian office by a specialist. It is not the voice of American shenanigans but the voice of the grand tradition from which academics have strayed.

Wooster, like all colleges, got its share of phonies or semi-phonies on its faculty. I never met the star-phony of my time—he came and left the year we were away on a sabbatical. The story, as it was told me, is that he was hired to teach and he came and took the campus by storm—until the day of reckoning came: he had forged his credentials. Not a degree given him was authentic. This is not so much a surprise as was the way he was taken in by the administration (and later by the whole campus). He reached his pinnacle and from such great height the fall was unbelievable.

I had one strange experience with a member of my department. His credentials were in order (so that I cannot charge him to be a phony). But both the president and I were suspicious of the many letters of recommendation: too many to be impressive. Some of them had gold seals, some notary public sworn-statements and one (I recall) was "authenticated" by an attached blue ribbon. He presented a manuscript-in-process so large and bulky that the president (maybe suspiciously) asked me to give-it-the-once-over. And he asked me later what I thought of it? My answer was simple: "No publisher will take all that stuff without editorial scissors all over the place. Don't worry about it." (The president may have then remembered that he had been an editor of the Oxford University Press and he at once relaxed.) This man was hired in August—a late appointment (characteristic of Dr. Lowry whose postponement of decisions was notorious.) We just had to take him.

He and his wife took the campus by storm. The wife was young and attractive and had "social graces." Moreover, she was a good dancer. The president who was a bachelor seemed to take to her, and the young professor was "in." He began to push his weight around in the department as if he was not subject to ordinary rules. For example, he disappeared from the campus days and days without notice. He told me he flew to Chicago and New York on important business. He and his wife entertained generously in their home and he was visibly proud of his library that looked somewhat like an old-fashioned bookstore, books piled high and all over the place. It was, indeed, impressive—to students.

He indulged in big terms, and with "an accent" which also was impressive at that time on a Wooster campus. His favorite expression had something to do with "the logarithm" which I remember had something to do with philosophy. I was told (this is hearsay) that he had some one audit some philosophy courses at Oberlin College (nearby) and that these notes were typed and used by him in certain of his courses. He had funds (somehow) to get secretarial help. He got himself mixed in with economics and gave lectures on the subject. He had had contacts with the motion picture industry and had traveled extensively in Europe representing something or other. To me he was Mr. X and as time went on I grew more and more suspicious of him. I saw with great alarm how he had taken over the president, the academic dean, the committee on faculty appointments, students, townsfolk; and I still knew there was "something rotten in Denmark." He brushed me aside after gentle enquiries and refused to cooperate in ordinary departmental routine affairs. He was simply "on his own."

Then the matter of his promotion came up. At Wooster, in those days the trustees made the official appointment at the recommendation of the president; the president conferred with the dean and the small faculty committee (close-mouthed to the point pleasing to Edgar Hoover). The low rung (in such matters) on the high ladder was the department chairman (then called "head"). According to the rules, as department "head" I, at least, must be consulted. (At one time, I was wholly bypassed by the president and when the announcement was made in the faculty meeting of a new appointee in my department, I stood up and enquired why I had not been consulted. The reply—after many whispers between the president and the dean—was: this man is being appointed to the religion department. And so I was fully eliminated—until after my retirement—when the thing was adjusted. This was Dr. Lowry in his later years, when he took matters pretty much in his own hands as did President Wishart before him.)

One night, at about eleven o'clock, the phone rang. It was Dr. Lowry. He asked my opinion about the promotion of this man—to a full professorship. I said to him that I knew he was quite aware of my opinion: I disapproved. Moreover, I reminded him that a "full professorship" meant permanent appointment and must be carefully done. I reminded him, too, that the American Association of University Professors was on record favoring any appointment to full professorship as binding unless some kind of open-court charges are made against an incumbent. And then, squaring away with my negative response I added: I shall give a minority report to the trustees; that he (Lowry) had the power to overrule me; and that I was acting in good faith.

Then, pleading with me, he said: "You are the only one standing in the way; I favor the professorship, so does the academic dean, so do the members of the faculty committee on appointments and most everyone on the faculty with whom I have had a talk on the matter."

"Dr. Lowry," I said, "I may be stubborn in your eyes but I cannot yield to the pressure. Something is wrong, dead wrong. Please understand that I know my limitations. I have no power. You have it with the trustees. You must act on your own as I act on mine."

The conversation ended with a formal "good night" on the part of both of us.

I knew that there was another pressure. The candidate swung a threat of invitation to another school with a larger salary offered and that the decision must be now. (Such is common in the business of hiring, firing, promotion, anywhere.)

After that, all I heard within the range of my limited sphere was that my colleague had resigned. I do not know of any loud mourning on the campus. There may have been. I stayed off the campus the following weeks except for teaching. What happened came as news to me much later. I can sum it all up in a short paragraph and then drop this incident as among the shenanigans which go to make up one's memory of bygone days. And it is this:

The president got a telephone call from one of his trustees. "Who is this fellow So-and-So—on your campus? He was here in Cleveland making a speech which I heard. I think he is some kind of —————."

This trustee was one of the very few who had a listening ear to campus affairs. I never spoke about the case to this trustee. I could have but I didn't. Dr. Lowry was very beholden to this trustee and (I know) would have gone out of his way not to risk the displeasure of this individual. Such a query could not be taken lightly. Moreover, it chimed in on the same wave length as my own. The appointment was not made and did not come before the trustees in spite of the "unanimous" support of the campus academics.

One day—many weeks later—the academic dean approached me on the campus. He held out his hand and said: "Thank you."

"For what?" I asked in total surprise.

"It's about that appointment. We are now certain you

were right and I think you have saved us a lot of potential trouble."

He mentioned no name. I named no name. And I now name no name. (I may add: my stock went up with the administration and stayed for a long while above par.)

Alumni meetings with faculty visitation each year was a kind of shenanigan which many enjoyed but about which some faculty members had misgivings. These meetings were arranged by the alumni secretary with the approval of the president. They were generally held as close to December eleventh as possible, the date of the historic fire of Old Main. (This fire of destruction is the date of the "New Wooooooooster.") Faculty members were chosen as representatives of alma mater—those who could be counted on as giving a favorable account of campus activities and acting as good public relations officers.

I went to some of such meetings and I enjoyed each and every one of them—with some reservations. I, for one, did not enjoy the "briefings" we had in the trustees' room prior to our assignments. The briefing consisted of mimeographed sheets on which favorable statistics would be set forth with notes on what favorable "happenings" are in the offing. We were given some financial statistics (which I did not understand). The president sat at the head table and the alumni secretary at the other. One knew that there had been previous meetings before this grand "send-off" of the ambassadors of goodwill.

Some faculty members were not asked to join this select company. I know of some who wanted very much to be asked but they were frankly not trusted to such an assignment. They were highly opinionated people who might give some unfavorable reporting. I myself was asked only a limited number of times. My assignments were generally near the home base. Favorites were assigned grand tours of New England, Chicago and even California (all expenses paid). When we returned we were supposed not only to put in our expense account but a general report of alumni questioning and the temperature of their attitudes. One did some counseling also with prospective students and their parents (since these were the days of fierce student recruiting for which special emissaries were engaged in such missionary work).

I never followed the sheets of instruction. I chucked them aside not even memorizing some of the statistics (enrollment, alumni response to last year's contributions, etc.). In my talks I gave alumni students campus gossip which they "ate up," of the antics of their favorite professors and an account of some of the shenanigans that were going on at the time (keeping myself in check *always*). This, they seemed to enjoy and no one ever asked about red or black ink in the college treasurer's reports, enrollment and campus courses. They all were sentimental (as they should be or they wouldn't attend such meetings). And their sentiments were personal, attached to people and places and "the old routines" of chapel cutting, romancing and the like. A few of these "ambassadors of good will" prepared formal lectures on the Renaissance or Current Events (one of whom was a specialist on the *New York Times* magazine and foreign affairs section—reports from where the material seemed to have come for the most part). Alumni do not want lectures and statistics. They want renewed friendships. And it seemed the "powers that be" never had the humor sufficiently to see all this.

I relate one typical meeting. My wife and I drove our family car some hundred or less miles from the campus for such a meeting. The "supper" was to begin at 6 p.m. at such and such an address. (Generally the locale was a dreary church basement.) We came to the appointed house a little ahead of the appointed time. There was some kind old lady (I seem to recall) who greeted us, not sure who we were and our business. We waited and waited. Finally, as the evening wore on (we had had no supper) some couples drifted in with "pot luck." (My, how I hate, despise, condemn, excommunicate pot luck suppers! I have been to too many ladies' aids and committee meetings in my day ever to get involved again. And church suppers are to me the lowest of lows—with people breathing down your neck as you tackle some strange dishes and shaking moist hands as you hold your bread.)

The evening wore on. Finally, the food was assembled and there was "grace" said by the local Presbyterian minister. Then the meeting. Who was to be on what committee for next year? Who would be secretary and chairman and vice-president and how much in the red is the treasury? Should the annual dues be raised from fifty cents to one dollar? When shall we have the picnic next summer? We must thank so-and-so for his fine work in getting the cards sent out. And so-and-so did a fine job last year with the alumni fund. And so on. By the time they were ready for my speech,

I was exhausted, angry, ill-humored, still hungry and ready for a martini (the language of our day but not the language then). I couldn't even smoke—which at that time was improper for a "good will ambassador." I generally chucked any notes and tossed off some kind of salad speech with the help of the Saint Who presides over Spontaneity. Then there were questions— mostly about some professor, does he still put his cat out at night and does the president still jerk up his trousers when he presides or is dull chapel still required and so on and on. This was fun and we generally ended on a note of some good will.

Outside it began to storm. It was snowing softly, gently, ominously. Already a blanket of the sticky stuff had glued itself to the ground. The driving was most hazardous. No one had suggested putting in the night where we had our appointment. Motels were not then heard of. It was already a late hour, perhaps after eleven o'clock. And there were miles and miles ahead of us, up and down curvy and lonely roads (no super-highways, then). The snow kept blinding the windshield and the wipers were crippled in their swing. How we made home I'll never know—except that Jehovah made the trip with us.

I vowed never to take another such assignment. And I never did. I would go Pullman if invited. I was invited Pullman only once—to Buffalo. And even that assignment was complicated since it meant sitting up into the wee hours and talking shop with the cleaning crew and waiting in a run-down railroad station for the light of day. And so on. I served my apprenticeship in such shenanigans and never heard a thanks from anyone (including those at academic home-base who sent out such home-missionaries). You see, alma mater (dear mother) is just not around to say anything—only to be sung to.

Gimmicks-courses are another case of shenanigans. I shall name one. Freshman English. Someone got the notion that instead of a standard refresher of grammar and writing there should be a Great Books course ("Liberal Studies") in which Freshmen will have the immediate experience of college instead of post-high school. So it was arranged. I was put on the committee to structure it. When I saw what was involved I got myself off. The new deal was to have many small sections presided over by faculty of whatever preparation. A geology teacher, for example, was assigned to guide students in Pláto's *Republic* with the poor Freshman participating, and Shakespeare's *Hamlet* and Waldon's *Thoreau* and Augustine's *Confessions, et al.* I know of no one college course requirement which sparked student gripes more than this course. Parents may have been impressed when the students wrote home that they were reading classical literature from the sources in their first year of college but students themselves under the auspices of incompetent people in the new assignment, teaching other incompetents, must have felt that the blind were leading the blind. I understand that pressure was brought on newcomers to the faculty that they were expected to take a Freshman English section. To demur would have spelled a limited appointment. The course was advertised as "a unique college experience" and *that* it was! When students came into philosophy classes (if they chose) they already had been brainwashed by others who went through Freshman English that philosophy too was a difficult and incomprehensible subject. Many of them (I believe) avoided philosophy as absurd (after their plunge into the cold waters of the classics).

I mention briefly a few more shenanigans.

Prayer Week came each year at an appointed time. There was an invited minister on campus and there were prayer meetings all over the place. Chapel was as usual required and evening meetings advertised. The campus was soaked with "religion." I got so I dreaded the week. Prayer, if artificial, is self-defeating. We even had a Sunday afternoon prayer meeting at the president's home. We all were expected to show up and anyone looking for a raise or promotion had better somehow appear. Even faculty volleyball was cancelled (except for a few of us who belonged to the unsaved). You never knew when someone would call on you to pray and it scared the daylights out of many, including myself. It all wound up with the following week called "Hell Week" when fraternities "scared the hell" out of candidates and all "———" broke loose. We went back to volleyball, shows and relaxation. Shenanigans? Yes. It all seemed like window-dressing to me—for those who were concerned over the assurance that this was a "Christian" college.

Another one. One day I was given a syllabus by a member of the religion department faculty. It was at the

Ford garage in town (curious memory?). I looked at it while waiting for my car. Then of a sudden I noticed material I really enjoyed! Until—I recognized the sentences and style: it was *my* material. No quotes around it and a large slice of it. No acknowledgement of source. I strode over to So and So, who was waiting for his car, and I said: "How come? This is *my* stuff."

And he said: "Is it?"

I got myself stirred to the point of losing my own religion.

"This is plagarism, stark naked" said I (in so many words). "You fellows will hear from me."

I went to the administrative offices and threatened the college with a lawsuit. (I do not know why I do such things when I get angry. But it was wrong, wrong, wrong [one more] wrong. And not even the ministers in the religion department are exempt from the law.) I heard that there were stirrings; that the college lawyer was consulted; and that copies were withdrawn. And so also my anger dissipated.

My next and last shenanigan account occurred at Ann Arbor, Michigan on the University campus. I had been invited to be one of four "Religion in Life" speakers. There were the rabbi, the fundamentalist, a Roman Catholic and myself (presumably representing Protestant liberalism). The arrangement was that I was to conduct some kind of informal seminar for about three days and that I was expected on Saturday. So I accepted.

I came on the campus after registering at a hotel. At the Student Union I saw my name in big black letters as scheduled for a lecture at such and such an hour on "Communism and Christianity." I went dead. My sponsor met me at the Commons. It was about 7 p.m. After preliminary conversation, I asked him about this lecture I was supposed to give. I told him I knew absolutely nothing about that topic. And he said he had nothing to do with it. Then he accompanied me to the hotel; there he picked up the phone and turned in a call. The gist of it was: he is here, at the hotel. Tomorrow at nine? Yes, he will be ready. So and So said, "Yes."

He turned nonchalantly toward me and said in a declarative sentence: "You are to preach at the First Christian Church tomorrow at eleven o'clock. There will be other clergy there. The service will be broadcast."

I died another death.

If I had known how to stutter I would not have been able to say another word. He was adamant. He knew nothing of the arrangements—except to meet me. I asked where I could get coffee. The hotel restaurant was closed. There was no coffee. I asked him politely to leave (fearful he would stay and stay).

"I'll have to get busy right now on this one," I told him, "and pull myself together."

I sweated out the night hours by a little table and a poor light. I tried to think and think. (I do not know now how my mind got itself expressed in some notes but by morning I had a few points down and numbered.)

Exactly at nine forty-five Sunday morning I stood at the desk in the hotel lobby. (I don't recall having had breakfast.) Suddenly, a little fellow came in, addressed me: "I am Reverend Grandstaff," he said.

I have never in my life failed to remember him nor his name. He was small in stature and his name was grandiose. Outside the hotel stood parked a Cadillac, room for ten or fifteen people. I never saw a car as big—outside a station wagon. He drove the car and his little legs could hardly reach the accelerator. The ride through Ann Arbor was, I am certain, beyond the speed limits. He told me he was Secretary of the National Council of Churches in charge of Radio and Communications. He said I would be broadcasting this morning.

I asked him about the technique of broadcasting. He pointed with his one hand over his head in the direction of the back seat. I looked back and there lay heaps and heaps of pamphlets. He told me to take one. And I did. It said something about broadcasting but my mind couldn't respond. I got no help.

He stopped at the rear of a modest-looking church. He literally ran ahead of me beckoning me on—we seemed to him to be a little late. Then he ushered me into his office. He put a telephone on his shoulder with some kind of contraption which allowed his hands and arms free play. He began dictating something to his secretary (a cute little something). And I heard him address the Tower located somewhere out in the county which was to broadcast the service. He paid no further attention to me. I was fit to be tied. There were wires all over the floor. Young people were coming in putting on their choir garbs. I was introduced to some clergymen. There was no place to go and I was in a state of utter confusion.

Suddenly, the Reverend Mr. Grandstaff came over and motioned to me to follow him. We walked toward an already-formed procession and moved toward the head of the line where there were some other clergy-men. He seemed to be either nervous or uncertain or distraught with sudden responsibilities. We walked slowly to the rear of the sanctuary-proper and then up some stairs onto the stage. I was motioned to sit at the right of Mr. Grandstaff and another clergymen on the left. The organ prelude was in full swing.

Then it happened. My bladder was asking for relief. It had gotten worse since the parade. I knew I couldn't possibly make it. So I leaned over to the "bishop" on my left and said "my bladder." (I could think of something else to express myself but I was in church up front and I knew I had to give it a kind of sacerdotal expression.)

"Ugh," he said, which I interpreted that what I had said had not been understood by him.

So I said: "I've got to go."

It worked. He stood up and said, "Follow me." We walked out.

Down the stairs in the deep caverns of the place he pointed to "the place." I didn't look to see if it was for me or my Aunt Tilda. I just walked in. I could hear the organist still playing the prelude. I wondered what would happen next.

The bladder was lazy and I had to respect its wishes. It took longer than usual. Why not? Look at the strain I had been under since leaving the hotel! He waited for me at the door. We both reentered the sanctuary. I could see on the faces of the people up front that they feared the worst. I had gotten sick (they must have thought). I had gotten stage fright (I thought they thought). The organist looked at me sympathetically and seemed to wonder if she dared to go into the hymn. We were already late in the broadcast. What would the world outside think of a prelude that was a prelude to several preludes!

The thing finally got started. One minister got up to pray after the hymn. Then Grandstaff leaned over and handed me a small piece of paper. I looked at it and it looked like an algebraic script. I couldn't make it out. It certainly wasn't funny. So . . . I leaned over and said: "11—29—11—49? What is that?"

And he said: "That's the radio-time you have for your sermon!"

All through the performance at the pulpit I was trying to remember the algebraic figures, wondering where I was with the world of mechanized time. It made me so tense that I could hardly think. (There was another occasion which I later remembered where the preacher had a loud tick-tock clock installed on the top of the pulpit. I was supplying the pulpit in his absence. This tick-tock thing set me wild with impulses up and down my frame. I didn't know how to shut the so-and-so thing off, and I wanted badly to disembowel it.)

Now back to the Ann Arbor service. At the conclusion, we entered into a recessional. As soon as I reached the exit I was met by a committee. They said they were to take me to dinner. I tried to beg off but "no" I had to go. I was supposed to say something or other at the dinner and I begged to leave early. Exhaustion took me over completely. I asked someone to drive me to the hotel downtown. I threw myself on the bed and fell asleep. Suddenly, it was Jehovah (I thought) who called. I was being paged by phone. A voice said I was expected to meet with a Presbyterian youth-group at five-thirty. I called a cab and went out for another round. How much can a human being with nerves take? These shenanigans still had not come to an end.

Monday came. I was scheduled to speak (so I was told) at a luncheon of a faculty group. I recall Professor Charles Stevenson was there. He was charming and seemed to sense something was "in Denmark" with me. (I told him later I was being murdered by the saints—that I couldn't even remember the name of Plato and for what he stood. Stevenson is the well-known philosophy professor at Michigan. He had married one of my Wooster philosophy majors which gave us a special personal relationship.)

I was scheduled for a round with the dormitory boys (some fraternity) for the evening and something for the morrow. I went to the former and we had an easy bull-session (more shenanigans) and then I went back to the hotel. I did give a lecture the next day on the subject "Communism and Christianity" in an interpretation I had myself never heard of before. And I guess I got away with it. (More shenanigans!) A few stayed after, asking me questions which I parried by asking questions in return (like Socrates of old).

The first chance I got, I just disappeared. I got into my car and headed for home. I had had enough. I said good-bye to no one. No one cared. I never heard from anyone connected with my Ann Arbor visit. Or, as Andy of "Amos and Andy" used to say: "I got nuttin' from nobody and dere ain't no more."

I have a precious recording of the Ann Arbor service which I sent for and paid a couple of dollars to own.

When I get weary from anything and everything and the recording is handy, I play it for a good laugh. It starts out with a prelude to end all preludes with some pauses here and there and the hymn of the morning comes unusually late for a standard orthodox service. The sermon is there and as I think about it, I am in no mood to remember or think about it—much less report it here.

THIS AND THAT

A book of this kind ought to have a section entitled as above. In one's files one has such a folder with such a title. Another and more exact heading would be: Here Is The Material I Want To Keep Or Tell Or Use Some Day And Now I Have No Logical Place For It Other Than Right Here. I have many such envelopes. When I look for something I can not find I go to these folders so marked and usually find what I am looking for.

There are numbers of incidents and events or topics which occur when one is writing his "memoirs" and if there is room he sits down and writes them out. Where to place them? They just don't find any scheme. So: This and That.

Here is one. Throughout my mature life, I have been a budget man—unashamedly. There is just so much income. You play fast or loose with it or you organize it. One of the standing comments of my sons when they chide their father is: "Have the rugs been paid for yet?" This meant in our family: no more stretching the budget until the bills are under control. To them it seemed to be in a state of potential financial disaster occurring under a reckless captain.

One makes his own style budget. Budget there should be: style this or style that. I give mine for what it is worth.

One knows—if one is a salaried person—what the annual income is. What is deducted for this and that for the government and personal income and city tax (or what not) gives the remainder figure upon which you make distributions. No need to have envelopes and place cash in them for each month. One needs only to list specific items of expenditure on a monthly basis: the sum total must square exactly with the net income (after deductions).

So a Journal is purchased showing, after initial page or pages, sources of income on a monthly basis: a list of apportioned expenses for the month. (This is ascertained by dividing net income by twelve—twelve months in a year.) You list the musts first; the next, the less-musts; and down to the "remainder" which may be little. An insurance policy premium is a must (divide the total premium in twelve parts and each month credit yourself with one-twelfth so that when the date of the premium comes due, the Journal shows this amount in the bank). You have in the bank in a checking account, the amount ready for the payment. Always a year in advance! (It may take some straining to begin with but it becomes easy once you are building up each month necessary capital for such payments.) Other necessities are: groceries, taxes, payments on a debt, car, house payment or rent, gasoline for car-operation, dues, donations, savings, sickness and drugs, fuel, utilities (telephone, water, heat, electricity, gas), clothing, weekly running expenses, hospital insurance, auto repairs, car insurance, house repairs, electrical appliances. Items which are perhaps not-musts but at least in a lower category are: periodical subscriptions, travel, a new something, minor repairs, laundry, yard care, gifts (charity), Christmas and "miscellaneous" and perhaps "entertainment." Any major new item which is not indispensable may be marked so-much-a-month so ready-cash in a year or two is available for cash price, such items as: new rugs, tuxedo, TV, radio, books, kodak supplies, new boat, eating-out, etc.

One Journal is purchased for each year with year numerals on cover (1969). The distribution of items is listed first after Income with specific amounts, on page O. (This is an Index page.) Then each specific item has its own page with the proper title and the amount per month. Anything listed shows that such amounts are in a checking account available when due. You write down the amount once a month on its own page and then keep adding. You subtract only when due and payment is made on necessities.

This kind of budget does not require that one write down each and every item spent. Such "every nickel spent" ends in disaster.

Our grocery money is in the hands of our family-head-grocery-buyer who is the lady of the house. On Fridays her cash for the week for groceries is available for six days in advance to spend *without* itemizing. She alone operates as she chooses (making money on it as she wills but always within the amount). We have learned from experience that for two people who eat extremely well, the weekly amount is sufficient without skimping. Food is forever a must for the living and Krogers and A&P and the rest operate on cash. Each Friday there is a renewal. (No questions asked: same amount dealt.) Since every three months brings an extra week, this week is also budgeted in the Journal so the check may be written and the cash ready in advance. (The Journal shows this accumulation.) This goes for general running expenses (an extra week every three months).

Running expenses also are limited on a weekly basis but not itemized. Each Friday the same amount for the week ahead is made available in cash. This covers gas and oil for the car, newspapers, casual donations, stamps, occasional paperback or book and/or magazines, small hardware items, sundries—and money left over may be spent the next week. But the budget must not be violated. (Only sickness, tragedy, tornado, volcano eruption, hail or high tide may intervene—never a "spree" unless it is made-up.)

Many people think of a budget-conscious person as "tight"; "penurious"; "screwball"; "dictator"; "Scrooge." But the fact of the matter is: it is unethical to ask someone else to pay your debts. A debt is an ethical obligation which the individual assumes. If he does not have the money, he should not incur the debt. This is ethics, good business, integrity, the code of a gentleman and good credit-standing in the community.

The secret of a good budget is the anticipation of needs. Whatever one pledges is a purchase—if there is no cash for it—it has to be paid eventually. Cash is cheaper than charge—a great deal cheaper. And to keep paying cash is to anticipate purchases—certainly large purchases. The sooner a family gets on this anticipatory way of financing, the sooner they will attain the feeling of reasonable security and peace and integrity.

Sickness and accident can upset any budget. But in some measure it may be anticipated by proper planning.

Years ago we used to pay for our Christmas presents way into the following August. Freedlander's in Wooster (general dry goods store) loved to see us come in month upon month. In those days, we were behind. We finally worked ourselves luckily ahead. To keep credit sound one may charge and then in ten days send the check. This keeps the name active and solid. Christmas Savings have been a God-send to many people—especially to those who have no self-discipline to "put-away" for the following year. We used to have it. Now we have our own "Christmas Savings" in our budget and it is a pleasure come November to play around with extra money for the season of joy.

Another little trick. *Once each year we balance our Journal for that year—to check with our checking account for mistakes in arithmetic.* If, for any reason, the balance does not show and we are "in the red" we have a page in the Journal which is headed "Emergency" and this monthly set-aside usually covers such sins. Always each month the statement from the bank must be checked with the checkbook balance. Otherwise there is trouble. We mark returned checks (when the bank statement comes) *in with the corresponding stubs*—the letter "c" in the stub which shows payments via the bank. When a check is written it is not necessary to run to the Journal immediately for proper deductions on the proper page; if the balance has not been deducted in the checkbook, this shows there has been no corresponding deduction in the Journal. (Rule: never deduct in stub of checkbook until marked in the Journal.)

These must check out sooner or later. So an evening now and then brings the checkbook and the Journal in harmony. They must be in harmony or there is no budgeting.

You either budget or you don't. You just don't play around with it. It is like dieting: either you do or you don't. There is no messing around. Two checkbooks in a family, one for the husband and one for the wife, would seem to be satisfactory if the wife has a separate income. But with one income the husband, (*who*, theoretically *is the man of the house*) should operate the business—unless he is feminine. Two people writing checks independently of the other, off the same account, are inviting trouble which eventually will need a lawyer to settle (especially if each is independent and temperamentally infallible). Mathematics has nothing to do with sentiment. It is hard, cold, cruel shuffling of numbers. A budget is not a sentimental relation between any two people however romantic they may feel; it is plain mathematics without love, religion, with favors to none.

It is plain fun to run a budget unless it ruins the details of life. As a monthly pattern by which to live it has no substitute. There is no work with it. It is sheer pleasure, especially the feeling that you know almost exactly how you stand from week to week, month to month.

And if you can spare it, it is nice to have a fund called "spendthrift" which permits the purchase of some unessential item which does not cut into the usual commitments (a thousand possibilities which may give special pleasure).

The reader may wonder why this topic enters into this book. Answer: 1) budgeting has been pretty much a part of my life; 2) it is presumed that many of the readers of this kind of book are college people starting out in life and a word to them on such a subject just might be appreciated.

I turn to another more prosaic topic. Faculty people are human beings and as such love attention. They will go to full lengths sometimes just to be noticed. Our town is (or has been) a small community—neither a village nor a city. The town gazette, called *The Daily Record*, is the binding union of whatever goes to make up a social unit of this size. Faculty people see to it that they are noticed from time to time in the local paper. This is legitimate if it is "news." But many rehearse their accomplishments in the press to the point of readers' nausea.

One faculty person has to come into print about himself just so often or (I guess) he is not well. We time him; some may even put up bets when he will appear next. The curious thing about it all: he never seems to have any news except to review his and his family's obituary of accomplishments over and over again; that he is speaking to this or that group; that he has one book out (everyone who reads the *Record* knows this since it is a reminder each year); that he is such and such a professor; and that he has a doctor's degree (and from where) and his sons and daughters are successes in this or that. And that, and that. He is in competition with a faculty wife who must see her name in columns just so often and her articles take on the status of no particular importance. One faculty member gives an account of their relatives and we almost know the names of their cousins and in-laws and where they are from and so on and on. We groan each time their name appears. Not one of such contributors has news of value; they simply wish to court notice and are hungry for attention. The newspaper management is generous in accepting their material or else it is anxious to fill space among the ads.

Then there are those who must report in more or less detail their frequent European trips on the assumption that local people need to be broadened and made aware of the limitation of their own county. Such articles downgrade the reader and upgrade the contributor with "much ado about nothing."

And on to another much more personal subject. If one is lucky enough to have a family one goes through that whole chapter of child care and responsibility. Today we read and hear everywhere from the experts on how to raise children. Some young mothers have Dr. Spock's book (or two) near the kitchen sink— always ready for counseling. Whatever his theories and worth (and many swear by him) I can report the theory of two non-experts who have gone through the process on the simple assumption that life is such and such and you just teach children to adjust themselves to situations and not vice versa. One does not need much theorizing beyond the elements of common sense.

We must not frustrate Junior! What a silly theory. If we don't, the world will. And the world is rough, rough, rough. To take frustrations is part and parcel of living. To try to keep children from them is to bring on an ultimate super-frustration in life when it comes. The child should learn the word "No" and very soon. There seems to be no reason on earth why a youngster should mess a house, sass a parent, stamp his feet when frustrated, monopolize conversation when elders are socializing, throw food on the floor when it is distasteful or scream or "show off." There is a world outside with its laws of behavior. You simply have to adjust: to your stomach, to the weather, to storm, to other people, to gravitation, to rules all over the place. Permissive education is fundamentally wrong, wrong, wrong. A father and mother need not sit down and have a little conference with Junior explaining all the facts of life. The youngster should be told "No" and the word must be golden (not counterfeit). Suppose a parent may be wrong with his "No." So is the world of opinion and authority quite non-infallible. But it still has to be learned and respected—the sooner the better.

We were lucky to have a family of normal offspring. Not everyone is that lucky. Nature sometimes plays embryonic tricks over which one has no known control. And it is sad. There is such a thing as luck: favorable genes, favorable confluence of events (breaks), etc.

We lost two children by early death: the one a son in infancy and a daughter in the beginning of her adolescence. Both experiences were hard to take. One just never gets over the hurt that one feels inside—like a scar that does not fully heal. The infant son was exposed to a tubercular patient (unknowingly) and the experts at the New Haven Hospital found no way to save him —(it was early in the days before some of the "know how" of present research). Our only daughter was in the prime of youth: attractive, gay and a sparkling personality of her own. When scarlet fever struck her, everything possible was done to save her. The football men on the campus volunteered and gave blood and there was a pall over the whole campus when the word reached the college community that she didn't make it. (It was the day before the new wonder drugs—only a year before.) Her jolly and vivacious personality was noticed by everyone crossing her path as she walked each school day across campus to high school. We didn't realize what a huge amount of sunshine she was shedding elsewhere. We knew she had a generous amount of it around us. She was the little mother to our brood and we could depend on her to take care of the brothers when we needed rest. (Today we call this "baby sitting.")

The mantle of Virginia's leadership in the family of our children fell to our eldest son. He, too, was dependable and he "fathered" his brothers when it was necessary to have a substitute.

Our family had ground rules—not from theory but from a kind of style. A loud whistle called the boys home almost immediately from play. Another whistle would not be heard for there was no other. Lateness to meals meant the risk of skipping the meal. We ate together, not cafeteria method. The icebox (not a refrigerator) was not locked nor was it a free-for-all. It, too, was respected and the guardian (the mother) was generous in spite of any non-raiding. Family birthdays were hey-days—begun with a surprise on the "unawakened" guest (who had been waiting hours for the surprise) with a procession before dawn—always before dawn—of the family singing(?) Happy Birthday and bringing breakfast, candles and simple presents. The birthday child was not expected to do any chores that day—not even the dishes. Opening the gifts was a ceremony and the blowing out of the candles by the guest was a prerogative. The whole process was a kind of *sancta* out of which a religion is made.

We played games together. But we did not try to play all games together. Kids have their own age-groups and this must be respected. (Some families are so knit together that the kids become sons and daughters rather than people—parents over-solicitous in arranging games and schedules and know-hows—which is sickening.) A family need not be scheduled to death and lose its soul.

We naturally learned the lesson of financial frugality. There was no theory about this. It was a fact of life: the income was simply limited. Period. Extra money earned was put away by the earner in his own drawer and no one was ever supposed to go to this secret holy of holies. Even I as a father (and their mother too) never peeked inside the unlocked drawer of any of them to meddle with their secrets. Their assigned privacy was respected and they knew it. Our youngsters were not put on a salary or "donation" by the week. What was needed was given without bookkeeping or dates. But our giving was in the small amounts consonant with family reality. It was a kind of communal living without destroying parents' authority. Major purchases required adult sanction (as the budget permitted).

It all added up to what may be called "normal growth." Punctuality was taught; so also integrity (never a promise made that had no possibility of fulfillment); punishment administered and not just threat-

ened; respect for elders; manners at table and social
hosting; orderly habits around the house and all rowdi-
ness outside; contacts with just anyone without consciousness of caste; the words "thank you" part and
parcel of gracious living. All this was not followed, of
course, perfectly. But the ground rules were there.

The PTA did not exist in our time. It came soon
after. I am thankful we were not involved in such an
organization. I do not believe in parents interfering with
teachers. Parents have their place and the world of
"professional" teachers theirs. We never felt it our
special duty to ask "How is Junior doing?" Junior
came home with his grades and that was that. We never
interfered. Once I almost went beserk when I heard a
teacher physically threaten one of my sons—but happily
I cooled. Seventh-grade arithmetic I still cannot do.
(How many rolls of wallpaper with so many running
feet will it take to paper three rooms each having so
many doors and windows measuring such and such and
one room with a slanting ceiling?) I gave up. Bless the
teachers who can do such stuff—admittedly important.

Parents today seem to compete with each other—
whose kids are doing better than the others? Each prize
or notice or membership in something or other is reported in the local gazette and the son or daughter of
So and So who live on such and such a street. And the
next family begins to bellow. I could name names but
this book is limited by certain rules of publishing.

Then there is the problem of "favorite" sons or
daughters. You hear this all over the place. I know I
was not a favorite son in my family. Nor was I the
rejected one. The answer here is something like this:

the older son gets into some responsibilities that the others do not inherit. He has priority chronologically and also by assignments of his age. Each offspring has his own personality. One tends to respond warmth with warmth. And as children get older some become more formal and austere and others remain as children toward their aging parents. To the latter, one naturally turns responses in what may be termed in a "favorite" way. It is almost impossible to treat offspring scientifically in balance. Where there is appreciation (more than formality) there is a flame that burns brightly and that is just that.

Fortunate is the man who has a partner whose interests are both in the kitchen (unashamedly) and in the fortunes of the "breadwinner." There are girls (many of them) today who think of kitchens as traps and not as careers. But what is more glorious in family life than a good table where mother's own cooking and arranging are highlights of family togetherness? The most noble career a woman can have is to be a woman, to be feminine. To be this, nature has favored women with many built-in attractions. To exchange this for some male characteristics is an insuperable loss which ofttimes (not always) spells family disaster. When children come home, at least mother should be there or soon-to-return (with a note on the table). A man's world takes a man from the home. To come home and find his sweetheart there to make him forget the troubles of the office is a dish hard to excel. The returns to the woman are so precious and many, that one does not talk about the balance between the tasks of a woman and that of a man: who does the *menial* tasks—the man at the office or at the writer's desk, or the woman tending the roast in the oven or polishing the silverware?

When it came to selecting careers and wives, the original family fades out—at least for a spell. Such decisions by one's children can be made only on a private and personal basis. In our case, graduate school seemed feasible since the atmosphere of the home and nearby campus was full of such rumors and possibilities. The War Years also had something to say whether or not to enlist immediately, be drafted or what else. In the case of one, it was medicine and medical training under government auspices which meant eventually a full stint in Korea where the action was. Our sons chose to go on to graduate school and marry at the same time. Their girls were willing to share the responsibilities and sacrifices of the rugged years in the postgraduate work of their husbands. They were willing to use packing crates or orange crates for furniture—to their credit. And they were willing to help in bringing in the financial bacon for the duration of the assignment. They and the parents saw the day when doctor's degrees were earned and joined in the festivity of sacrifice and victory.

As life moves on, families find their own unities and the old homestead, like General MacArthur, tends to fade away. This is difficult for parents to take—but it probably is the fate of ninety percent of them. Lucky are the parents who may remain together and find new circles of friendship and interest and fun. The fact of the matter is that a woman makes or breaks the man and whatever he may or may not accomplish has much to do with the woman with whom he shares his life. Lucky was my fate. And each one must speak for himself as time wears on.

TWICE OVER THE ATLANTIC

It was somewhat late in the spring of 1954 when a visitor dropped in one afternoon at our home. It was my good friend John Williams, minister of the First Presbyterian Church in Wooster (about whom I have already written). He came to tell us that he and his wife were planning a trip to Europe. Wouldn't we go along with them? Surprised and amused at the idea, I called loudly to my partner who happened to be at the other end of the house: "How would you like to go to Europe?" My first query was either not heard or it was so shocking that I got no immediate response. The second time I called with the same question I heard her say: "Sure. That's great."

And thus without planning or even thinking about such a matter as a long trip to far distant lands, the thing began to take shape. I had no idea that money would be available even after the Williams and we began to make preliminary plans. And we had no idea of how to plan or just where we would go and how—and even why.

The thing snowballed so quickly and the whole thing seemed so unlikely, I wonder to this day where and how we got the push. It was a kind of snap-judgment which demanded my finding the funds which I thought were quite unavailable and which also to my surprise seemed quite available at least for a modest vacation.

Then came the awful shock. Mr. Williams took ill suddenly and with what turned out to be a long illness and the trip was cancelled. How it became revived I just do not recall. One thing comes to the light of my memory: the insistence that we should follow through with a trip on our own. It was a tough decision. Late in that same spring it was suggested to us that we join a conducted tour. The American Travel Company of New York City (ATC Tours, Inc.), Ben Gottschalk, Director, took us on their list. William C. Holmes who had been a student of mine was our tour conductor. He personally set up a schedule and made late registrations and reservations for us—even though there would be some inconveniences. It turned out that Bill Holmes, experienced as he was, proved to be the perfect guide and companion in Europe.

And so came about our first crossing of the Atlantic in the early summer of that year with reservations on the United States Lines, cabin class, with a special bus to pick us up in London and to take us to Stratford to join the tour (already begun). We therefore were in the hands of experienced people with dates and places and reservations assigned by the headquarters in New York City. When we saw the itinerary we decided at once that we were fortunate since there was not a single place on the schedule we didn't want to include: the tour included a little of England, Scotland, Norway and Sweden and then across the English channel down through the continent as far as Rome and Naples.

It was Mr. Williams who introduced me to a new type of camera and the gadgets which go with the thing and to the whole new era of colored slides. This was the day when every Tom and Harry began to show such slides in their homes and I was unwittingly "taken in" by the fever. Two thousand of them for this trip and (perhaps) twenty-five hundred on a later trip. (To this day, I shudder when I hear someone say: "Come over and see our slides." This always reminds me of the stereoscope they had in my earliest years when one held it to the eyes and saw two black-and-white pictures at the same time and someone would give a long lecture on the image which came to view. No improvement over the ancient family album of photos. I recall the boredom of it all. I recall the times I have been caught for whole evenings in some home in the hey-day of colored slides on the screen—a day in which I was about to enter when this first crossing of the Atlantic took place.)

There were two such crossings. How the first one came about I have already given an account. The second one in 1956 was carefully planned. The occasion was a sabbatical and the plan was to spend the year either in Scandinavia at Uppsala University or at Cambridge in England. (I have already mentioned the circumstances earlier in this book.) The second pilgrimage was planned by the Wooster Auto Club for two people, my wife and myself. Mrs. Glorene Bechtel supervised every detail with professional know-how and loving care. We were to be met by professional representatives and our hotels were reserved from June to our destination in Sweden with places and time schedules tailor-made. Our first trip had whetted the appetite for more leisurely second visits and new places. The tickets were drawn up and all we had to do was to keep track of them and present them in person on the days assigned. The trip didn't seem so costly once we had it all paid for in advance. And I can report that every person appeared as guaranteed—even bus and taxi services. The one thing required of us was that we remain healthy and fit. Nothing could be postponed or changed without affecting the remaining days and weeks of the trip. This meant no night galavanting and care in eating. The days were rugged and we saw to it that we had the necessary rest and sleep. Our daily routine consisted of one dedication: I would keep track of the pictures taken by jotting down the time and the place and the scene and I would keep track of the tickets for the following day and keep financial score of the extra expenditures and the mailing of the films for processing. She had the assignment of writing up notes in a modest journal, a diary with special information gleaned that day. This meant a "study-hour" each evening.

It is to such a journal of three volumes I can now turn as I set down some of the recollections of our tours.

I choose in this reporting not to follow a deadening chronology which is as interesting as a railroad timetable. I choose to reminisce casually (mixing up the two grand tours) and re-think places and people and events which pop into mind, regardless of when and in what sequence they occurred. And my inclination takes me, for better or worse, immediately into some spots in the middle of Norway as a starter.

Lillehammer is a cultural center which many American tourists miss, perhaps because it is not on the usual tour-spots advertized and perhaps because it lies outside the usual rail-cross-Norway-route from Bergen to Oslo which connects west and east coasts. Lillehammer is in the north-central area approached either from Oslo on the southeast or from Trondheim (the ancient capital of Norway) on the northwest. Here is located the famous Sandvig collection—an open-air museum much like the folk museum in Oslo—specializing in farm buildings, water wheels, workshops at a place called Maihaugen; here is located the Nansen School, the academy of humanism (founded in 1939); in this vicinity at Aulestad, a few miles northwest, is located the former home of the great nineteenth-century poet and novelist Bjørnstjerne Bjørnson (1832-1910), author of *Arne, Beyond Human Power* and the poet of the Norwegian national anthem—now a national shrine; and here in Lillehammer itself is the home of Sigrid Undset (1882-1949), famous novelist.

Our visit to the Undset home—a fifteen-minute walk from our hotel—was most fortunate for us since we were given a tour of the home and gardens by her son (on the morning of July 24th, 1956). Everyone knows something about this author who wrote *The Axe, In The Wilderness, Kristin Lavrandsdatter, The Snake Pit.* Her typewriter at the desk with the sheet of paper on it was just as she left it shortly before her death; the garden which she loved was run down and unkempt; the house was an old but attractive building not too far from the center of town. We were given information about the family and briefed on the character of the author: a devout Catholic (in the midst of a strong Lutheran tradition), lover of nature and of the folklore of her beloved country. She had traveled to America and loved the Berkshires and particularly Massachusetts. Her manuscript on birds was not finished although much work had been done on it. Her schedule: she slept late in the mornings and stayed up most of the nighttime writing. Since she expressed the wish that her home would not become a museum, her son expressed his hope that the Catholic Church would take it over in return for a life pension for himself and his sister. Although divorced from her husband, the church allowed a special dispensation in her joining the establishment.

My wife and I were treated to some kind of strong drink before leaving. We accepted gladly. It was our undoing. Our stomachs refused the infusion and we were made semi-invalids the rest of the day.

Our visit included the open-air museum, the famous Sandvig collection at Maihaugen (a folk museum). We visited Aulestad (the Ostre Gausdal Valley), the Bjørnson home (already mentioned). The grand-daughter of Bjørnson was our guide. She told us of the great commitment of her grandfather to his beloved Norway and how he inspired the patriotism of his people for their country, culminating in the peaceful separation of Norway as a country from Sweden in 1905. He inspired self-confidence in the peasants, an outspoken opponent of social injustice and violence. He became a "free thinker" leaving the Lutheran church. His friends were Grieg and R. Nordrok. Nordrok's interest in folk tunes influenced Grieg and he (Nordrok) is known as the musical composer of the Norwegian national anthem. Aulestad is now the center for contemporary artists and writers who,—following Bjørnson's example,—settled down among the farmers in this beautiful dale. Other friends of the national hero were Ibsen and Ole Bull, the violinist and the moving figure in the contemporary theatre. We inspected the farmhouse, saw his study, the bear rugs on the floor, the beautiful china in the dining room, the gifts of silver plates, the stoves and the fireplaces, the carriages and sleighbells and caught the atmosphere of calm and peace which seemed to pervade the place.

The Nansen school in Lillehammer is a big house done over for use of students, mostly girls, supported by voluntary gifts in memory of the great idol of the Norwegian people, Fridtjof Nansen, explorer and power of inspiration for great ideals. Students were forty in number, mostly of high-school age who attended classes although living off-campus. What interested me especially was the information that both philosophy and psychology were taught here even though these were the younger level of Norwegian students.

Thus is the culture of this beautiful city. And with it the proximity to the countryside of Gudbrandsdal (upper and lower) wherein so much of the Peer Gynt legends abound—the land where the reckless Gynt drove his reindeers in outburst of imaginatively swift rides and became a part of the folklore of Norwegian children and of their ancient forebears. "Peer Gynt" is supposed to be buried near Harpefoss (although we did not see the alleged grave).

Before we left America we had it planned to visit the highest rock-mountains of Norway—a place where tourists seldom stop off to see. Arrangements were made to board the train at Trondheim and stop overnight at a little village by the name of Otta. I recall this place by the fact that of the few buildings besides the hotel and the railroad station there was one: a bookstore! Imagine: in this off-center stop: a bookstore, well stocked with hard-cover books. In Europe, people not only read but also buy books! It is with many of them a passion. They not only browse but they come out with books packaged. At Otta lies the center of Sigrid Undset's tale of *Kristin Lavrandsdatter* (which we learned later). This place offers tourists their immediate contact with direct travel to the Galdhøpiggen and the Jotunheim mountains of Norway, with the dips and the peaks, the valleys and even (if you go high enough) the forbidding glaciers of Norway. Here the Peer Gynt stories of folklore in Ibsen's great drama find their source in the mystical folds and contours of a rugged countryside. My anticipation of this visit was one of the greatest of any of our tour: for here was Norway in her generous display of granite splendors. Enroute to Galdhøpiggen we stopped briefly at Vågå (1100, bell tower, 1400, a Catholic church for 400 years) and Lom (1150) and saw two of many "stav" churches which date back beyond the Christian invasion (*circa* year 1000) of religious influence. The "stav" churches combine both pre-Christian and post-Christian symbols in their architecture and for tourists and artists and students of culture here are mines of information and inspiration in an unwritten pre-history. Norway's *stav kirker* are medieval masterpieces in wood, taking their name from the upright timbers, "the staves," basic to their construction. Ship builders were carpenters and the old Viking ships may have been the inspiration of their art.

A private cab called for us at Otta early in the morning. (We had had this arranged in America.) The date: July 23, '56. Elvester, our destination. Our names at the small but inviting inn were in the date-book but we were told that it would be inadvisable to try to ascend the Galdhøpiggen that day. We protested the announcement. Would we (we were asked) substitute another trip in the morning—to Sun Hill? A party was being readied for it. "Yes, we would." But we still insisted on Galdhøpiggen. The morning trip seemed dangerous, eight of us seated in a jeep with yawning valleys almost directly below us and only a few feet in the rocky road to spare us from a catastrophe. It was a hectic ride although beauty abounded everywhere. The Big Mountain (Mr. G.) stuck itself straight and towering in the distant sky and we wanted more than ever to ascend it. When we returned to the inn, we were told that another jeep had been gassed up for us with a special driver to take us to the glacier which drapes the Big Mountain. Yes, we were to see Galdhøpiggen. A jeep with driver would carry us all the way up to the ice-line.

The road winding and narrow (at times) ended at five thousand feet above sea level with another two thousand feet to the top. One just does not see any more impressive scenery anywhere. And the atmosphere was for us happily clear of clouds so we could see the farthest distance which the earth permits with its globular structure. One could see our path winding upward below any cloud lines. (We were told that it began to pour rain about the time of our descent but we enjoyed a cool crystal-clear skyview above the gathering clouds.) Breathing was noticeably difficult for us unaccustomed to this height at such a quick change. The glacier looked ominous and forbidding. The wind blew lustily and we were glad when the driver of our jeep motioned to us that the descent must begin soon lest we would be caught in what may be a threatening storm below. (We were reminded of the Swiss and Italian Alps of our 1954 tour by the Galdhøpiggen view and overcome by awe of the majesty of height and distance and our own finiteness as human beings.

Our return trip was uneventful and the little inn awaited us with open arms and treated us as somehow victors over something. Next morning the cab driver was to return us toward the road that led back to civilization. Norway is a country only for the rugged and sturdy and we were proud to have an encounter with that part of Europe that brought forth our own sturdy ancestors who gave us good blood.

The old capital of Norway was called Nidaros (on the banks of the river Nid). There stands the magnificent and renovated cathedral, again in the state of renovation (its first structure dating back to 1066-93). Nidaros is now Trondheim and the area is brimful of legend going back beyond Olav Tryggvason (a young and powerful Viking chieftain, the founder in 995). A convert to Christianity he set out to "unpaganize" his subjects. Trondheim is but some four- and a-half hours away from Otta (by train).

Our visit to Trondheim (July 19, 1956) came about by our planned cruise up to the top of Norway as far as Kirkenes near the Russian border. Trondheim was the port of return call from this coastal voyage since we planned to take the train route on to Sweden via Oslo; and, again, we planned, if possible, to visit the birthplace of Jacob Nelson, father of my wife. So it was that after a tour of the ancient capital to see its famous Cathedral, its folk museum, its 200-year wooden castle (the *Stiftsgården*, residence of the Civil Governor, largest wooden house in all Scandinavia), flower market, and the like, we began in serious purpose to enquire how we might find transportation to Leksvik about which we had heard father Nelson speak so glowingly and always with a kind of homesickness. I recall his description of the large house, the scenic creek that passed in front of it, the forests, the fences—a pastoral scene too vivid for him to keep secret. He had left home as a very young man and staked his future with other emigrants toward America, the land of opportunity. And he never returned to his homeland. "Mercer" (Wisconsin), he said, reminded him so much of Leksvik. And he would hit his cane against the chair and go on and on in glowing reminiscence. So . . . naturally we must find Leksvik somewhere near Trondheim.

Our enquiries led only to frustration. The only route to Leksvik was by water. Boats crossed the fjord only on a slim schedule. There was no other way. It is on an island eigtheen miles away. Tourists are few to such a place and hence facilities of travel were slim. My wife and I took a cab to Trondheim's port and I made enquiries of an elderly gentleman who sat and watched the sea-gulls. Then, suddenly, came the suggestion: go over to the little house yonder and ask the man inside; he knows more about such things. And this I did. In my poor Norwegian I explained to the little man (who looked at me with amusement) of our anxious desire to be taken to Leksvik and he got across to me the suggestion that he might call the captain of the tourist boat about how things stood. I shall never forget how the conversation went. To sum it all up in a few words: The man at the other end of the phone had a tourist cruiser seating seventy-five people. It was his only boat. Would I want him for the trip and for one day? What would it cost? I translated the *kroner* into American money and told him to hold on while I consulted my wife. She heard the price and said that it was altogether too expensive. I knew full well that she wanted to see her father's old home and the expense did not matter at all to me even though it did to her. Without one minute's hesitation I responded: Please come tomorrow with your boat and take us to Leksvik for the day and we will pay your price. (I have often thought of the cost of this trip: two people hiring a 40-foot cruiser powered by an engine ensconced a deck below, seats for seventy-five people, two small boys who waited on the captain, a whole day's rental—what mattered the cost? In terms of American dollars the whole deal was extremely reasonable.)

So for the day of July 20th, 1956, I find these words in her diary: "This is a day long to be remembered" at the heading and at the conclusion "after a full day, a very happy one." The cabin cruiser was named "Tripp." It was a rough sea and we were afraid the bonamine (bonine) pills would not function. But they did. Two hours of ups and downs and sideways, both of us kept bursting out laughing at the incongruous situation of *our* renting for a whole day a big cruiser with a Norwegian captain and sailing a sea once the home of the ancient Vikings! Little did we realize then what only recently I have learned: it was this very fjord about which I now write that Bertrand Russell writes about in his late autobiography:

"In the same year that I went to Germany, the Government sent me to Norway in the hope of inducing Norwegians to join an alliance against Russia. The place they sent me to was Trondheim. The weather was stormy and cold. We had to go by seaplane from Oslo to Trondheim. When our plane touched down on the water it became obvious that something was amiss, but none of us in the plane knew what it was. We sat in the plane while it slowly sank. Small boats assembled round it and presently we were told to jump into the sea and swim to a boat—which all the people in my part of the plane did. We later learned that all the nineteen passengers in the non-smoking compartment had been killed. When the plane had hit the water a hole had been made in the plane and the water had rushed in. I had told a friend at Oslo who was finding me a place that he must find me a place where I could smoke, remarking jocularly, 'If I cannot smoke, I shall die'. Unexpectedly, this turned out to be true. All those in the smoking compartment got out by the emergency exit window beside which I was sitting. We all swam to the boats, which dared not approach too near for fear of being sucked under as the plane sank. We were rowed to shore to a place some miles from Trondheim and thence I was taken in a car to my hotel. . . . Some amusement was caused when a clergyman supplied me with clerical clothing to wear till my clothes had dried."

Pp. 11, 12 *The Autobiography of Bertrand Russell, 1944-1969* (1969). Reprinted by permission of Simon and Schuster (New York).

It was strange to come upon a taxi in this isolated island. But there it was. I asked that we be taken to the *prästgården* (the home of the minister). It was a good hunch. In a matter of an hour, the hospitable minister's wife had us in tow, sought out by telephone neighbors who might remember the Jacob Nelson family and gave us a tour of the old Lutheran church and the cemetery which surrounded it.

The church register, called the *Kyrkobok* for Leksvik, dated 1880, was too recent for our use. Our lead came when the cab driver found someone in the parish who had a book and under the name of Fagerkind there was the name of Jacob Odin Fagerkind and the notation of his vaccination in 1864 when he was 1 ¾ years old. The lead: the Fagerkind home and estate must be found! While arrangements were quickly made for such a visit, we were touring the church (built in 1664). Lights hung from the ceiling had small foot-long boats as decorations, duplicates of the type in use in yesteryears' centuries. A balcony surrounded the inside of the church with hard light-maple benches without backs offering worshippers no view of the main sanctuary— probably the place reserved for the farmhands or the proletariat (my guess). The organ was hand-pumped. The minister's wife did the honors of pumping while

I played some numbers which came to mind. The key to the church door was a foot long; the door closed by its own weight with a pulley arrangement. Wood and coal stoves were the means of heat. The view from the churchyard overlooking the Norwegian fjord was unforgettably beautiful.

And so to the estate of the Fagerkinds. Still standing and deserted was the old two-story homestead, 200-years-old, with some of the painted designs still visible. It stood majestically on a little knoll overlooking a small creek. And there were the tall pines—even as Jacob Nelson had said. And there were the wild flowers which seemed to vie with each other to be picked and taken to America! The old mansion was about one-hundred feet in length with one end seemingly reserved for animals. The grass was tall and there was no sign of a path, suggesting that no one had come along to enquire about anyone or anything, no contemporary interested in its history—*except today:* a daughter who by the quirk of fate had been chosen to return to it with some message of the new generation in far-off America, which can claim a stake in its silent heritage. It was a moving experience for both of us and we had little to say, for we knew nothing more than what our memories could tell us from the lips of the Norwegian emigrant who had left it many years before; and moreover, our emotions did not call for words to describe the deep and moving impressions of this lonely place which had kept its beauty amidst many of the hard winters that had beat upon it.

We returned to Lina Osnes' parish home to find her husband, the Lutheran minister, awaiting us. The hospitality was doubled and we had to beg off their insistence on our staying for *kaffe* and even overnight. Our captain was waiting at the harbor and we had no choice but to return to the port of entry. I wished so much to talk with this fine clergyman who revealed a kind of "class" of an Uppsala University (Sweden) graduate in his conversation and demeanor. Here was this fine little family pleased to serve their Lord in a modest parish three Norwegian miles from the main coast; satisfied to work his little farm and enjoying no modern conveniences and experiencing no special handicap or sacrifice. I noticed he had an attractive study, its walls lined with books and my wife noticed that Lina had an attractive kitchen where undoubtedly she reigned supreme.

And so we rode the waves and returned to Trondheim on the *Tripp* with emotions elevated. We hurried, after landing, to the *Stadts Archivet* (City's Archives) to try to pick up information to fill in the highlights of our eventful day but found the place closed. It was still light and the day was not ended by far. So, on the spur of the moment, we decided to take the train to visit Hell, a forty-five minute ride! How could we ever live with ourselves if we did not visit Hell, Norway? This was our one chance and we knew it.

I recall saying to the ticket agent in my poor Swedish: two tickets to Hell *and return*. I made sure that there would be a return. Hell (we were told the following day) means a hole in the mountain. We saw no hole. The people there looked normal. Only *we* felt *hopefully* out of place! And full of the American tourist spirit, we remembered so many of our friends back home in America who might be interested to learn we were now in Hell. So . . . we spent the early evening hours at a souvenir shop buying and autographing postcards: remembering our Puritan friends especially (some of whom we knew were vacationing at the Bible camp at Chautauqua, New York and others who might be pleased to know that we had finally come to the place appropriate for us). For the sake of the record: we returned to Trondheim the same night—and it was still light. Moreover, our friends in America, when we returned, particularly remembered our cards from Norway and anxiously awaited our report of *the one spot* of our entire European journey, asking perchance if we had information they could not possibly have, not having been accorded a visit to Hell. It was nine o'clock. What a day! How much more could two human beings endure than a day such as this?

The *Stadts Archivet* clerk next morning hauled out from the vaults *Kyrkobok* 1854-1863 and on page 155, No. 14, the following notations appeared which I copied down: Lexvigen Födelse (Birth) daten 1st Januari 1863 Jacob Odin, Daabs (baptized) datum Feb. 15 1863 (six witnesses) Om aegte (legitimate) fodt (born)—blank after the words: eller noegte fodt (which would say "illegitimate"). This information came from Leksvik Sognepraest Ministerial Bog No 1854-1863. To this was added "Ders Föraldres (Parents) fulde Novn (full name) borgerlige Stelling og Ophildsted Hüvedmend Nils Olsen Fagerkind og Olava Ols dotter. In another record book marked Fagerkind (Leksviken parish) there appears the name Nils Olsen 1818 Husmand med jord (earth). Under the Nils Olsen name there appears the name of four children plus one adopted. Second on the list is recorded Jacob Odin Nilssen, 1863, gjästergut. And then a note Enkeman (widower) Nils Olsen Fagerkind 41 yrs old och piga Lava Olsen Neveraas 32 years old were married October 27 1859. All of which adds up: Earthowner (land gentleman) Fagerkind married young maiden Lava Olsen Neveraas and these were the immediate ancestors of my wife.

A few sentences now about the *de luxe* North Cape trip.

On the evening of July 9th, 1956 our cab in Bergen took us to our boat the "Nordlys" (62 1st-class and 128 2nd-class passengers) for the long trip north to the top of Norway with many stopovers and some bus rides, including Trondheim, Tromso (which is the place to buy a blue fox cape and a cormorant coat and a medium-size white bear skin—paid for by a personal check and no questions asked), and, of course, North Cape. I climbed (part stairs and part on knees) to the top of North Cape (July 14th) and was rewarded with an impressive view of the harbor and the ocean and the little ship that brought us to this out-post of the world. Then on to Kirkenes around the top of Norway to its most eastern part—a stretch of Lappland—guarded, from the other side, by Russian soldiers warning foreigners not to trespass or else face capture.

The midnight sun is described in our diary: "Then the most beautiful sight of all begins—the sun comes out and shines on all the mountains and fjords and we run from one side of the boat to the other to see the sights. It was indescribable and we saw the sun set and rise at the same time. It did not touch the horizon. We sailed up the Tromso channel and passed the big whaling station and saw the Lyngen mountains in all their glory. To the south we saw the Lyngenfjord . . . It was midnight: a real fairyland one will never forget. How nice the sun came out for us. (Many tours of this crossing of the Arctic circle and beyond are not lucky enough to view the splendor when the clouds intervene or the rain shuts out the panorama.) What a day!" (July 12-13, 1956). The captain set up a party: to solemnly initiate us into the company of those who had made the crossing of the imaginary line that brought us into the land of the midnight sun. Neptune was present in costume. There was a ritual. We were baptized afresh. And certificates (dated July 12th, 1956) were formally presented.

On our first Atlantic trip (June 22, 1954) we were given our first introduction to Norway in a visit to Bergen (founded 1070). Bergen was quite isolated from eastern Norway, particularly Oslo, because of the mountainous country until 1909 when the Oslo-Bergen Railroad opened up cutting through the seemingly hopeless barricades. Bergen's earlier commerce had been via the ships at sea. As one enters the city from the docks, one passes the famous storehouses (and museum) of the German Hanseatic merchants who for many years controlled shipping, exacting tolls and living a somewhat isolated life from the conquered Scandinavians. The Germans invaded Norway in 1940 and took over and destroyed what they wished while the Norwegians fought underground successfully though at great cost (all the way up the coast). One sees the scars of the invasion and one recalls Hitler and the German machine and now the famous motion picture starred in by Kirk Douglas depicting the period of humiliation.

One is lucky if the weather is good to view Bergen ("the rainiest city of the world") from Floyen, 1050 feet high overlooking the city, reached by cable car and only a few minutes from the city. The view of the harbor is memorable in its beauty especially at sunlit evening. The restaurant at the top is memorable for its cuisine, especially for sea food—one restaurant one never fails to recall when European eating places *deluxe* are mentioned.

A visit to this city lacks fulfillment unless one visits the home of Edvard Grieg (born 1843) "the Chopin of the North" which can easily be reached by cab. The place is called "Trollhaugen" (hill of the trolls). Here Grieg spent happily the last twenty years of his life. Here music flowed freely and appropriately through the woodsy acres of trees and brush uncut as he wished. Here he played his Steinway for his Norwegian friends and visitors seated near the door of the veranda. Here Nina (his musical wife) and Edvard are buried in niches in the stone abutment adjacent to the expansive waters below. There stands the very special little hut in the woods where he found inspiration and meditation for his musical soul.

Speaking of Grieg one cannot help reminding oneself of the famous Norwegian Ole Bull (born in Bergen in 1810), himself a musician and a Norwegian patriot. It was Ole Bull who recommended Grieg to study at Leipzig where Grieg did go and came under the influence of Mendelssohn and Schumann who, no doubt, sparked his career. It was Ole Bull who brought Henrik Ibsen in 1851 to Bergen recognizing in this inexperienced young man even at the age of twenty-three a potential for success in the field of dramatic art. Crude was Henrik at that time and meager was his salary (about $6.00 a week). Ole Bull seemed to have a way with him to spot people and advise and encourage them. His scheme for a National Theater was established in 1845 (opened in 1850) and the place is still a shrine for Bergen visitors. It was Ole Bull who probably inspired Longfellow's love of Scandinavia. He met Longfellow in his visit to America in 1843 and (it is pointed out) he is brought in to the picture in Longfellow's *Tales of a Wayside Inn*. Oslo vies with Bergen in proclaiming Ibsen as its unforgettable hero and, of course, Christiana (now Oslo) has the edge since the playwright not only spent the later years of his life there but received the plaudits of his people so generously given and so humbly received.

A trip to Norway must include the fabulous transcontinental ride from Bergen to Oslo (or vice versa). The scenery on the western side past the fjords and into the mountains and the little farms on the hillsides, the sight of glaciers and the expanse both in length and depth are unforgettable—wholly comparable to the scenic Swiss and Italian Alps. The railroad extends some three-hundred miles from end to end and penetrates through some two-hundred and seventy tunnels, (two of which are more than five miles in length) and rises to more than fifty miles above the timberline.

On midsummer's eve on our excursion across Norway by train, leaving Bergen and along the scenic Hardanger fjord, we came to the city of Voss (first tour, 1954). Voss is memorable to me for two reasons. It was there I learned first-hand how risky it is to address Scandinavians as if they were altogether foreigners to us when not only do they speak good English but they dress like the many tourists who visit there in summer. I wanted very much to purchase a Swedish or Norwegian dress (costume) for my wife as a grand souvenir. Not knowing my way around in the town I planned my attack. Two ladies came strolling down the street. I practiced my Swedish (although we were in Norway). Finally, it came from my lips all ready rehearsed and memorized. I said to the smiling ladies: "Ursäkta mej, kan Ni tala om för mej var jag kan köpa en Svensk eller Norsk klädning för min fru?" Now this was not Swedish at its best. I got through the sentence all right and waited a few seconds for the answer. It came and it was: "Sorry, we don't speak Norwegian." And they went happily on and I stood there frozen like a statue. I let them believe I was a native and let it go. "So," I said to my partner, "we do look like a couple of Norwegians." And we both laughed and felt complimented.

The second reason I recall Voss, turns me to write some parenthetical paragraphs as follows: I suppose it is not uncommon for persons to recall hazardous experiences in life which almost cost them life or limb. One such in my life occurred in Voss. We were about to watch the ceremonies of midsummer evening, June 23rd: the crowd had gathered in costume and I was getting my kodak ready when suddenly I found myself out of film. What to do? Scurrying here and there and finding no solution, I got in a cab and asked the driver to take me to a film shop. I had no idea where he was heading nor the distance. It was quite a ride. I recall that he stopped where there was a cluster of small shops. I paid him and ran to the one most promising. The door was heavy to open and reluctant, perhaps semi-locked. At any rate, it opened and I lunged through. Suddenly my body lurched downward. There was no floor. There was only deep darkness. I had come into an open and yawning cavern the end of which I could not see. Somehow, I grabbed something on my way down and held, camera and carrying-case dangling around my neck. My arms somehow held me until I could swing my legs upward and pull my body up. Lady Luck had declared that this was not my rendezvous with death and allowed me to rest my torso on the floor above. How I succeeded I shall never know. Imagine my reactions when I sat there: alone, in the dark, at someplace in Norway, unknown, with no one there to give help, my wife two or three miles away, not knowing where I was. I finally collected myself. I walked away wondering what to do, where to go and whether there may be another cab since the whole town "had gone to the fair" to celebrate the one major festivity of the year.

Another paragraph on similar experiences. I recall (during my student days) my nearly drowning off the shore of Catalina Island in California when I was trying to swim in the expansive beach. I felt myself go under, my feet touching nothing but water, my strength ebbing and the shore line only a few feet away, with a current pulling me away and with no one there to observe my plight. Lady Luck pulled me out of that one and I still have the awful feeling of utter helplessness as I tried desperately to gather the last ounces of strength to reach shore. And another: Walking alone one Sunday afternoon in Northern Michigan (along the shore of Lake Superior some forty miles from our summer home) I suddenly felt the whizz of something ominous over my head—perhaps inches—and simultaneously heard a shot. Yes, it was a bullet. It barely missed me and I am certain my skull was not tough enough to cause it to glance off. I was later told that some tourist (up there we call them "ten day tourists") had been out trying out his gun and then came Bronson (Ferm). A complaint later to the sheriff of the county by my host was filed, but it no longer mattered for Lady Luck had interfered.

Our next overnight stop (after Voss) was at Finse where we walked to the Hardanger glacier at late eveing enjoying the cold and the strange sensation of light where darkness is supposed to be.

I suppose at Oslo the thing we recall most readily from our two visits there was the visit to the Vigeland Fountain and statues. Gustav Vigeland (born 1869) worked on this project some thirty years. And I particularly remember the philosophy which seemingly underlay this gigantic piece of sculpturing: in the upward thrust of human passions and struggles there is only turmoil and the twistings of fate from which all men suffer. At the top there is no suggestion of solution—only an abrupt cut-off representing (I suppose) the ultimate despair of man for any solution. It may be that I did not interpret him correctly but I am certain he was engrossed by the plot of evolution with a conviction that evolution has no solution other than its own momentum.

The tireless Vigeland spent time and talent at the reconstruction of the cathedral in Trondheim and it may be that this gigantic offering at Oslo was his answer to the tradition represented by the ancient temple.

And of course, at Bygdöy with its collection of Viking ships, farmhouses, Stav churches—a sanctuary near Oslo reached by steamer—there is in the *Ridehus* (rooms furnished in different styles and periods), Ibsen's study just as he worked in it in his latest years—years which brought him not only physical but mental failures even to the point of difficulty with remembering the alphabet. "I" · he said, "who was once a writer." Bygdöy houses the polar ship *Fram*, the 800-ton wooden-vessel which survived three polar expeditions. This ship was built for Fridtjof Nansen and reached the farthest northern point of any ship up to that time—1893-1896. Roald Amundsen used it for his expedition in 1910-12 when the South Pole was reached. (The Nansen and Amundsen polar equipments are on display at Holmenkollen near Oslo, a museum full of old acquisitions including ski exhibits.) Also at Bygdöy is the famous *Kon-Tiki* museum which displays Thor Heyerdahl's raft which drifted the Pacific in 1947.

This chapter would be incomplete without at least a passing report of our search for my own immediate ancestors. Now that we found my wife's Norwegian ancestral shrine—what would we find about my own? We were at Uppsala covering the ancient shrines and centering our attention on the University and the cathedral (dating back to the 13th century). The Uppsala area is memorable: Flustret—student atmosphere with delicious cuisine, university library, the castle, the home

of Carl von Linne' (Linnaeus) in the country-place
called Hammerby (Linnaeus said "everything comes
from an egg") and the Linnaeus gardens in Uppsala
where the digitalis plant is growing, *Gamla* (old) Uppsala with its burial-mounds of ancient Kings and the
castle at Skokloster (by boat from Uppsala), a castle
once a medieval cloister, the most magnificent of European castles we were privileged to visit.

By means of telephone communication with the
K.A.K. (*Kungl Automobil Klubben*) in Stockholm,
arrangements were made for us to find a tour-guide and
an automobile to take us on a sentimental journey to
my father's and my mother's birthplaces. My information was sparse but it did include names of places and
enough directives to make the search promising. Sweden, as we know, is divided into provinces and parishes
(*socken*). Swedish-American immigrants (I recall) always mentioned to each other when introduced to
friends in America, the name of their province and perhaps their own *socken*. This was revealing. Even the
Swedish accent betrayed the province. Skåne, in southern Sweden, is sometimes considered by other Swedes
to be foreign, particularly by the accent of its people
(*Skånsk*). Lund University, founded in the 1660's (it's
Cathedral begun in 1085) is situated in Skåne, ten miles
from Malmö, the port of entry to Sweden from Copenhagen, Denmark (16 miles away). My mother was a
Smålänning, which is to say "from Småland" in the middle of the country. My father was from Nerike not too
far from Småland but they had to come to America to
meet (of all places, in Chicago).

This was the chief reason for hiring a native chauffeur

and a private car. To find these places by buses or trains would have been ridiculous. So off we went: what turned out to be a 1500 mile trip in a period of seven days. Our guide was well informed. We recall his name: Björn Bark-Lindgren ("Bark" to us), a pre-med student who was then not altogether pleased by his professional prospects in a socialist country and longed to migrate to Canada if not to America.

We shall always especially remember Hotel Gillet in Uppsala. It was there I was handed my mail one morning at the desk in the small lobby: a letter from America. It was a surprise beyond any expectations! Mr. Armstrong (about whom I have already had much to say in this book) sent me a short note insisting that my wife and I visit Greece on this trip. Such an extended tour we had not planned. The letter contained a substantial personal check. All this meant a series of telephone calls *while traveling* to KAK in Stockholm to set up new arrangements, itinerary and reservations.

So it was on the morning of August 27th, 1956 when we left Hotel Gillet. (We had finished wide travel in Scandinavia: Visby (Gotland), Finland, Sigtuna, founded in 1000, with its ruins, once Sweden's chief political and religious center now a humanistic center—approached from Uppsala.) Our destination now was Örebro where I knew my father had gone to receive pre-university training at its celebrated university. I wondered as I walked the campus situated in the very heart of the large city, if I was walking actually in his footsteps and if the buildings could talk what they would say. It is a beautiful city but hardly so metropolitan when my dad was there as it is now. The old castle still stands. Our meager data in our search for his birthplace and early environment took us on a twenty-five-mile drive from Örebro to Tislinge Church, the *prästgård* where we luckily found the *kyrkoherde* (minister) Löfgren at home and very hospitable toward us. Indeed, consulting his *kyrkobok* (church-book) he found records of the Ferm family: father, mother, one sister and four brothers. We were taken on a tour of the twelfth-century (its front part) church next door, now a white stucco building, modest and yet impressive. A foot-long key opened the door to the shrine we had longed to see. The rug had swans as a design and we were told that each spring the swans stop here on their way north never to return. The old baptismal font stood in the back of the church (quite unusual). I felt a kind of inner assurance that it could tell us of my father's baptism if it could speak. (Frankly, I was surprised to find the name *Ferm* in the parish records—believing that the name was an army name recently acquired. However, I learned in Stockholm that the City Telephone Directory there listed fifty-three Ferms, seven Fehrms and one Ferhm.)

A few miles away we saw the name of the place we especially wanted to see in print. There it was, the modest sign: "Garphyttan," where my records show was my father's birthplace. What we found, with the help of a Mr. Gerhard Olson, a native, were the remains of this and that which, pieced together, made us certain that this was the place. There stood the old "fabriken" (plant, factory) probably successor of a more modest building. We followed our guide to the spot (he said) where the blacksmith shop used to be: a mound near a creek and now overgrown with bushes; and then on to the house where eight families lived at that time and probably the place (or very close to it) where Olof Wilhelm was born—my dad! Side stairs earlier on the outside of the house led to an upper story where work clothes hung (said our guide). The land-owner lived in a separate building and it remains quite unchanged from what it was years ago. We saw hills of slag which the workers had dumped from their back-packs and if we had had time we might have picked up remnant pieces which perhaps would attest to the fruits of the laborers. No wonder (I thought) that my dad projected for himself an education at some available school when the day of opportunity came and no wonder, too, that he caught the spirit to emigrate to America, the land of golden opportunity. No wonder, too, that he began his first job in America someplace where he could pit his strength and his trade toward a livelihood. This, thus, explains his contact with the rough and hard labors in the steel mills of South Chicago (or in that area) and the hidden desire in his breast of continuing his education when available at the (then) little Lutheran College in Illinois. Some Lutheran minister turned him to focus his ambitions to seek more education that he might some day join the Lutheran ministry. (These hard earlier days may have contributed to his early death [1911] at fifty-eight, when his heart failed almost suddenly in the prime of life and not too far from his alma mater who had spurred his ambitions toward a successful professional life.)

Then, on to Lerbeck and the church (rebuilt, 1783) and its cemetery for more information. The Ferm relatives are scattered in this small parish and we stood at

one grave marked Mathilda Ferm and were told that
she was recently buried (1926)—a person well-known
in the community who had operated a *konditor* (con-
fectioner's shop). It was beginning to get dark so we
left the spot only to return in a few days to seek out
more information and to take us to other and later homes
of my grandparents: one at Skyllberg—(the 300-year-
old manor-house) and another at Rönneshytta—somewhere nearby lie the bodies of my grandparents. Not
too many miles away we stopped at Töreboda where
we found, at their cozy home, the sister of my wife's
stepmother Kristine Johansson and her husband. And
all the time we were there the lady cried and cried; she
was so moved and bewildered and perhaps even happy
by the sudden experience of someone from far-off America who had come to visit even for two hours and share
in the news of relatives so far, far away. Töreboda is
about a four-hour drive from the city of Borås where
another long day ended—August 29th.

North of Örebro is Värmland. I asked Bark to give
us a day there. Why? For two reasons: First, I had so
often heard in my earlier days from the lips of Swedish
immigrants how beautiful Värmland is and how great
was the emigration from that province to America. Indeed, we found it to be so: lakes, forests, meadows, hills,
vales—no wonder there are so many folktales and folk-
songs associated with this area. And secondly, this is the
ancestral home of the Swedish novelist Selma Lagerlöf
(1858-1940). We must visit this shrine.

Her grave is at Östra Ämtervik in a beautifully-kept
cemetery. From there to Mårbäcka, her forefathers'

home, is but a short distance. On August 28th we visited both places.

Her family had been a family of clergymen. She, herself, (I learned) was a cripple. Compensating for this she wore one heel lower and the other higher. Her ancestral home is Mårbäcka in Värmland, an estate of some size which the generations held in possession by the family. It was lost some time during her early life there. Meanwhile, she had a literary bent and wrote essays on the folklore of the area. *Gösta Berling's Saga* was the book resulting from manuscripts put together. And, in 1891, this novel brought her a prize and fame. In 1909 the Nobel Prize for literature was awarded her. Her books were translated in thirty different languages and eventually she became the first woman-member of the Swedish Academy. It is said that she bought back the Mårbäcka estate from the Nobel prize money of some forty-thousand dollars and built the beautiful rambling manor house that stands there now preserving some of the original home. Her study is book-lined wall-to-wall and the place is priceless for its beauty of home and gardens. In her major novel her ancestral home figures a part while the nearby Rottneros Manor with its present display of acres of gardens and flowers is the "Ekeby" in the story.

Our search for ancestral shrines continued on September first; our goal was Småland. We had been in Jönköping, capital of the old province of Småland, taking a tour of the famous match factory *(tändsticker fabrik)* and we headed by auto *(bil)* for *Gyllene Uttern* (Golden Otter) Castle on Lake Vättern. This lake is about eighty-miles long, the fourth largest lake in

Europe—intersecting the famous *Göta Canal*. Here we stopped at a beautiful Inn; registered there for a cabin in the woods as our home plate for the duration of the search. We remember the beautiful Swedish meals at this Inn, especially the baked salmon and we remember too, the wedding, in the little chapel, of the bashful Swedish couple who had for their attendants: the preacher, the organist, two others and ourselves.

Our notes said that *Vireda* Church *socken* is the birthplace area of my mother. And sure enough we found the country church nestled comfortably amidst the rolling hills—not too far from our home base. Although a Lutheran church, the evidence was forcefully clear that this place dates back beyond Reformation times into the heyday of Catholicism. The building dates back to 1300 although re-done and immaculately cleaned and in perfect repair. Paintings on the ceiling date from 1755 and still look freshly painted. (It seems they had the quality of oils that withstood washing—the last washing in 1938.) Of course, there were additions to the building but these seemed minor. The sexton gave us a tour supplementing his expositions of each painting with a kind of sermonette. The baptismal font dated back to 1112; the crucifix on the altar of 1212 and the *predikstol* (pulpit) to 1663.

When Sweden was a great military power Count Per Brahe, the Elder (1520-90) and Count Per Brahe, the Younger (1602-80), governor of Finland, owned a large section of this part of Sweden in their day. Their castle ruins on an island on Lake Vättern are visible from the *Gyllene Uttern* inn. The organ for the Vireda church was given by the Brahe family (1755) and still stands in the choir loft. Pastor Tore Lord, the *kyrko-herde* of this *socken* and his family gave us the welcome treatment and so much help in matters concerning our personal interest. Among the things he told us he said that the favorite Psalm of his parish was that of Number 169. And dressed in his *prästrock* (minister's suit, one exactly like mine which bedecked my body at a Luther-an convention of ordination in 1919 in Lindsborg, Kan-sas in America) he pointed out this and that—and I re-call his entering into the sanctuary and from the pulpit read the Old Testament *Vireda* Psalm for the benefit of the son and his wife of one of his 19th century parish emigrants who had now returned to pay homage. He brought the *kyrkobok* to the church and there in clean and visible and beautiful penmanship was the record on one of its pages of the family names of my mother: be-ginning with the father, Anders Andersson, and his wife (my grandmother), Gustafva Andersdotter and the names of six children, aunts and uncles of mine, most of whom I personally remember from visits to Chicago, to Chariton, Iowa and in Nebraska. My mother's name was fourth on the list and it was plainly written: "Au-gusta Mathilda" born 1859 the 22nd day of the first month. I took a kodak picture of this page marked Slät-hult: Mellangårde and the surprise of my life came when Eastman Kodak Company developed and safely deliver-ed the film to me to have as a remembrance of finest quality. (I am looking at the original slide now as I write these lines.) We visited the graveyard and then were invited in to meet the pastor's family in the cute but ample home provided by the parish for *prästfamiljen* (minister's family).

Släthult (we were told) was only a short distance from the Vireda church and we drove off to look for it, I in an emotional pitch, riding high and with anxious impatience. There was the modest sign along the country road: Släthult! And I took a kodak picture of it. We accosted some neighbors in the village and came upon two middle-aged persons, Märta Wangstrom and Stora Hulbrunn. After consultation (with others) it was agreed that up the hill a ways was the home of my grandparents. We walked to the spot where the house once stood with no timbers preserved. There were the four stone boulders each in place showing the exact size of the building and with persons as markers I took my picture. The countryside was very much as my mother had said: rolling hills, boulder rocks, some woods, with a good view of the countryside from their home.

Two more places to see and our sentimental pilgrimage would be fulfilled: Nobenas (not too far from Släthult) was the grand estate where my grandfather was an overseer (*rättare*) now turned into a hospital; and there was the caretaker's house where my maternal family once lived before the exodus to America. (In this country the family name became Slattengren.) And as a souvenir of the perfect day, we purchased a small brass candelabra at the *Gyllene Uttern* Castle inn, which graces our dining room as an every day reminder of Småland and of our visit there.

To top it all off, the next morning (the final lap of our pilgrimage which was to end at Stockholm) we stopped a few minutes at Gränna (not far from the *Gyllene Uttern*) to see the little town so famous for its *polkagrisor*—the sweet, sweet candy that we used to munch

on and in our minds always associated with Christmas:
the kind that comes resembling sticks with handles (like
canes) and with a winding red stripe running down the
whole length never to be sucked away. A tidbit *par excellence* known to Swedish people everywhere and a
delicacy at celebrations and parties. Vadstena Castle
with its moat, bleak and dreary (of Gustav Vasa fame),
the church and Abbey (of St. Bridget fame) were on
our route to Stockholm and the remembrance of this
town of medieval traditions lingers on as a highlight
visit of our trip.

And in Stockholm we bade goodbye *(lycka til)* to
Bark, our mentor, who by now is a practicing M.D.
somewhere.

The City of Stockholm, "the Venice of the North"
is a tourist's Paradise. The reader may be assured that
we made the most of it on our many visits there and in
the adjacent areas: Drottningholm Palace, for example,
nearby, the impressive *Storkyrkan* (Cathedral) in the
old part of the City, City Hall, NK or Nordiska Kom-
paniet ("name it, we have it"—department store),
Swedish-speaking Chinese waitresses serving chowmein
in one of the tidy restaurants, *Skansen* (outdoor establishment), the palace and the ceremony of the changing
the Guard and hundreds of other fascinating places.
But, this would take a whole chapter. Stockholm is a
must for anyone.

One of our planned tours was to take in the famous
section of Sweden known as the *Dalarna (Dalecarlia)*
which is Sweden in its most Swedish caste. Lake Siljan
is its center. And there is so much Swedish atmosphere
here that one cannot tell about it on paper. There is

Leksand, a tourist center with its picturesque church with a Russian-style steeple and Viking-simulated boats which on festive occasions are seen approaching the shore and (if you are lucky) you will come upon a funeral procession with pallbearers carrying the coffin of the deceased on their shoulders as the bells toll. And you visit shops and mingle with tourists. Then there is Rättvik, another popular tourist center on Lake Siljan, with its medieval church and historic reminders of how the Dalecarlians responded to the call of their country in times of crises, driving off "foreigners" (particularly the Danes).

Then farther north on Lake Siljan is the city of Mora. On July 30th we reached this spot by steamer and were taken to our hotel and given the bridal suite and the red carpet treatment. (Because we were Americans? I do not know.) One memory stands out from this visit: our tour of the principal home of Anders Zorn (1860-1920). I knew his name well. For in my earlier years I had seen the name of Zorn on church-altar paintings and regarded this name as somehow associated with religion. Mora is the birthplace and burial place of Anders Zorn and there is his museum full of impressionist paintings. In one of the smaller buildings there is a collection of his works. To my surprise we found that the building was full of paintings of female nudes. Poses of all sorts. What I recall most is my standing (after a brief tour) at the entrance and watching the looks on tourists' faces when they suddenly found themselves in a kind of shock: nudes, nudes, nudes. This didn't quite fit in with the Zorn of famed altar-paintings also perhaps in the minds of visitors. At any rate, it was amusing to

watch people trying not to show their interest and pleasure to others in their party—all the time practicing the
art of side vision. (In those days there was more modesty, seemingly, than in the days in which we now live.)

It would be beyond the scope of this book to give a
full running account of other places and of the heaps
of other experiences in our two crossings of the Atlantic. On the other hand, it would seem to be remiss not
to mention some of the places and a few of the memories which rise quickly to the surface of one's mind as
one reminisces.

Our second tour brought us by ship to the outer harbor of Cobb in Ireland on June 21 (1956). A tender
met the big ship and brought us to shore. And then on
to Cork where arrangements had already been made in
America for a private car to take us across Ireland as
far as Dublin. There was no other way than this really
to see Blarney castle (and kiss the Blarney stone), to
see the greenest greens of the Irish summer landscape,
the beautiful rolling hills and the ribbon roads winding
around them and to enjoy the colorful fuchsia blooming
generously along both sides of the road. One hundred
miles to Killarney and a stopover to drive leisurely
around the lake in a jaunting car(t) and next day on toward the river Shannon and to Limerick city and the
area where (we are reminded) the limericks of poetry
had their origin (five-line-verse form of two rhyming
couplets and a-half) and passing the Tipperary mountains on toward Dublin. What a privilege to see Trinity
College, the second oldest in the Western world, and

to see the modest home of George Bernard Shaw (born 1856) and the place where the Abbey Theater once flourished (building burned in 1951), not to mention to pass by the famous Guiness brewery which covers some 600 acres. Then to Belfast and the Parliament buildings.

And then on to Glasgow, Scotland (where the Cairds [Edward and John] taught their well-known idealistic philosophy at the University), the Robert Burns (1759-1796) country in Ayershire (his cottage at Alloway) and on to Edinburgh with its Princes street, flower clock, Holyrood Palace, John Knox home, home of the famous David Hume marked with a modest inscription and later, on to Aberdeen across the two-mile bridge (River Tay) and a taxi to Balmoral Castle and then back to Sir Walter Scott country, Abbotsford House and then north to Oban and by boat to Iona (a bleak island with an ancient Abbey and full of uncovered history). Loch Lomond in Scotland is a big lake (28 sq. miles) in a folklore country (sea monsters, witches, et al).

Then down to the English Lakes (England) where Wordsworth and other poets and novelists were inspired by a nature philosophy—and no wonder. Eleven lakes and a tour around them. And Keswick of lead-pencil fame and then on to Newcastle quay for the boat to Bergen.

No one should miss Gotland (the ancient walled city of Visby) and the countryside. The sea-resort hotel Snäckgärdsbaden is memorable.

Nor should one miss Finland with its beautiful and modern city: Helsinki (architects' paradise for striking buildings—especially churches), with its University, Stockmanns' beautiful department store, wharf, Olympic stadium (built in 1950) from its tower a view of the city. Helsinki is overnight by boat from Stockholm. A private car-tour to Porkalla (occupied by the Russians during the last war and recently returned to the intrepid Finns) was a memorable experience: a lonely place of sickeningly-blue cottages—at our time of visit—a no-man's land of small villages without human beings. And by car to the home of Jan Sibelius (born 1865),—his home called "Ainola" in Yarvenpaa—whose music will survive the centuries: an old-fashioned big house with its gardens and woods and pathways and "sauna" (Finnish bathhouse) and his maid to conduct our tour. (He was ninety years old at the time of our visit and very feeble.) His home is not far from Helsinki. And then there is *Storkyrkan* (the towering cathedral) in the middle of the city of Helsinki, seating some two thousand people. The service on Sunday high-mass was in Swedish and we understood what it was all about: but it was dull, dull, dull, with the minister's wife attending the preacher by opening and closing the gate to the altar. Attendance: thirty people counting tourists most of whom left during the service! Passed the home of Alex Kivi, greatest name in Finnish literature, writer of old folk songs. And then a visit to the famous cemetery which for the Finns is a holy shrine, beautifully kept and full of memories of their recent patriots who fought with their hands to defend their little homeland. There stands the impressive monument to General Mannerheim near his grave (died 1951). The beauty of it all: Finland with its lakes and forests and sturdy people. (Our visit August 17-19, 1956.)

The SAS (Swedish air line) is the best. Our trip (Sept. 7 1956) from Stockholm to Geneva (stopovers at Copenhagen and Frankfurt) was a "first flight" for us and it was comfortable and exciting. Geneva is an old city and is not only beautiful but historic. The monument to the Reformers is imposing: Farel, Calvin, Beza, Knox, Luther and Zwingli. By a wiggly cable car we were hauled up part way to Mount Blanc—a harrowing experience. Then (Sept. 9) a TWA flight to Athens over Mt. Blanc and a short stop in Milan, Italy and a short stop at Rome. The plane circled the entire city of Rome at low level for the benefit of its passengers. (From the air we recognized many places from our earlier tour of 1954.) And, boarding the same plane, coming into Athens at night and seeing the Christmas-tree-like lights of the ancient city brought a lump to my throat: ancient Athens about which I had read and read through many years: the home of the Sophists, Socrates, Plato, Aristotle and all. Though not of Greek descent, I felt like an adopted son.

Athens is the center of so many outlying trips: one to Delphi in the mountains (Parnassus) where halfway up the precipitous and narrow roads, is the marker "the center of the Universe" near the temple of Apollo (home of the Apollo cult) and higher up the Roman amphitheatre almost at the top (which one cannot resist climbing). Here at Delphi came the pilgrims for advice, ancient leaders daring not to make war without the advice of the oracle (through women mystics who had emissaries of information and gave out prophecies based on their latest scout information under the guise of Deities). Another side-trip: to Corinth, in our judgment, the hottest place on earth. Sand, sand, sand, forbidding even though hugging ocean breezes. Our entrance to ancient Corinth brings the memory: a solemn warning to bus passengers not to take pictures of the Corinth canal; a memory of one person who did, the click of the camera which was noticeably audible to keen ears on the bus and a breath of suspicion passing around, the guilty party sitting stone-eyed and now the proud owner of the film claiming it to be one of his best in his huge collection and living to tell the tale. Corinth reminds us that Paul's two letters to these "foreigners" (the Jewish grotto is pointed out among the ruins) are among the four Pauline letters today regarded as quite authentic (that is, Pauline in authorship) as over all the rest of "his" letters in the New Testament which are regarded either as questionable or very doubtful as to his authorship. It was a long ride back and forth in one day from Athens to Corinth.

And, of course, a visit to Eleusis and the place of the Eleusynian mysteries (no one knows what they were—held twice a year with the big initiations occurring in November). Devotees forbidden to speak about them; Pluto's kingdom is entered into through a large hole in the ground (which is visible to the tourist).

Passing through Thebes, I grew intense with excitement and pleaded with the bus driver to stop for a picture. Neither he nor I seemed to be able to communicate. With help, I got the message to him. And suddenly he stopped the bus along the narrow road. I hurried out with my kodak. There was nothing to see—*really*. I snapped my shutter. Result: when I got back to the States my picture of Thebes was a lonely telephone pole: all that was there for me to see after what once was a mighty empire! The driver thought surely I was a nut and, no doubt, the passengers who were tourists not excited by such a name as Thebes and looked at me with disgust.

Having taught Greek philosophy for so many years, naturally Athens was pored over day after day on our stay there (Acropolis and all). Plato's Academy was a disappointment—only an empty and sandy vacant lot (probably used now for car parking). But Plato never did emphasize the material world too much. The world was for him essentially spiritually oriented and so it was proper to stop and just think about "universals." And the *Agora* (the market place): where democracy once flowed freely and where the Sophists argued and Socrates debated and Mrs. Socrates had to go after him to come home for supper ("his" tomb amidst the nearby olive trees). And the *Agora* where Aristotle must have walked and got his idea of Peripatetic Philosophy (walk and talk). And Piraeus, the port which teases one with the call to visit the ancient historical islands of the Aegean Sea—a prized trip I probably will never experience and I knew it while I enviously watched passengers board some of the vessels in port. A typical cosmopolitan port, with the chaos of peoples and baggage and a generous display of disinherited port-inhabitants who probably were wondering what all the fuss was about.

And then by plane to Istanbul, Turkey—the place of mystery. Our hotel was full of porters with their hands out for tips; and thousands of displaced peoples exhibiting their poverty and frustration, walking aimlessly on the city streets. And the beautiful mosques with devotees unashamedly squatting on the bare floors with their children, pleading with their Allah and no doubt hoping something or other. And the acres of caverns (under the streets) filled with crowds and merchants and small shops, salesmen almost grabbing you for a sale. And the Bosporus and the ships and the feeling of (by proximity) the current Russian "menace."

And then by plane (Sept. 20) over Thessaly and along the Adriatic Sea with Yugoslavia visible on a beautiful sunshiny day and with excellent food and on to Vienna (four hours from Istanbul). Vienna, the Austrian capital and one of the most beautiful, friendly and cultured cities of all Europe. Our first experience in Vienna: visited St. Stephans Cathedral (14th century) and found ourselves *unwittingly* joining a tourist group walking through the cathedral and, uninvited, staying with them. Before we realized it we found ourselves "caught" in the catacombs below the church. And I with my claustrophobia! It was a memorable experience: following a strange crowd and gasping for breath in the black darkness (with only a dim light held by the leader) and told that we were passing by the bodies of dukes, sealed caskets, intestines of Hapsburgs in large containers and piles and piles of bones, some neatly arranged and some helter skelter. (Mozart is supposed to have been buried here but his body was taken away); and finally, we reached the open air and the light of day in some alley! Moral: don't follow the crowd, especially if you have no ticket! The day ended with *wiener schnitzel* and *apfel kuchen,* German fried potatoes and *Hof Brau.* Memorable! memorable!

The Schloss Schoenbrunn, 200-year-old palace, with gardens covering two square miles, is beautiful in a lovely setting—outside of Vienna. Franz Joseph, fairly recent emperor, ruled from here for some sixty-eight years—his iron bed exhibited (to symbolize his participation in the hard rôle of his soldiers), memories of Maria Teresa, Napoleon (who occupied the place), and so on in endless numbers of rooms. The Blue Danube looking gray. The Vienna Woods—vineyards and chestnut trees mostly. Belvedere castle (outside the city walls) and of course the Opera House. Beethoven houses (he moved many times) and the home of Franz Schubert.

Then on to incomparable Salzburg (Mozart birthplace), a clean and orderly city, and about four miles away to the memorable Hellbrunn Palace (built 1613-19) and now empty, which had hidden water spouts to tease and entertain and frustrate guests (a prankster-host's idea of a good time)—which, by the way, almost caught me (because I did not obey the guard) with an unscheduled baptism.

Berchtesgaden (area of Bavarian Alps) is but a bus drive away and this means the Eagle's Nest of Hitler (reached by a one-way hazardous drive—from Obersalzburg—on a narrow road through five tunnels to the top and then by private elevator 400 feet through a rock tunnel to the very top). What a view: the Kehstein mountains in the distance and "perhaps the broadest and grandest panorama in Europe—a vast expanse of countryside." Here, he and Chamberlain (and the latter's umbrella) met at the Nest and agreed to something. At Obersalzburg (below) there are some slight remains of the famous Hitler hideouts (foundation stones only) which were destroyed by Americans in the hope of stamping out his memory.

Then, on September 24, on to Munich, Germany (founded 1158) next to Berlin the largest city—a memory of World War II—badly damaged with innumerable sights and historical associations, not the least the one which originated in October 1810 and now called the *Oktober Fest*—which was in its first days of celebration the day of our visit: the celebration of a crown prince's wedding. A half million people congregate for this one and the old *Hof Brau* (restaurant) generates its beer freely from barrels, and the horses displayed in the streets are the largest and the orchestras playing throughout the night hours are the loudest. A perfect time to see Munich, to see people in their merriest mood and to tune the ear to deafening noises as only crowds can achieve. (One beer house under construction is said to be slated to seat 8,000 people!) *Frauen Kirche* (the Cathedral) of two towers is impressive.

Then on to Augsburg where the famous Augsburg Confession was proclaimed in 1530 and to see the modest plaque (which we searched for hours) on the former Bishop's Palace "*Confessio Augustana*". Luther visited this town in 1515 in a disputation with a cardinal. This tribute to Luther and his cause was all we could find in this (probably) Roman Catholic town except the double Catholic-Protestant Churches (one building —St. Urich's). A city within a city (Augsburg) which was built by the Fuggerei is still intact and is said to be the oldest social settlement in the Western world.

Heidelberg (on the banks of the Neckar) is about four hours from Augsburg by train. Its international reputation of interest is its famous castle on the high hill (reached by the funicular), its University (founded in 1386) in the valley below with some of its old buildings still in use. Heidelberg University has historic academic stature and, most of all, a famous faculty it has attracted through the many years. The little *Güldener Hecht* (students' inn) has atmosphere. The town streets are quaintly narrow. The friendly greetings pass from strangers to strangers: *Bitte schön, Heute Abend, Guten Abend, Aufwiedersehn.*

It is one hour from our last stop by train to Worms. At the station we took a cab to our hotel. The ride was (unknown to us beforehand) across the street! Famous here is the monument (designed by E. Rietschl)—world known—erected in 1868 to honor Martin Luther—the place where Luther was asked to retract his writings against the papacy. The building which saw the Diet of Worms in 1521 was destroyed in the 1600s and on its site stands the Church of the Holy Trinity (1709). For the world to see, the statue offers Luther's famous message: *"Hier Stehe Iche/ Ich Kann Nicht Anders/ Gott Helfe Mir!/ Amen."* The edict of Worms (1521) condemned Luther and sought censorship on his publications and those of others. The names of his intimate friends are engraved and so also the names of the friendly "states" and their Coat of Arms and the Towns which joined in the 16th century Reformation. And many more symbols. Also the four precursors of the Reformation: Waldus (French), Wyclif (English), Hus (Czeck), Savonarola (Italian.) (The date of our visit:

September 27th–28th.) The Wittenberg Bible of 1526
and many other contemporary documents are to be seen
in the Luther room at the Museum. Ruins from the last
World War speak their solemn pieces. The Luther Gate
stands through which the Reformer passed at night ar-
rested by his friends and taken to the castle of Wart-
burg—so the legend.

The railroad follows the Rhine river with its picturesque scenery: many old castles on both sides of the
river, bombed towns, fertile country, boats loaded with
coal going in both directions. We left Worms at 9:40
and arrived at Bonn, 12:30. The Cathedral showed the
bruises of war. The University was easy to find—at the
end of the park. Ludvig von Beethoven's (1770-1827)
statue graces the center of the city. Marketplaces are
attractive. And the shrine: Beethoven's home, containing his piano (equipped with extra strings and one extra pedal to make more sound for his defective hearing)
and organ, some of his musical manuscripts, his hearing
aid and other personal articles, the room in which he
was born, garden (very small). And, of course, the
new government buildings *(Bundeshaus)*, Capitol of
West Germany and the residence of the Federal President.

And on to Cologne *(Köln)*, next day at noon. Our
hotel across the street from the magnificent cathedral:
breathtaking in size, tradition, architecture. It suffered
bombing but repairs continue to cover up the scars. In
1948 the cathedral celebrated its 700th anniversary. Its
interior is 66,592 square feet. A sight to behold from
within and without! It dominates the landscape. A fer-
ry across the Rhine brought us to an international ex-

position of photographers in a huge building at Messe.

In the early morning of September 30 we headed for Ostend, Belgium. A ride of confusion with no certainty that we would reach our destination, passing through Liége, Brussels, etc.—and then finally to the dock and the boat at Ostend. After more confusion we landed at Dover, England (overnite), after passing the famous White Cliffs of Dover, so real to us from war songs. They were striking, indeed.

Then, on October 1, we headed by train for London (quick change) with destination Cambridge. Our Cambridge visit was one of the highlights of our "second crossing." It is an unbelievably beautiful area with campuses in the plural, colleges in the plural, gorgeous buildings, a quaint countryside, a creek called "the River Cam" with cows grazing on the other side. Our hotel had academic atmosphere, leisurely people sitting around, a place old and comfortable and "style." It was "University Arms"—one place of refuge we would like to enjoy again and again. Then two days of walking, walking—entering hopefully *each* and *every* campus: Jesus College, St. Mary's Church, King's College (the most impressive we have ever seen—not for size but for sheer beauty), Downey College, Pembroke, Emmanuel, Queens, Clare, Magdalene (Peppys collection)—not to mention all of them. The University Library (well guarded) with student patrons in short robes for identification—huge, impressive. Memories tingle ever-after when Cambridge is mentioned. Cambridge calls to mind many of the stalwarts of England's best scholarship who either were students or professors there or both. (To us the whole complex out-did Oxford University—its ancient rival.)

And then back to London with a tour of the British Museum (fabulous), Dickens' home, Winter Garden Theatre and on and on. (The theatre plays we saw on a previous London visit were positively boring: was it British humor which lacks spark or was it our mood, or was it a reputation from past centuries—or what? Our rating of London theatre is "F" and we saw more than one play.)

Trafalgar Square (the hub of London) on the evening of October 3rd (for the 'nth time) was our last London spot on our second crossing. Feeding the pigeons and watching the ever-restless crowd and glancing over in the direction of the fabulous Art Building, (the National Gallery)—we went to our American Hotel to rest up for the next day (October 4, 1956) which was to take us to the London airport and by air (BOAC) to the international airport at Prestwick, Scotland. Then the night-crossing of the Atlantic to Gander, Newfoundland and finally New York where our son Robert met us and we drove to New Haven (where he was a graduate student) for a short visit and a much-needed rest and then headed for our summer-retreat in Mercer.

The remaining account is exceedingly brief. This chapter is long and the reader is weary. But "two crossings" mean at least a quick briefing on *the unsaid places of the first tour* which was made in company with a group and under daily supervision of a guide. And here the story ends as quickly as it can be told:

1954—the month of June: Warwick Castle (after the Shakespeare visit at Stratford-on-Avon); Oxford and Eton; Windsor Castle; London: Westminster Abbey (fabulous), Piccadilly Circus and the theatre district, the London Tower, St. Paul's Cathedral (of Dean Inge fame midst the banking places), the Thames, Covent Garden, Royal Opera House, London University, Buckingham Palace and the Changing of the Guards, British Museum, National Gallery, King's Cross Station express to Newcastle and across to Norway . . . .

. . . Leave Oslo by train for Sweden (June 28, 1954); by train to Gothenberg and a relaxed time at "fun-fair" Liseberg Park (fabulous); on to Kronberg Castle (Hamlet); to Copenhagen via Hällsingborg and Elsinor (Denmark). In Copenhagen, the fabulous entertainment spot in the heart of the city, Tivoli Park, with its flowers, orchestras, family entertainments (similar to Liseberg Park) and also the Castle nearby and the park benches where Soren Kierkegaard used to brood; Little Mermaid; Georg Jensen's silver factory; Carlsberg Brewery and Glyptothek; Thorvaldsen's Museum; the view from the Round Tower with its wide ramp to the top overlooking Copenhagen's church towers and associated with the famous astronomer, Tycho Brahe (b.1546); Grundtvig Cathedral, and so on and on.

By train across the Danish Island and embarkation to Germany on a Baltic steamer (July 3) and on to Hanover and by motor to Enschere, Holland and on to Amsterdam (canals, famous Rijks Museum, one of the very greatest in Europe) then on to Antwerp, Belgium and to Brussels (Grand Palace); to Bastogne (where General Patton fought with his army); to Luxembourg and on to Nancy (France), (palaces, parks) and on through the Vosges Mountains to Switzerland. Lunch, dinner and overnight at Basel on the Rhine (visit the famous Cathedral) and recall my partner's enthusiasm for their baked goods. Then next day to Lucerne (covered bridges, lake-ride, evening with Swiss yodelers and dancers); then the Brünig Pass to Interlaken (the towering Jungfrau by rail half-way up); next day (July 12), to Zurich, Switzerland's largest shopping center; then on to the Principality of Liechtenstein, and to the Tyrolian village of Feldrich and then via the Arlberg Pass and St. Anton to Innsbruck (cable car up the mountain). From Innsbruck (July 13-15) (beautiful) cross the Brenner Pass into Italy. A memorable stop at Verona where "Juliet's balcony" inspires reflections on romance and the evening performance of opera at the ancient Roman arena (moonlight) inspires more romance; and on to Padua and Venice (July 16) (canals, gondolas, Doges' Palace, Bridge of Sighs, St. Mark's Square, pigeons) and on to Bologna (seat of the oldest university in Europe), then to Florence (leather goods, shops built over the Arno River, art galleries and more art [galleries Palazzo, Uffizi and Pitti], the great Cathedral); then on to Siena with its unusual Cathedral (black and white marble) and the famous square with memories of ancient splendor of parades and then on to the Eternal City of Rome.

Five days in Rome: July 19-23, 1954 leave memories among the many peaks of pleasure. Too many places to mention besides Vatican City, the Old Appian Way, the Colosseum, the Tiber, catacombs, the busy stores, the midnight operas sung by inhabitants at continuing hours, Villa d' Este (hundreds of fountains), and on and on. But there are three experiences which stand out from the visit. One is the experience of loneliness on being lost, the other, the wish at the Fountain and the third, the ascent of the sacred stairs.

On the tram I was told in the crowded car by my partner (who was far up front) to get off at the fountain. This I did (at the sight of a fountain). None of my party got off. I was alone and lost. (Rome has thousands of fountains!) To be lost as a total stranger and without language facilities is an experience of claustrophobia. The name of our hotel would not come to my memory. I decided to wait for the rescue party and stood near some fountain. The entire rescue party was out to locate their fellow tourist. And the short of it: I was found because I stayed put and my rescuers got their bearings by finding the route of the car. Moral: don't get off at *any* fountain in Rome! You are doomed (unless you may be a Roman)! The other: *Fontana di Trevi* ("three coins in a fountain" fame). Drop a coin into its stirring water and you are assured of a return trip to the city. This my partner and I did. And sure enough: after leaving Rome we did return unexpectedly. The bus broke down and our party was hauled back to Rome to see Rome once again—for a few hours! The other incident takes longer paragraphs.

For years I had heard the story of Martin Luther (the monk) ascending the holy stairs in Rome (the promise of an indulgence from penance for a thousand years) and in the midst of the climb, stood erect and walked down—in protest of the low estate of the Establishment. (This was in 1511.) Such an act of defiance deserved punishment. In the Guide Book, I spotted the note on the Scala Santa (Sacred Steps)—twenty-eight of them in a place called the *Sancta Sanctorum* across the street from the Lateran Palace, the Chapel of early popes. (These are the stairs believed to have been in Pilate's Palace, those which Christ ascended to be judged and descended to his scourging and death.) Not telling my partner where we were going, I followed the printed directions in the Guide and we got on a car. We got off at a designated place. Asked "where are we going?" I replied *"this is it.* You'll never forget this one."

We entered the building. A monk stood at the door. I motioned myself toward the stairs which I saw immediately on my left and joined the pilgrims ascending on their knees. My partner whom I thought was following me was delayed by the monk. She was told by sign language that she had to have a head-cover and sleeves. She was, accordingly, bedecked by the monk who seemed to have such supplies (for a coin). Unbeknown to me, she followed belatedly in the pilgrim procession. I felt it too holy to look back. The stairs were hard, hard, hard. I slipped my soft-covered tour Guide Book under one knee and then the other for fear I would develop "maids' knees" or perhaps calloused knees. My ascent was very slow. The traffic of the "saints" ahead prevented my passing anyone. At any rate, the elderly fat women blocked the way. I knew that something good would come into my life by my suffering this indignity and the pain of walking on knees. Meanwhile, my wife not knowing the holiness of the place had started to ascend on her knees mimicking the others but she had no pad. It was too much. So, after a few tries, she stood up and walked down (like Martin Luther) to the horror of the monks below. She was taken, not prisoner, nor spanked (which she may have deserved) but shown to a hidden stairway which went to the top and told in Italian politely to "beat it." Still I worked my way to the top, religiously dedicated to the knee-operation. Finally, at the top there was a spot everyone was supposed to kiss. I came to it and looked down the small hole on the last stair. I shuddered to think of the millions of microbes. *This* I could not do. So I went the full distance with partial religious commitment and then rose to full upright position at the top and to my amazement there stood my "Mrs." waiting to greet me. I thought I had reached the Beyond! How could she have passed me? I saw her not and here she was smiling a welcome arrival. I think I said "Holy God, Holy Mother, how can this be? A miracle! A miracle! There are such things as miracles." And she supported my wobbly walking, saving the explanation until I was ready for a scientific account of what had happened and letting me believe in a miracle that had just taken place. (Thus, has come my philosophical explanation of all miracles: if only we knew how things operate we would be less inclined to settle for the shortcuts of miracle explanations—or something.)

A very short distance from the Victor Emmanuel II Monument (monstrous) there is a little church which we found in Rome. How? I do not recall. But just inside the door and to the right was a monk cadaver dressed in his robes, exhibited in a glass case for the devout to view. Gruesome. And luckily, I saw a living monk at the stairs (farther back) with a tin cup. I asked "Do we go down?" Whether or not he understood he seemed to bow "yes." I put something or other in the cup and my partner and I descended into the basement. The sight of it all I shall never forget! Monk skeletons (assembled) all over the place and where the full skeletons were absent human crania were displayed. There were ankle bones, leg bones, knee bones, arm bones, hip bones, hand bones, chest bones, bones, bones, bones, arranged in neat piles or hanging in doorways as decorations. Living monks walked around in company with their dead predecessors. I do not know the theory of it all. But it was perhaps their assurance of bodily resurrection and a constant reminder of the rewards of monkery (some kind of immortality?). Though it was very improper, I slipped my kodak out from under my coat and took pictures by the artificial light furnished visitors. And would you believe it? These are some of my best pictures in my huge collection. For those who doubt my reporting all I need to do is to show these slides without any running commentary. Fantastic! And all this not far from Vatican City (which, of course, tolerates beliefs of the dedicated faithful).

I suppose that next to Scandinavia I shall have to vote for Italy as my favorite European country for two reasons: (1) it has such a grand tradition in so many areas, particularly art, government, music, virile history, organization, individuality, climate (with changing seasons from extremes), topography—not to mention the sheer beauty of the Italians (figure and complexion), their warmth and spontaneity, and so on. (2) But the second is as important: I was named "Vergilius" probably by my dad who must have known something of the virtues of the Italians unless he hoped I would be much less in kind (unlike a father). I proudly carry the full Latin name and my regret is that somehow I never really got to appreciate the classic Latin and the literature beyond the four years then required in secondary education. The use of it (along with Greek) in my professional career has been generous and I like to think that I had fairly good preparation in the classics—so fundamental in the study of the history of Western Civilization. Anyhow, "Vergilius" I was meant to be and I gladly accept the term—having seen the country from the top of its leg to almost where its foot begins.

On July 24th we went south by bus to one of the choicest parts of the whole of Italy: to Naples and Pompeii. The latter is about seventeen miles from the former. And, of course, every school boy has read of the burial of Pompeii by a volcanic eruption in 79 A.D. The molten lava has preserved intact many evidences of the routine life of that earlier day which recent excavations have revealed and continue to unfold. It still presents a sad picture and the threat of nature. With a good guide one learns much in a little time. What most tourists do not know is that there is one little locked room amidst the ruins which reveals some of the more or less intimacies of ancient life in sculptured form. I was pre-advised of it and paid the guard the required fee and was taken along with some others (including, to my surprise, some of the women of our party) to the locked room. Our guide knew about it and we just winked at each other.

Two hours' drive south of Pompeii is Sorrento (famous for table laces and linen, embroidered shawls and silks). Cut into the rocky hills lining the shore, this spot offers a wonderful view of the bay. Sorrento is idyllic and I could wish to return there and stay and stay and stay. Across Naples Bay is the Isle of Capri—a quaint village—just the spot for tourists. A launch picked us up (pre-arranged) and took us into the famous Blue Grotto—a memorable experience. Back to Sorrento to motor via Naples (July 25th) for the long trip north, back to Rome. Enroute we saw the famous Monte Cassino which was almost completely destroyed during the war (and now rebuilt). Another full day at Rome and then on to Pisa with its famous leaning Tower, Cathedral and Baptistery. And then next day, following the rugged coastline, we stopped at Rapallo, Italy's Riviera area, where we enjoyed a swim in the Ligurian Sea. Overnight. Then on to the French Riviera: via Genoa, San Remo to Monaco. Evening at the Casino at Monte Carlo (the center of the Riviera) and a full day with a visit to the little castle and the overlook view of the town and the bay. Then next day to Nice and to Grasse (famous for perfumes) and on to Cannes and a swing north to Avignon (the castle of the Popes in Captivity —a gloomy pile of rock, indeed). Then on to Valance and to Lyon and to Bourges viewing there the magnificent Cathedral. A most beautiful section of southern France is the cluster of feudal castles in the Loire Valley (vineyards) which no tourist should ever miss, including Chateau de Chenonceaux. Overnight at Tours (150 miles southwest of Paris). And through the Loire Valley to Chartres to view the most beautiful cathedral of them all at Chartres. One could spend endless time here. My own impression of the cathedral was: here is supernaturalism incarnated in an elegant structure thrust high against the sky and over man,—with nature and man (naturalism) taking the lower seat. For this Cathedral looks up. If it looked around it would hardly see the tiny squatters' huts huddled around it—and one would ask: do not man and nature count too?

Paris is unique. And one cannot begin to see its treasures and those of its environment on a hasty tour. But we were given from August 4th through the 9th (on this tour) and, with good health and professional guidance, we experienced a generous overall view.

The notes remind us of some of our visitations: Castles of Versailles and Trianon, the Louvre, Flea Market, flood-lit Montmartre, Fontainebleau, Eiffel Tower (with an unscheduled walk down from the second level to ground on a narrow steel stairway, bringing on dizziness), the Opera House, the river Seine, Notre Dame (colossal), Museum of Modern Art, the Concierge (oldest prison in Paris where Marie Antoinette was jailed), the church of the Madeleine (near our hotel), Tomb of Napoleon, Arc de Triomphe, the Sorbonne (University of Paris) where Henri Bergson and Louis Pasteur (among so many others) held lectures, Grand Palais, Luxemborg Gardens, Pantheon and not to forget: the *Folies Bergère* (musical revue extravaganza). August 9th: Farewell Dinner: *La Doucette, Place Gaillon.*

And on August 10, 1954 "By Special Boat Train" for Departure on *SS Flandre.* New York, August 16, 1954.

DAYS OF RETIREMENT

Retirement comes if you live long enough. Someone tells you, you are no longer wanted where you are and they say politely, "Sorry, these are the rules." And you don't answer back by saying how good you feel, how much you need more money, how lonesome it will be. The notice is final and admits of no exceptions.

With rising costs of living and with no real preparation for the Day of Doom, one begins to take serious stock of himself and his immediate family (his Mrs.) and wonders how he'll make it with the salary check no longer in the hands of the mailman.

Of course, you have some modest insurance set up by the college to which both it and you have been contributing through the years. Of course, you have some little pension here or there (the church, a policy, some savings). But all this is too sparse to carry on, even with the sacrifices of modest living.

I found out to my amazement that one would have to have three thousand dollars invested at five percent to have a ten dollars *net* income a month (deducting for Federal taxes). Thus to have a hundred dollar income net per month from an independent source, one must have thirty thousand dollars in invested five percent savings. (This is figured at today's interest rate of insured savings and can be verified by anyone having had seventh-grade arithmetic.) And then: mounting real estate taxes, food costs and some minor pleasures as gas and oil for the car, and repairs, etc., on and on—where do you go from here?

This report is not a complaint. It is only a confession of a blow that hits you of a sudden. Against this blow we had good life insurance which works on the theory that death would bring winnings to someone. But meanwhile you have to live until you die! Simple, isn't it? What's the point of an estate-when-you-die when you need it when you live? So we pondered and pondered.

I said: this report is not a complaint. It is, no doubt, the fearful conscious experience of many thousands who live in our contemporary unstable society with predictions so impossible. We had two things going for us: good health and at least a "sound mind and body." I was lucky to receive a phone call (a thorough surprise) inviting me to a visiting professorship for one year. This would give a breathing spell so we would know how to rearrange the whole financial structure. (Clergymen are finding their problem accentuated by having lived in parsonages and when retirement comes there is no home except precarious rentals. We had no such problem since home ownership in our book was a part of the sacrifices we made during the time of the monthly salary to pay off mortgages.)

Off to Sweet Briar College—a women's college, quite well known with acceptable standards of excellence and situated in the foothills of Virginia, not far from the Blue Ridge Mountains. It was a wonderful year. We escaped the isolated campus each weekend, touring the battle grounds of the Civil War (attending the one-hundreth anniversary of the surrender at Appomattox nearby and Lexington and Manassas and all). From our apartment window we watched the girls down below, riding their horses, with the mountains in the background. Our little village, six miles away, was Amherst —the closest shopping center, typically Virginian and the only point of social excitement which was nil. One of my students one day told me she would not be to class on Monday since she was going home for a visit. I told her I thought she should be in class but then she had freedom so far as I was concerned. Then she said: She was going home to Puerto Rico for the weekend and I promptly added with feigned enthusiasm: I am going to Amherst over the weekend.

This was not uncommon. Many of the girls seemed to have come from affluent homes although affluence did not seem to interfere with their academic work. I piled the assignments on and there was no grumbling. The campus was dead most weekends; the dances with the boys at other colleges was the rule except for boys descending on the place for certain weekend festivities and the usual love-ins or love-outs all over the hideouts on the campus. One usually respected their privacy at the lake area since one never knew when one might come upon a blanket rendezvous.

It all seemed to us an unnatural situation. Girls' colleges, no doubt, had their *raison de être* in years gone by when there may have been parental overprotection. There is something strangely missing in classes with no tenors or potential bassos responding in class. One almost has to fight the tendency to be a soprano or alto in lecturing. Politeness seemed never to have been disrespected. The sad feature seemed to be that many girls

who were ready, willing and able, seemed not to have
potential dates. Their weekends were lonely. There may
have been a reason: pulchritude is not guaranteed by
affluence.

With a faculty majority being women and a noticeable sprinkling of the faculty men being somewhat on
the feminine side, it seemed, at times, to be an exhibi-
tion of a glorious matriarchal society. The president,
a widow, was not as masculine as I had expected but she
would not be president if she were altogether of the
qualities of tenderness, shyness, reservedness. She was
altogether independent, self-sufficient, proper and cool.
She and I got along (from my side) but I think she
found me a little too informal and maybe too independent. My new book, *Inside Ivy Walls* (just published),
seemed to disturb her! (I am very prejudiced and the
reader will discount my impression here. The president
of a college is a man's job in a still man's world. And
I don't blame her for being a woman. She, in my opinion, would have been happier to have a lectureship in
American history or government—her field of specialty.) The community on the hilltop consisted of a
generous number of women-professor-retirees and this
in itself made for a kind of social segregation that comes
with advanced age and an atmosphere of Sunday afternoon dullness.

The unmistakable trend today is moving straight
away from women's and men's colleges. It is healthier
and the ones who would agree with me are the students
themselves rather than alumnae, women presidents (if
there are any left?) and overprotective parents. So that
is that—as *I* see it. (I would—I am certain—not give my

life to a girls' school. I recall that when the great Roman Catholic scholar, Alfred Loisy, became *persona non grata* in his church because of his writings challenging Catholic fundamentals, he was given his punishment by being sent to teach in a girls' school and this always seemed to me to be appropriate for the church and at the same time a cruelty.) Remember: for everything one may say, there may be exceptions. My Virginia experience—as wonderful as it was—left me somewhat with a feeling of pity for the men who (for whatever reason) are committed to teach and associate only with women.

One example: Friday afternoons in all colleges are simply dead do-do. The woman dean and the madame president (the year I was there) seemed to think that important committees of the faculty might well meet on Friday at four. I demurred. Not only am I psychologically dead then but I have a mounting pressure for wanderlust. "T G I F" students sing. And I, too. (THANK GOD IT'S FRIDAY.) I skipped these meetings believing a professor emeritus deserves special privileges. This, I am sure, the dean and the president didn't like but my salary and my future did not depend on my total submission. Can you honestly imagine efficiency and wisdom decided on anything on a Friday afternoon? Well, most *men* cannot imagine this. And that is that.

Wake Forest College (Winston Salem, North Carolina) became a University during my two-year stay as visiting professor of philosophy. Winston Salem is a charming city with lots to offer, including Old Salem and Salem College, a girls' school dating back to pre-

revolutionary days. The area offers many cultural opportunities.

The liberal arts' college is located on a wide expanse
of land donated by the Reynolds people (Reynolds tobacco—"Winston tastes good like a cigarette should").
The family estate is a park in itself with a lake and adjacent to the main campus. All of it together is now
Wake Forest. Ten years prior to my coming, the college was located in a small village of Wake Forest,
North Carolina—on a beautiful campus. The decision
to move meant many difficulties: including torn sentiments and disputes. Called to be leader was a Baptist
clergyman, Harold Tribble (systematic theologian and
liberal). He ruled with a gloved hand which was one
qualification necessary in such a time. His skin was
tough; his early regime was full of controversy on the
part of the discontended and of partisans. But he led the
school into the front ranks among denominational colleges. Its medical school rates with the best in America
with hospital facilities near the center of the city, growing in effectiveness and prestige. Among the noted college alumni is the golf champion Arnold Palmer whose
sentiment for his school can hardly be matched.

I came there knowing no one. The president (I am
certain) was the prime mover in extending me the invitation for an *ad interim* appointment. The two years
(plus) there were exciting to us since we found we had
moved into what seemed to be the best in the southland.
Fellow faculty members lived in semi-affluent homes
near the campus. The college buildings were of similar
architecture. The parking places ample and orderly.
The concerts and platform-speakers were of the best.

The big coliseum nearby offered space to a mass audience of nine thousand; and now a new football stadium costing in the three millions has been recently dedicated. Athletics play a top role especially with the alumni who think of Wake Forest on a par with nearby Duke and North Carolina University athletes.

The philosophy department was in the process of change: the head, Dr. A. C. Reid, having just retired after decades of service. His following among alumni brought unusual gifts to the university: of endowments, cash, estates, a library and a professorship. I had been briefed very little on the situation—only to know that things were somewhat delicate and uncertain. I soon saw the problem but decided that at my stage in life I would be content with a modest number of hours of teaching and the least number of responsibilities as acting chairman.

We came away with life-long friends from among the faculty and were it not so late in life, we 'might even have considered Winston Salem a haven for retirement. Some events seemed strange or peculiar to us. For example, the awful gap between the Baptist Church which sponsored the university and the existing faculty and student body: the one, the majority conservative beyond belief and the other for the most part educationally oriented in competition with the academic world. Between the two stood the president whose heart had been given to his new appointment which he saw was a commitment to academic standards no matter how the clergy roared at him. He did a grand job and his stature will be appreciated in the perspective of time. We could not get over our surprise concerning the practice of public prayer before football (and other?) contests. I thought it was embarrassing and out-of-place all around. But the chaplain handled the business well both for the players, the partisan rooters and for Jehovah (and shall I add: for the church constituency loyalists who on denominational campuses like to snoop around to see that everything is in ecclesiastical order).

One semester we spent at Heidelberg College in Tiffin, Ohio. Over the phone the invitation came as a surprise: would I fill in for a professor on a semester's sabbatical? Since the genial dean at Wake Forest was notoriously slow in making up his mind about faculty reappointments and other decisions and having heard no word as to his plans, I accepted immediately. (I was honored and embarrassed by students at Wake Forest turning in a public protest in not asking my stay and criticizing the administration. Yet, it was too late. I had made the decision.)

Terry Wickham was then president of Heidelberg and I found him a quiet and effective person moving behind the scenes. It was under his administration that the beautiful circular college library was built, unique, indeed, and worthy of a trip to see. (The hole was dug the semester I was there.) The dean, Dr. John Krout, was a most unusual person. (I first got this impression when he talked with me over the phone inviting me to come: his businesslike procedure and the professional know-how.) For some time Dean Krout had been the right-hand man of President Eisenhower when the latter presided over Columbia University. The dean had no end of stories about the Eisenhower administration and one could laugh far into the night just recalling some of them. Among the more serious stories which I recall is the time when Eisenhower came to Heidelberg to deliver a speech at the insistence of Dr. Krout who was a Tiffin native. The White House was trying to contact him. The Heidelberg people concerned with the message thought such matters could wait and did not notify "Ike" until the evening was well spent. Then the pressure was on. "Ike" must call the White House immediately. The message finally got through when the speaker's car had reached a small junction (was it Bucyrus, Ohio?) where the east-bound Pennsylvania train was to be boarded. So, in the lateness of the night, "Ike" had to call President Truman from an outdoor pay station near the depot to respond. (Did he have to borrow the exact change? What did the operator think when a White House call was put in from such a lonely pay-station?) It was, indeed, Truman. The president (seemingly of a sudden) had decided he wanted "Ike" to go abroad to command (I believe) the North Atlantic Treaty Organization forces. This brought about Eisenhower's early resignation at Columbia.

Dean Krout also told of how afraid Eisenhower was of the Columbia faculty. (They, indeed, were quite aware of his misplaced appointment to an academic presidency and whispered their amazement around the campus halls.) Eisenhower was quite aware of his limitations at Columbia. It was one evening early in his administration that he heard the dean speak at a faculty banquet. He was so impressed that he at once summoned the dean to become an associate in the president's office, to take care of what is now called the work of the "provost." When faculty meetings came around Eisenhower froze. He feared and hated them. (Who doesn't?) Dean Krout suggested to the President that he might do well to take an occasional lunch at the Faculty Club—mix with the professors. One day the "provost" posed this question as "how about today?" Ike answered: "Please, come home with me. Mamie will fix up some sandwiches."

This was a command. Then, after a modest lunch, Ike took the "provost" up to the attic of the president's home, donned a white robe and exhibited with enthusiasm some of his unfinished paintings.

At Tiffin we moved into a downtown hotel. (There were no other possibilities.) A "broken-down" little old fellow answered my query at the desk if we were expected. He responded affirmatively. So I asked for help with the baggage. He came along with me and helped pile our things on the cart to take to the elevator. He worked like mad, sweating and grunting. I felt sorry for him. When we were through, I offered him a tip. He hestitated and then took it. Later, when I came down to the desk in the small foyer there was the same man dressed in a suit and tie, behind the desk. He now was assuming his real role. He was the "owner" of the hotel!

I tell this incident since it gave us an impression that never left. Indeed, it was a broken-down hotel on its wiggly financial legs. Our apartment on the third floor overlooked the gray and dirty roofs of nearby buildings. Ours was the "choice" apartment available and we had no choice. There was no kitchen sink and no kitchen.

There were crude substitutes. A look down the fire escape was a look down the Grand Canyon. I shuddered at the thought of a fire in such a building, especially for those who occupied the third floor. I even thought such thoughts as: Is this the way the Ferm story will end? Stuck in this firetrap or carried down this precarious outside fire escape?

The students at Heidelberg were wonderful. We laughed together and we studied together and I lectured. My last chapel speech was delivered there—twice by request (not that it was so good but because they had two chapels [like masses]—for those early birds and the latecomers). I cannot remember a thing I said—nor surely can those who came.

While I resided at Sweet Briar and later at Winston Salem, I took the notion that I would take some lessons in guitar playing. A piano in a faculty apartment building was quite unthinkable. So was guitar playing. But one need not practice with a pick. Why not just the fingers? So it was. On certain days of the week I wrapped my Gibson guitar in a blanket and carried it out to the car (I did not want the neighbors to know any thing about this extra-curricular activity.) My teacher in Lynchburg (Virginia) was a violin teacher who (I guess) would take on students in any related instrument. I learned little from him. I made no progress and lost interest. When I came to Winston Salem I noticed an ad in the newspaper that a beginning guitar class was being organized at the YMCA. I had no guitar. My Gibson was in Ohio. That made no difference. Perhaps I might learn something. The class met on Monday nights for nearly two hours for six weeks. There must have been

some thirty kids, ages six to sixteen. Naturally I was
grandpa kid *par excellence*. They looked at me as a
foreigner. The teacher was a typical dashy young fellow who not only played popular music very well but
also knew musical theory. I went steadily each Monday
night and listened. He talked all theory, with blackboard
chalks talks. Then he suggested to me that I buy a Jap-
anese-make guitar cheap for eighteen dollars at the
Camel Pawn Shop. He said it would do, to get going.

This I did (without a case). I had quite a time keeping this package in disguise with neighbor faculty people coming and going into our campus apartment building. When the strings were tightened the thing was
quite tolerable but not alluring. I found that for the
life of me I could not understand the young teacher's
drawings on the board—until it dawned on me much
later that he was left-handed and I read his drawings
in the opposite direction. Like Paul's conversion on the
road to Damascus one day I suddenly saw the light and
a new world opened up unto me.

There are two ways of playing a guitar: one is the
hard way and the other the easy. The latter way requires
the use mainly of four strings, with the thumb holding
on and doing little else. The hard way is to play all six
strings which, by the way, really makes music! My
teacher was teaching us the hard way: barring with the
first finger all across the board and then changing the
remaining fingers on other fret positions. Try this some
time. It seemed actually impossible. I told my teacher
(who did it freely) that only a chimpanzee could hold
the first finger down with the strength of an ox and then
let the other fingers of the same left hand fall here and

there with the strength of an ox on other properly related positions. Well, he promised that I would be doing it some day and told me to practice, practice, practice. Moreover, he taught us that this method was the one method for strumming (which I wanted to learn) and that once we knew one key the other keys followed suit. It worked!

But it still was all theory. Either you get arthritis with this kind of manipulation or, if you have arthritis, you get rid of it in the fingers. Once I had transposed a left-handed teacher into a right-handed pupil (myself) and with practice, practice, practice, I got so I could hum a simple melody and strum accompaniments. I almost cried when for the first time I chorded "Way down upon the Swanee River" and added such tunes as "Blue Skies"; "Vaya Con Dios"; "Try to Remember"; "Moon River"; "Far Away Places"; and so on. What beautiful chords on a six-string guitar, especially the ninth, the four-string diminished chords, the sevenths, the sixths—and certainly on a Gibson. I learned to read off piano sheet-music where guitar chords are given. But alas, too many other interests came into my schedule (such as the last two books) that I have lost the dedication that comes only with the help of a good teacher.

When the class ended, he took me on privately at his Bohemian home. Out of the YMCA class only two survived private lessons: a nine-year old and I (I almost said ninety). Some time in my retirement days I shall take up strumming—especially in northern Wisconsin where only the birds and the chipmunks will wonder and perhaps be disturbed. At least only one other human being will hear and perhaps protest: my wife, but her tolerance is generous.

My teacher disappeared from Winston Salem and he took with him things he should have left behind (so the neighbors say). I miss him and feel sorry: such talent, such Bohemian informality, such full and relaxed living. I hope he changes and comes back somewhere that I may again take up lessons where we left off.

Another deep secret in my life and I will be very brief. I had the accordian bug-bite at one time and secretly took lessons on that instrument. My teacher was a semiprofessional Italian player and he gave me a taste for the classical as well as the polka variety. I bought a splendid instrument and as the years went by, it seemed heavier and heavier to carry. I now haul it on a wheelbarrow to the car and take one heave and get it into the trunk. An accordian is not too difficult for the right hand since it is like a piano keyboard. But the buttons to press: too many and too close to each other and fingers too big and farther out of sight and known only to a practiced touch. But for peppy music and "swing" you just can't beat this one. I'll ask for one to practice on when and if I get to heaven. For the "saved" in merry mood, there is no more suitable instrument for sheer joy and genuine participation than accordian music.

Not all of life is sweet and rosy. There are times of illness—almost always unpredictable and frustrating. While living in Sweet Briar and on a weekend journey to Roanoke, Virginia, I was suddenly seized with the most excruciating pain in the lower middle of my spine. I could hardly move around the motel where we stayed.

Then pains came at the side of one knee (of all places) and then on the heel of one foot (of all places). We continued our journey—but headed to home base. The college physician thought it was some thing or other and I thanked her (!!). (The physician at Sweet Briar College, too, was a woman.) Finally, I knew I had to have help. At Lynchburg there were two physicians recommended by friends. It was plain luck that I "chose" the one nearest the drugstore and that he was in the mood to take on a new patient ("without a month's appointment"). I was not in his private office very long before a look at me and my posture and few other mysterious symptoms he said "You have Osteoporosis."

This was frightening.

"Is it curable?" I asked.

"No" he replied, "but it is normal for your age."

(This chapter is on "retirement years" and this story therefore is appropriate.)

"You have arthritis. There is no cure. I can stop it. But you must promise to do exactly as I say."

A mysterious shot was given me and then I was put on a two-week office-visit schedule, indefinitely.

Pain makes choices easy. If it is first class you obey and are willing to make the required sacrifices. I was way overweight (said he) and must lose forty some pounds post haste. This meant a diet following his printed directions. I was to be weighed *in his office* by a nurse each visit and if I did not follow his directions I was not to come back. This was it. Dieting is very possible if you realize the alternatives. (He told me some of them and I knew he had me in his professional trap.)

I relate this story because I have only words of sincerest thanks to Dr. C. E. Keefer who professionally made me into a new person. My weight at the time of the attack was one hundred and seventy pounds. But I must go down closer to my weight as a young man which was about one hundred and thirty.

The schedule was rigorously followed. The first two or more weeks nothing happened. And then slowly and regularly my weight sagged about one pound a week. Then there were the exercises. Arthritic people must exercise early in the stages of the onslaught. (By the way, people came to him from all over the area, people bent, people maimed, people looking haggard, people of all sizes and shapes, cripples and what not.) The office looked like a menagerie of pathetic human specimens. He studied them and he made them follow his commands. No pussyfooting.

My exercises I give here in grateful appreciation of what they *and the diet* did for me and as a gift to my readers who happen on this book and who may suffer similar onslaught. *These exercises each day, morning and night. Each day!* Lie on your back on the hard floor; arms and hands at side; raise hands and arms backwards touching the floor beyond the head; return hands and arms to floor. Back and forth fifty times. (But you begin with just a few rounds of this and work up to the maximum. When I started I couldn't possibly touch the floor with my hands back of my head.) Follow this with a five-pound weight placed over the stomach. Move the five-pound weight (sack of sugar, for example) up and down fifty times using stomach muscles only. Begin modestly and work up to fifty after a few weeks. Then, fifty times of the following: turn over, lie on your belly, hands and arms down parallel with the body; keep them down and do not use either hands or arms; raise head and shoulders from the floor without any help. (It stretches the spine to the seeming breaking point.) The chin must sooner or later reach a considerable distance from the floor; return head and shoulders to floor gently. (Start with a few such raises; then work up; count and rest. Eventually you will do the fifty but with at least five rests.) This kind of stretching gives you the feeling of well-being—ultimately. Each time you do it you feel like a novitiate and think you cannot finish. But it limbers the body like nothing else.

The physician told me I was flat-footed. (I was insulted!) There is a "cure" for this and it is the following exercise.

Take off your shoes.

1. Hold on to something (for balance). Stand with feet somewhat apart. Raise both feet up simultaneously with weight on heels; then as you return the feet to the floor, turn the feet on edge (outward) and in that position wiggle your toes and rest your feet (on edge) on floor and continue wiggling your toes. Then return both feet to normal position (flat on the floor). Repeat twenty-five times in succesion. (Not too many times to start with!)

2. Raise both feet on the balls of the feet (lifting the heels) as high as you can; then return feet to the floor (slowly) while turning both feet (outward) on their edges and wiggling your toes; then return both feet to normal position (on floor). Repeat twenty-five times

in succesion. (Go easy. Only a few times to begin with!)

3. Turn both feet on edge (outward); hold in this position and wiggle toes; then return *the one* (the left) foot to floor (normal position) while wiggling toes of the other foot (the right). Alternate: now both feet on edge (outward) wiggle toes and then the right foot on the floor (normal position) while wiggling toes of the left. Alternate back and forth following the same routine—twenty-five times. (Go easy.)

Result: I have today feet which are arched which means that only the heels and balls of the feet touch ground.

You now can bounce!

The above exercises should be done in the morning as you are prepared to come out for breakfast and then again at night before retiring.

"Never, never, miss these exercises, never" he said to me when I bade him good-bye upon leaving the area of my professional assignment.

I have continued them for more than four years with only a hiatus during a period of the flu. (If I forget the exercises at night, I will awaken and think of them and resolutely jump out of bed and do them—to the consternation even of myself.) My diet, of course, was my major therapy.

Result. I am superstitious and don't want to say too much. I can say that my weight came down to below one hundred and forty pounds and I have never felt better since I was a kid. I have a bounce. My breathing is better; my stomach is flat "like the boys"; I can bend down and pick things off the floor without getting diz-

zy; I have more pep; I look thinner (some think I look
a bit on the sickly side and my friends whispered that
I was on my way out into eternity); I eat well but I eat
now with an unstretched system of inners so that I do
not have that awful hunger which tempts one to overeat
and feel so miserable.

Diet: no sugar at all (we have not had the sugar-bowl
on the table for four years—except for finicky company). This is not a command because of diabetes; it is
the comand from my Lynchburg physician who holds
that the great American curse is the consumption of
sugar. "Remember" he said, "sugar is poison." We get
sugar in the natural foods and this suffices. And all the
starches must be frowned upon; pies, potatoes, bread,
pizza, cake, etc. When you get your weight down, you
can sin a little now and then. Even a saint should sin
or he would be a kind of "pill." But not during the
downward process: never. To begin with the diet: meat
three times a week without the fat; chicken and fish un-
limited; fruit always welcome in season and plenty of
it. No cheating when reducing. The cheating can come
later when the body stabilizes itself. But not until then,
no, no, never and that includes candy, sugar substitutes
"for sissies" (he said). You diet and eat well. You
shrink. You again come to look like a human being. No
measuring of calories. Just *some* food "off limits"; no
starvation; just a change in bad habits picked up from
parents who used to say: "clean your plate before you
get anything else" (which is sinful). A small glass of
one *fresh* lemon (without sugar) and with half a glass
of water is a *must* each morning before breakfast. (If

lemons are expensive so is medicine!) You here have your daily vitamin C.

And then, weigh *each day* with sparse covering of the body. Each day. Not once a month—ever. Each day. The pleasure of victory is wonderful and more wonderful is the pay-off: you are younger, more vigorous, healthier and can walk (if not run) with normal people alongside of you. And for arthritics (who have been diagnosed early enough) the thing seems to be "under control" without prophesizing a cure.

I bless the name of Dr. Keefer. This was Lynchburg. This was Sweet Briar. This was an academic year of return to a fuller measure of life. And it came from pain. And pain came from not only growing older but from the abuse of the body and acting like a living porkchop.

Ashland College in Ohio—only eighteen miles from home base in Wooster called me to their service very unexpectedly. The phone rang in Mercer. There was a telegram asking me to come for the year—and a letter followed. The president is Dr. Glenn L. Clayton, a go-go man with proper academic qualifications. He had me there one summer and for off-campus adult classes in philosophy years ago. This was a "return home." The place has gone through fantastic changes. From a small Brethren school, it now numbers over some twenty-five hundred students, drawing many of them from the east coast, affluent with cars and from many varieties of religious and cultural backgrounds. Buildings (a campus today of thirty-four) seem to sprout each year. My schedule was made convenient to me. The salary was competitive. Classes are small. Philosophy (two courses) is a liberal arts degree requirement. His management includes the invitation to senior retired professors to join his faculty after their service has been terminated by compulson elsewhere. So, there are many of us there: from Oberlin, Western Reserve University (Cleveland, Ohio), Ohio State, not to mention some of the eastern graduate schools. I was given the privilege of living at home and of absence from committee work and special assignments—with the concurrence of the kind and understanding dean of the college, Leslie E. Lindower. I needed only to lecture and tend to my own business and to counsel students where individuals are not numbers but are people. It is an arrangement that makes retirement-teaching—in a good small college—as close to paradise as one can get this side of the Great Divide.

Again, how lucky can one get?

INDEX